No Peace
without Justice,
No Justice
without
Forgiveness

No Peace
without Justice,
No Justice
without
Forgiveness

COMPILED AND WITH AN INTRODUCTION
BY BRENDAN LEAHY

VERITAS

First published 2005 by
Veritas Publications
7/8 Lower Abbey Street
Dublin 1
Ireland
Email publications@veritas.ie
www.veritas.ie

ISBN 1 85390 986 6

10 9 8 7 6 5 4 3 2 1

A catalogue record for this book
is available from the British Library.

Cover Design by Colette Dower
Printed in the Republic of Ireland
by Betaprint Dublin

Veritas books are printed on paper made from the wood pulp of managed
forests. For every tree felled, at least one tree is planted, thereby renewing
natural resources.

CONTENTS

INTRODUCTION:
A POPE FOR ALL

Mention Pope John Paul II as a man of peace and each of us can cast the mind's eye over a vast memory bank of images. Here's just a few of them:

- Pleading for peace in Drogheda in 1979.
- Crouching in attentive listening in a prison cell as he offered forgiveness to Mehmet Ali Agca two years after the assassination attempt on his life.
- Moving among the destitute and dying, hand in hand with Mother Teresa, during his visit in 1986 to Calcutta.
- Welcoming warmly the representatives of world religions invited by him to come together in Assisi in October 1986 to pray for peace.
- Receiving Mikhail Gorbaciov in the Vatican in December 1989.
- Going in 1997 as an aging man on the courageous and risky trip to the martyred, war-torn city of Sarajevo.
- Crossing directly during his visit to the Holy Lane in 2000 from the Al Aqsa Mosque to the Western (Wailing) Wall of Jerusalem, moving on then to the Holy Sepulchre, thereby embracing in the same journey of love, Jews, Muslims and Christians.
- Donning Bono's shades as he met the U2 leader, ally in the international debt-relief campaign.
- Speaking out for peace before the second War in Iraq and declaring 'war is a defeat for humanity.'
- Releasing two white doves from his appartment window in the Vatican surrounded by some children just a few weeks before his death.

I attended the Assisi event (mentioned in several of the messages contained in this book) and its message of peace remains stamped in my memory. In many ways it was a true masterpiece of Pope John Paul II's pontificate. It captured much of what he wanted to say about peace: we build a culture of peace by coming together in mutual acceptance and respect and by sinking the roots of all our relationships deep into the terrain of freedom, justice, truth and love.

Above all, peace must be understood against the vast horizon of God, the unlimited source of freedom that enables us to inject real forgiveness and honesty in relationships. Believers in particular are called to unite in building the peace that God wants.

Peace is far more than the absence of war. It is the work of justice; it is also the work of love that knows how to forgive. It is more than renouncing ideological intimidation and violence; it is active promotion of a civilization of love and all that goes with this – joint action and cooperation between individuals and peoples, nations and religions.

Large and small gestures contribute to education in peace. But the inspiring spark of all our efforts needs to be personal and collective conversion of the heart. *I* can do something about peace. Together *we* (interpersonally, internationally and interdependently) can 'begin again' to commit ourselves to take new steps along the way of peace. The Assisi event was the message of peace made visible.

The Pope and the Berlin Wall

Pope John Paul II follows in a line of Popes spanning the twentieth century that worked for peace. In 1917 Pope Benedict XV defined the First World War a 'useless slaughter'. John XXIII's last encyclical was dedicated to peace, while Paul VI's words in the United Nations became a resounding cry from the heart of the wounded twentieth century: 'War never again.'

In taking over the 'pilgrim's staff of peace' from Paul VI, the Polish Pope came onto a world scene divided into two blocs following the tensions that lingered after World War II. What

Churchill defined as the 'iron curtain' saw one bloc allied with the Soviet Union while the other looked towards America. Walter Lippman coined a phrase 'cold war' to describe the resulting friction. This 'cold war' was to last up until 1989 and the collapse of the wall of Berlin.

Each bloc represented, in a sense, two ways of trying to create the earthly city with two different lifestyles. Pope John Paul played no small part in the first 11 years of his pontificate in laying the foundations for a major world turnabout and the collapse of Communist regimes. From his first encyclical, *Redemptor hominis,* he took up the theme of the respect for human rights and linked justice and peace as cause and effect (n.17).

His repeated underlining of the need for justice, freedom, truth and love resonated far and deep. As Cardinal Sodano put it: 'The fall of the Berlin Wall was nothing short of a collapse of a spiritual way that was much greater than the material wall. The material wall had divided the German capital in two with a barrier of 154 kilometres, but the spiritual wall was much longer and it was eventually knocked down thanks to the constant work of John Paul II who never ceased to cry out against the absurdity of that system and plead for the right of people to freedom and, so, to social peace.'[1]

A Pope for all peoples – initiatives for unity and peace

Pope John Paul II's contribution to peace went well beyond the issues symbolised in the Berlin Wall and its collapse. His outreach was universal. There were two sides to his commitment – teaching and practical activity aimed both at avoiding conflicts and promoting peace. While this book looks above all at his teaching contained in his messages for the Annual World Day of Peace, it is vital to recall how his teaching was always accompanied by action and practical initiatives.

He was very conscious of the more than 150 armed conflicts since World War II and the continuing states of violence, including the forgotten wars in various parts of the world. He sought to build peace wherever he could. It is not surprising that in 2000 the *Economist* magazine called him 'a Pope for all peoples'.[2]

He worked on several levels. Firstly, the Vatican Secretariat of State and the many pontifical representatives throughout the world mediated day by day in myriad political and social circumstances his mission of peace. During his long pontificate 82 new apostolic nunziatures were opened bringing the number of states with which the Holy See has official relations to 174. He wanted the nunziatures to be homes of international dialogue. The Pontifical Council for Justice and Peace was dedicated to promoting the Church's social doctrine and activity particularly in relation to peace and the promotion of the vision of the world as a united family of peoples at peace with one another.

In the course of his more than 103 international journeys, he availed of personal meetings with heads of state and government, academics, leaders of society and peoples worldwide to encourage a culture of dialogue, peace, unity and fraternity. He spoke of peace and all its conditions in assemblies such as the UN in New York, UNESCO in Paris, FAO in Rome as well as in the various international bodies in Geneva and Strasburg.

His condemnation of anti-Semitism and racism is well known. In 1986 he was the first Pope since Saint Peter to enter the synagogue in Rome. In humility, respect and a spirit of dialogue in the Jubilee 2000 Year he visited some of the symbolic places of the Palestinians and Israelites, two peoples in conflict. In a veritable tour de force he moved from the Palestinian refugee camp of Deheisheh to the Mausoleum Yad Vashem, from the Mosques to the Temple and the Western Wall.

Apart from his constant concern for such areas as the Holy Land, he also championed the cause of peace in the Balkans, Iraq and Central Africa. In the context of the 1994 ethnic conflicts in the region of the Great Lakes (Rwanda, Burundi and the Democratic Republic of Congo), for instance, with the terrible fratricidal wars between Tutsi and Hutu that resulted in millions dead and two million refugees within a few short months, Pope John Paul II spoke out while the international world powers remained passive.

His contribution to conflict transformation in Latin America should not be forgotten. It was his mediation in war between Argentina and Chile that resulted in a Peace Treaty in 1984 that still stands.

More recently, we saw him mustering his failing energy to do all he could to prevent war in Iraq. He attempted direct mediation by sending Card. Roger Etchegaray as his personal representative to Baghdad and Cardinal Pio Laghi to Washington to bring messages of peace to the respective presidents Saddam Hussein and George W. Bush. He invited them to reflect before God and their conscience on possible solutions that would safeguard the primary good of peace based on justice and international law.

When war broke out on 20 March 2003, he kept the Nunziature open in Iraq even during the bombing. It has been noted by observers of international politics that the Pope's repeated, passionate interventions meant that the war was not seen by Arab peoples or adherents of Islam as a war of Christians against Muslims, nor as a Western religious war against the Muslim world.

A personal commitment

The roots of John Paul's personal commitment to peace are deep. In his message of 2002 he reminds us of 'the events of history which have marked my life, especially my youth...the enormous suffering of peoples and individuals, even among my own friends and acquaintances caused by Nazi and Communist totalitarianism.' He opens his heart to us when he says, 'I have often paused to reflect on the persistent question: how do we restore the moral and social order subjected to such horrific violence?'

A visual image of his harsh personal experience with all its dilemmas is partly captured in a recently released film *Karol: The Man who became Pope* directed by Giacomo Battiato and produced by Pietro Valsecchi (with the Polish actor, Piotr Adamczyk, playing the lead role). In describing the background to so much of Karol Woytyla's convictions about war and peace, the film brings us to realise more deeply how much as a young man, a young priest and then bishop, Karol Woytyla experienced at first hand the darkness of totalitarian regimes. It also portrays how he came to perceive the need to underline freedom and especially religious freedom and to focus on the important role of young people and families in building up a new culture of justice, truth and love.

In his last book, *Memory and Identity*, Pope John Paul returns to the theme of his personal experience and offers his own experience of the need to forgive: 'I have had personal experience of ideologies of evil. It remains indelibly fixed in my memory…We were totally swallowed up in a great eruption of evil and only gradually did we begin to realize its true nature… Both the Nazis during the war and, later, the Communists in Eastern Europe, tried to hide what they were doing from public opinion…Yet it is hard to forget the evil that has been personally experienced: one can only forgive. And what does it mean to forgive, if not to appeal to a good that is greater than evil. This good, after all, has its foundation in God alone.'[3]

After the assassination attempt on his life he also spoke of how he now knew suffering in a new way and this time too he provided eloquent testimony in extending forgiveness to his would-be assassin.

The messages for the Annual World Day of Peace, therefore, provide us with no mere theory but rather words crafted from inner convictions, the fruit of experience distilled through reflection, prayer and meditation on God's plan of salvation.

Anyone who would be interested in charting Pope John Paul II's views on social–political developments throughout his pontificate would benefit much from also studying his addresses given each year after Christmas when he met with the Diplomatic Corps of the Holy See. They provide an overview of world scenarios and suggest actions that could contribute to world peace. Again the passionate personal concern is evident.

Annual messages for World Day of Peace

Each year to mark the World Day of Peace (1 January), Pope John Paul II, continuing a tradition started by his predecessor, Pope Paul VI, issued a message on some aspect to do with peace. Cardinal Sodano who worked closely with the Pope says of these messages: 'They are almost a Christian syllabus of peace.'

In the messages published in the first years of his pontificate, John Paul took up major themes such as education for peace (1979), truth (1980), freedom (1981). Then he moved on to consider more specific issues such as dialogue (1983), solidarity (1987), religious freedom (1988), respect for creation (1990) and conscience (1991). Some of his messages focus our attention on particular categories of people who suffer from lack of peace: minorities (1989), the poor (1993) and children (1996). Others highlight particular agents of peace – young people (1985), the family (1995) and women (1995). In his messages he stresses the importance of the unity of believers in building peace (1992).

The 2002 message was particularly incisive in the dramatic context of world events post 9/11 and talk about a 'clash of civilizations': 'no peace without justice, no justice without forgiveness.' In this and the remaining messages of his last years of life, he wove the threads of his many years' teaching about peace into a reflection on what we need in order to build a civilisation of love.

In his messages, he often talks of 'going to the roots.' He himself does this in a style of writing true to his philosophical training, especially in the area of phenomenology, which attempts to go to the roots of issues by extensive reflection on the various facets of any given question. He approaches the topic of peace from different angles inviting the reader to turn over in one's mind along with him what's involved in peace, what's its cause, what's required to build it, what needs to be done now by me, by you, by us, by the communities, local, regional and international.

The general structure of each message can be divided up roughly as follows. Initially, there is a review of some major issues facing the world. This is followed by an analysis of the specific aspect of education for peace that is being proposed in the year's message with a consideration of how this aspect could contribute to the contemporary search for peace. Generally, there is an appeal to those in positions of responsibility. Each message concludes with a section dedicated to Christians providing brief but quite stimulating insights into Jesus and the theme of peace. Constant reference is made to the Letter to the Ephesians' statement that Jesus Christ 'is our peace' (*Eph* 2:14).

Pope John Paul II's social teaching concerning peace

The messages contained in this book have a 'home' in one of the most significant developments in recent years within the Catholic Church, namely, the huge development in its social teaching.[4] Recently, a new compendium of that teaching has been produced. Pope John Paul II brought new vigour and insight to the promotion of that teaching. Not least in the social teaching concerning peace.

We hear echoes of its principles throughout the 27 messages, principles such as the primacy of the human person, subsidiarity, the common good, the importance of political, civic and social participation, the universal destination of goods and the preferential option for the poor. We also hear Pope John Paul II's typical emphases – the dignity of each human being and his or her human rights, the need for social solidarity and the belief that war is always a defeat for humanity.

Mention must also be made of another context that shapes Pope John Paul II's engagement with the topic of peace – Vatican II. Documents such as *The Church in the Modern World* (*Gaudium et Spes*) and *The Declaration on Religious Liberty* (*Dignitatis humanae*) that he himself played a large part in drafting provide the renewed bases for the Church's contemporary outreach to share in humanity's joys and hopes, grief and anguish. It was Vatican II that reminded the Church that it itself is called to be a reconciled and reconciling community, a people whose identity is to be a 'sign and instrument of unity with God and unity among humankind'.

The four pillars of peace outlined by Pope John XXIII are a further source of Pope John Paul's reflections: freedom, justice, truth and love. Yet, as we have seen above, he doesn't simply come with principles from above. He allows the situations of the contemporary world to speak to us. The cry of the more than one billion four hundred million people who are living in a situation of dire poverty cannot but prompt us to move from words to action. It also urges towards a reconsideration of the models that inspire development policies.

Pope John Paul observes too how peoples and nations today seem to be striving in new ways towards unity and peace on the levels of politics, economics and culture. He desires, therefore, to engraft onto this popular movement a profound education for peace, dialogue and articulate belief in an international juridical system. What's needed is a culture where we recognise ourselves and others as 'fraternal beings'.

The deepest well-spring of all his thought, however, is the arch of divine revelation witnessed to in the Bible from the Book of Genesis to the Book of Revelation. Put succinctly, the Biblical story is one that tells of a human family created by God to exist in interdependence, harmony and distinction within unity. As children of the one Father, created in the image and likeness of God, we are all brothers and sisters created to be a gift to one another. History is humanity's journey to correspond to that plan.

God's road-map of salvation for the human family culminates in Jesus Christ. The gift of the Spirit poured out upon humankind ensures that we hear the inner voice deep within each of our hearts that directs us towards unity and peace. The reconciled space that has opened up in Jesus Christ demands of Christians especially that they engage in extending pockets of reconciled humanity so that all humankind, while respecting the created diversity of cultural and ethnic belonging, may live according to God's plan of the unity that brings peace.

War and the dignity of human life

Throughout the messages, Pope John Paul II repeats his conviction that war is a defeat for humanity. He delves into this issue in a number of ways. First and foremost is his passionate proclamation of the dignity of all human life in the context of a culture of death that seems, in the extreme cases, such as suicide bombers, to hate human life. But there are myriad forms in which the dignity of human life is ignored due to lack of social solidarity, poverty and deficient models of development. A particular contemporary feature of the culture of death that grieves the Pope is the tragic ideological justification of abortion in the name of civil progress that has taken hold also in democratically elected parliaments. He pleaded that we recognise moral and cultural sovereignty, above all, the sovereignty of the human person.

He also puts before us the devastating implications of war, both immediately during and subsequent to conflict. He stresses that in war it is the civilian population, especially children and women who suffer the most. War results in poverty and poverty, in turn, breeds war. Not only that but war gives rise to macabre scenarios, the memory of which can damage people's ability to relate, thereby giving rise to further crises at various levels.

Appropriate attempts at mediation and pacification by international and regional bodies, including non-governmental humanitarian organizations, and religious bodies, are viewed by Pope John Paul to be of the greatest importance.

The Polish Pope is no naive pacifist. In his message for the Year 2000, he recognises that it is legitimate and even obligatory to take concrete measures to disarm the attacks of an unjust aggressor where political efforts and non-violent defence prove to be of no avail. He adds, however, 'these measures must be limited in time and precise in their aims. They must be carried out in full respect for international law, guaranteed by an authority that is internationally recognized'.

Pope John Paul II advocates the fullest and best use of the

provisions of the United Nations Charter. In a plea for a renewal of international law and international institutions, he also remarks that the United Nations itself 'must offer to all its Member States an equal opportunity to be part of the decision-making process'.

The reader will note how often the Pope picks up on the new phenomenon of public opinion against war. He sees it as a sign of something new emerging in human history, a new consciousness of the need to resolve humanity's problems together. He often reiterated his opinion that the media and communications' network play an important role in this.

In an address to the Diplomatic Corps on 13 January 2003 some months before the second war in Iraq began he spoke of war as a 'defeat for humanity' and pleaded for renewed international arrangements that can ensure peaceful co-existence between individuals, nations and peoples:

> 'NO TO WAR'! War is not always inevitable. It is always a defeat for humanity. International law, honest dialogue, solidarity between States, the noble exercise of diplomacy: these are methods worthy of individuals and nations in resolving their differences...War is never just another means that one can choose to employ for settling differences between nations. As the Charter of the United Nations Organization and international law itself remind us, war cannot be decided upon, even when it is a matter of ensuring the common good, except as the very last option and in accordance with very strict conditions, without ignoring the consequences for the civilian population both during and after the military operations.

Timeliness of the messages for peace

The internationally recognized human rights advocate, Miroslav Volf, has written that 'It is not what the mainstream sociologists who followed in the footsteps of Karl Marx, Max Weber, and Emil Durkheim were predicting over the past century or so, but it happened. Instead of slowly withering away or lodging itself quietly into the privacy of worshippers' hearts, religion has emerged as an important player on the national and international scenes'.[5] As a world religious leader, Pope John Paul knew how much the world is looking expectantly to the various religions in matters concerning peace.

Recent terrorist developments and reference to an emerging 'clash of civilizations' has accentuated the need for religions to witness to an unlimited passion for the cause of peace. Pope John Paul II had that passion. He lived and spoke as a religious leader offering perspectives and insights that could enlighten those with other social, political and cultural responsibilities. He invited and joined with followers and representatives of other religions to work and proclaim peace.

His message is indeed, therefore, timely. As world leaders came together in New York in September 2005, at the largest gathering ever of political leaders, to celebrate the sixtieth anniversary of the United Nations, there was a palpable sense of the political and social need for new directions in pursuing what links peace, security, human rights and development. It has been said that many of today's approximately twenty major armed conflicts going on in nineteen locations worldwide are chapters of a 'global civil war'. International relations and domestic politics are increasingly taken up into an almost permanent mobilization that goes along with the 'global war on terrorism'.

Pope John Paul II promoted dialogue on all these concerns. During the early 1980s his messages focussed on issues resulting from the East–West tensions such as the arms race and need for disarmament. How much we still need to hear his words on nuclear non-proliferation and disarmament of weapons of mass destruction! His constantly voiced esteem for the United Nations and yet clear recognition of the need of its renewal are well worth re-meditating.

From the mid-1980s onwards the Pope increasingly highlighted the growing North–South divide as well as East–West world divide. The theme of social solidarity emerges more and more strongly. He repeatedly refers to the complex issue of poverty that results from and often leads to war. He pleads for reduction in poorer countries' international debt. Recent events such as the Live-8 concert, the 'Make Poverty History' campaign and other initiatives aimed at tackling world poverty, indicate something is stirring in humanity's consciousness in this regard.

Readers of these messages will note that Pope John Paul is offering us new political categories that should inform our dialogue concerning peace. He is inviting world leaders and all of us to let categories such as forgiveness, mutuality, solidarity, interdependence, option for the poor become dominant in our language and action as we describe and go about transforming our political and social landscape. And these categories speak to all, not least to us on the island of Ireland.

Reading this book

I have already outlined the general structure of the messages contained in this book. I believe they can be studied in a number of ways.

They can be read as meditations. By entering, as it were, into dialogue with Pope John Paul on the various themes, the reader will discover perspectives, insights and many nuggets of wisdom that throw light on contemporary world issues.

The messages can also be analysed thematically in order to learn more about the Church's social teaching concerning topics such as the conditions for peace and the just war theory as well as Pope John Paul II's views on development policies, international debt relief and international bodies such as the United Nations and the international criminal court.

Individual messages could be used by pastors, teachers and others as discussion documents. They would be suitable, for instance, for meetings of young people, women's groups, peace and justice/reconciliation groups and family groups. Teachers might integrate some messages or sections of them into religious education or programmes covering civic, social and political education.

To assist the reader, I have provided an introductory summary to each message. The purpose of each of these short summaries, printed in italics, is to give something of the flavour of the message that follows.

Pope John Paul II's concluding word – peace, forgiveness and love

This book took its title from the 2002 message for peace. It focuses on justice and forgiveness. A few years previously, in the course of the Jubilee 2000, Pope John Paul celebrated a ceremony seeking forgiveness of the Church's misdeeds throughout the centuries. It was a highpoint in a process of the healing of memory that he had begun several years previously. The 'healing of memory' that involves forgiveness was an important theme for him. We see it again in the 2002 message we read:

> True peace therefore is the fruit of justice, that moral virtue and legal guarantee which ensures full respect for rights and responsibilities, and the just distribution of benefits and burdens. But because human justice is always fragile and imperfect, subject as it is to the limitations and egoism of individuals and groups, it must include and, as it were, be completed by the *forgiveness which heals and rebuilds troubled human relations from their foundations*. This is true in circumstances great and small, at the personal level or on a wider, even international scale. Forgiveness is in no way opposed to justice, as if to forgive meant to overlook the need to right the wrong done. It is rather the fullness of justice, leading to that tranquillity of order which is much more than a fragile and temporary cessation of hostilities, involving as it does the deepest healing of the wounds which fester in human hearts. Justice and forgiveness are both essential to such healing.

It was his hope that such healing of historical memory and

forgiveness will spread as a culture also in the political arena within nations and between nations. Peace is the work of justice, yes, but it is also the work of love.

Politics is the 'love of all loves' because it is at the service of all our networks of interrelating. And the white light of love has many colours. The messages of this book are glimpses at the various shades and colours of the love that builds peace through justice and forgiveness. They offer food for thought and action to all of us, political participants in building a new universal fraternity. In his last message for peace, the Pope wrote in 2005 that overcoming evil with good is a fight that can be fought effectively only with the 'weapons of love': 'When good overcomes evil, love prevails and where love prevails, there peace prevails.'

All of this is possible because there is an original unlimited source of forgiveness – the infinite mercy of God. For Pope John Paul II, the God who is Love has a second name and it is mercy. He dedicated his second encyclical to that very theme that was so central in his whole outlook.

At the end of his life the various strands of his magisterial teaching and gestures concerning peace became more concentrated in a suffering distilled to the point of silence that touched many hearts. It was no longer his words and teachings about peace that struck as much as his very being that had become a word, a teaching: love conquers all.

Notes

1   Card. Sodano, 'Al Servizio della Pace', *Regno-documenti* 19/2003, p. 593.

2   *Economist*, 25 March 2000, p. 47.

3   Pope John Paul II, *Memory and Identity* (London, Weidenfeld & Nicolson, 2005), pp. 15–17.

4   The Pontifical Council for Justice and Peace, *The Compendium of the Social Doctrine of the Church* (Dublin: Veritas, 2005).

5   See Miroslav 'Forgiveness, Reconciliation & Justice' in Raymon G. Helmick and Rodney L. Peterson (eds), *Forgiveness and Reconciliation: Religion, Public Policy & Conflict Transformation* (Philadelphia & London: Templeton Foundation Press, 2001), p. 27.

1 January 1979

'TO REACH PEACE, TEACH PEACE'

In taking over 'the pilgrim's staff of peace' from his predecessor, Pope Paul VI, John Paul II notes the new phenomenon of public opinion that no longer tolerates the justifying of war. He points to the need, however, of a long and patient education for peace between peoples, within each country, within each neighbourhood and within each person. Such an education involves a new way of seeing world situations and looking to examples of everyday builders of peace, both individuals and families. Education for peace means re-shaping our categories of thought by learning the new language of peace in our social and political communications. Gestures of peace are, of course, essential to an education for peace. In light of the 1979 United Nations' Year of the Child *the Pope notes the original contribution of children and young people. Having lived under communism, the Pope appeals to leaders of states not to be prisoners of ideologies but rather to 'open up new doors to peace' and 'weave the political, economic and cultural fabric of peace'. He mentions issues such as the arms trade, disarmament, the need for new institutional frameworks to preserve peace. In the last part of his message he outlines the Christian vision of the world as one family of brothers and sisters. He concludes with a strong note of hope: 'Work for peace, inspired by charity which does not pass away, will produce its fruits. Peace will be the last word of History'.*

✳ ✳ ✳

20

To all of you who desire peace:

The great cause of peace between the peoples needs all the energies of peace present in man's heart. It was to the releasing and cultivation of these energies – to the training of them – that my predecessor Paul VI decided, shortly before his death, that the 1979 World Day of Peace should be dedicated:

'To Reach Peace, Teach Peace'

Throughout his pontificate, Paul VI walked with you along the difficult paths towards peace. He shared your anxiety when peace was threatened. He suffered with those engulfed by the misfortunes of war. He encouraged all efforts to restore peace. In every circumstance he kept up hope, with indomitable energy.

Convinced that peace is something built up by everyone, he launched in 1967 the idea of a World Day of Peace, with the desire that you would take it over as an undertaking of your own. Every year since then his Message offered to the leaders of the nations and of the international organizations the opportunity to renew and express publicly that which legitimizes their authority: the enabling of free, just and fraternal human beings to progress and co-exist in peace. Widely differing communities met to celebrate the inestimable benefit of peace and to affirm their willingness to defend and serve it.

I take from the hands of my revered predecessor the pilgrim's staff of peace. I am on the road, at your side, with the Gospel of peace. 'Blessed are the peacemakers.' I invite you to celebrate the World Day at the beginning of the year 1979, placing it, in accordance with the last wishes of Paul VI, under the banner of teaching peace.

I. A HARD TASK

An irrepressible aspiration

The attainment of peace is the summing-up and crowning of all our aspirations. We sense that peace is fullness and joy. To

21

achieve peace between countries, many attempts are made through bilateral or multilateral exchanges and international conferences, and some people take courageous personal initiatives to establish peace or to ward off the threat of a new war.

Confidence undermined

But at the same time, we see that individuals and groups never bring to a conclusion the settling of their secret or public conflicts. Is peace therefore an ideal beyond our grasp? The daily spectacle of war, tension and division sows doubt and discouragement. In places, the flames of discord and hatred even seem to be kindled artificially by some who do not have to pay the cost. And too often gestures of peace are ridiculously incapable of changing the course of events, even if they are not actually swept away and in the end taken over by the overbearing logic of exploitation and violence.

In one place, timidity and the difficulty of carrying out needed reforms poison relations between human groups in spite of their being united by a long or exemplary common history; new desires for power suggest recourse to the overpowering influence of sheer numbers or to brute force, in order to disentangle the situation, and this under the impotent and sometimes self-interested and compliant gaze of other countries, near or far; both the strongest and the weakest no longer place confidence in the patient procedures of peace.

Elsewhere, fear of a precarious peace, military and political imperatives, and economic and commercial interests lead to the establishment of arms stockpiles or to the sale of weapons capable of appalling destruction. The arms race then prevails over the great tasks of peace, which ought to unite peoples in new solidarity; it fosters sporadic but murderous conflicts and builds up the gravest threats. It is true that at first sight the cause of peace seems to be handicapped to a crippling extent.

From words of peace...

And yet, in nearly all public statements at the national level or that of the international organizations, rarely has there been so much talk of peace, detente, agreement, and the rational solution of conflicts in conformity with justice. Peace has become the slogan that reassures or is meant to beguile. In a sense, we do have something positive: the public opinion of the nations would no longer tolerate the justifying of war or even taking the risk of an offensive war.

... to convictions for peace

But if we are to accept the challenge presented to the whole of humanity confronted with the hard task of peace, we need more than words, whether sincere or demagogical. The true spirit of peace must make itself felt in particular at the level of the statesmen and of the groups or centres that control, more or less directly, more or less secretly, the decisive steps either towards peace or towards the prolonging of wars or situations of violence. At the least, people must agree to place their trust in a few elementary but firm principles, such as the following. Human affairs must be dealt with humanely, not with violence. Tensions, rivalries and conflicts must be settled by reasonable negotiations and not by force. Opposing ideologies must confront each other in a climate of dialogue and free discussion. The legitimate interests of particular groups must also take into account the legitimate interests of the other groups involved and of the demands of the higher common good. Recourse to arms cannot be considered the right means for settling conflicts. The inalienable human rights must be safeguarded in every circumstance. It is not permissible to kill in order to impose a solution.

Every person of good will can find these principles of humanity in his or her own conscience. They correspond to God's will for the human race. In order that these principles may become convictions in the minds of both the powerful and the weak, and in order that they may come to imbue all activity, they must have their full force restored to them. At every level, this calls for long and patient education.

II. EDUCATION FOR PEACE

Bringing Visions of Peace Before Our Minds

1.   To overcome this spontaneous feeling of impotence, an education worthy of the name must have as its first task, and produce as its first beneficent result, the ability to see beyond the unfortunate facts in the foreground, or rather to recognize, in the very midst of the raging of murderous violence, the quiet progress of peace, never giving in, untiringly healing wounds, and maintaining and advancing life. The movement towards peace will then be seen as possible and desirable, as strong and already victorious.

Rereading history

Let us first learn to reread the history of peoples and of mankind, following outlines that are truer than those of the series of wars and revolutions. Admittedly the din of battle dominates history. But it is the respites from violence that have made possible the production of those lasting cultural works which give honour to mankind. Furthermore, any factors of life and progress that may have been found even in wars and revolutions were derived from aspirations of an order other than that of violence: aspirations of a spiritual nature, such as the will to see recognition given to a dignity shared by all mankind, and the desire to save a people's soul and its freedom. Where such aspirations were present, they acted as a regulator amid the conflicts, they prevented irreparable breaks, they maintained hope, and they prepared a new chance for peace. Where such aspirations were lacking or were impaired in the heat of violence, they gave free play to the logic of destruction, which led to lasting economic and cultural retrogression and to the death of whole civilizations. Leaders of the peoples, learn to love peace by distinguishing in the great pages of your national histories and throwing into relief the example of your predecessors whose glory lay in giving growth to the fruits of peace. 'Blessed are the peacemakers.'

Esteem for the great peacemaking tasks of today

Today you will contribute to education for peace by highlighting as much as possible the great peacemaking tasks that fall to the human family. In your endeavours to reach a rational and interdependent management of mankind's common environment and heritage, to eradicate the misery crushing millions of human beings, and to strengthen institutions capable of expressing and increasing the unity of the human family on the regional and world level, men will discover the captivating appeal of peace, which means reconciliation of human beings with each other and with their natural universe. By encouraging, in spite of all the current forms of demagogy, the search for simpler ways of life that are less exposed to the tyrannical pressures of the instincts of possessing, consuming and dominating and more open to the deep rhythms of personal creativity and friendship, you will open up for yourselves and for everyone immense room for the unsuspected possibilities of peace.

The light of many different examples of peace

Just as it is inhibiting for the individual to feel that humble efforts in favour of peace, in the limited area of each one's responsibilities, are nullified by the great world debates which are held prisoner by a logic of simple relations of force and the arms race, so it is liberating to see international bodies that are convinced of the possibilities of peace and passionately attached to the building of peace. Education for peace can then benefit also from a renewed interest in the everyday examples of simple builders of peace at all levels: the individuals and families who by controlling their passions and by accepting and respecting each other gain their own inner peace and radiate it; the peoples, often poor and sorely tried, whose age-old wisdom has been forged on the anvil of the supreme good

25

of peace and who have succeeded in repeatedly resisting the deceptive seductions of rapid progress obtained by violence, convinced that such gains would bring with them the poisonous seeds of fresh conflicts.

Yes, without ignoring the drama of violence, let us bring before our eyes and those of the rising generation these visions of peace: they will exercise a decisive attraction. Above all, they will set free the aspiration for peace which is an essential part of man. These new energies will lead to the use of a new language of peace and new gestures of peace.

Speaking a Language of Peace

2.   Language is made for expressing the thoughts of the heart and for uniting. But when it is the prisoner of prefabricated formulas, in its turn it drags the heart along its own downward paths. One must therefore act upon language in order to act upon the heart and avoid the pitfalls of language.

It is easy to note to what an extent bitter irony and harshness in making judgments and in criticizing others, especially 'outsiders', and systematic contestation and insistence on our claims overrun our speech relationship and strangle both social charity and justice itself. By expressing everything in terms of relations of force, of group and class struggles, and of friends and enemies, a propitious atmosphere is created for social barriers, contempt, even hatred and terrorism and underhanded or open support for them. On the other hand, a heart devoted to the higher value of peace produces a desire to listen and understand, respect for others, gentleness which is real strength, and trust. Such a language puts one on the path of objectivity, truth and peace. In this regard the social communications media have a great educational task. The modes of expression in the exchanges and debates of political confrontations, both national and international, are also influential. Leaders of the nations and of the international organizations, learn to find a new language, a language of peace: by its very self it creates new room for peace.

Making Gestures of Peace

3.   What is set free by visions of peace and served by a language of peace must be expressed in gestures of peace. Without such gestures, budding convictions vanish, and the language of peace becomes a quickly discredited rhetoric. The builders of peace can be very numerous, if they become aware of their capabilities and responsibilities. It is the practice of peace that leads to peace. The practice of peace teaches those searching for the treasure of peace that the treasure is revealed and presented to those who produce humbly, day by day, all the forms of peace of which they are capable.

Parents, educators and young people

Parents and educators, help children and young people to experience peace in the thousands of everyday actions that are within their capacity, at home, at school, at play, with their friends, in team work, in competitive sport, and in the many ways in which friendship has to be established and restored. The International Year of the Child proclaimed by the United Nations for 1979 should draw everyone's attention to the original contribution of children to peace.

   Young people, be builders of peace. You are workers with a full share in producing this great common construction. Resist the easy ways out which lull you into sad mediocrity; resist the sterile violence in which adults who are not at peace with themselves sometimes want to make use of you. Follow the paths suggested by your sense of free giving, of joy at being alive, and of sharing. You like to utilize your fresh energies – unconfined by *a priori* discriminations – in meeting others fraternally without regard for frontiers, in learning foreign languages to facilitate communication, and in giving disinterested service to the countries with least resources. You are the first victims of war, which breaks your ardour. You are the hope of peace.

Partners in social endeavours

Participants in professional and social life, for you peace is often hard to achieve. There is no peace without justice and freedom, without a courageous commitment to promote both. The strength then demanded must be patient without yielding or flagging, firm without throwing down challenges, and prudent in actively preparing the way for the desired advances without dissipating energy in quickly fading outbursts of violent indignation. When confronted with injustice and oppression, peace is led to clear a path for itself by adopting resolute action. But this action must already bear the mark of the goal at which it is aimed, namely a better mutual acceptance of individuals and groups. It will be regulated by the desire for peace that comes from deep within man, and by the aspirations and the legislation of peoples. It is this capacity for peace, cultivated and disciplined, which provides the ability to find even in tensions and conflicts the breathing spaces that are needed for developing its fruitful and constructive logic. What happens in a country's internal social life has a considerable influence for better and for worse upon peace between nations.

Statesmen

But, we must insist once more, these many gestures of peace run the risk of being discouraged and partly nullified by an international policy that failed to find, at its own level, the same peace dynamism. Statesmen, leaders of peoples and of international organizations, I express to you my heartfelt esteem, and I offer my entire support for your often wearisome efforts to maintain or reestablish peace. Furthermore, being aware that mankind's happiness and even survival is at stake, and convinced of my grave responsibility to echo Christ's momentous appeal 'Blessed are the peacemakers', I dare to encourage you to go further. Open up new doors to peace. Do everything in your power to make the way of dialogue prevail over that of force. Let this find its first application at the inward level: how can the peoples truly foster international peace, if they themselves are prisoners of ideologies according to which justice and peace are obtained only by reducing to impotence those who, before any examination, are judged unfit to build their own destinies or incapable of cooperating for the common good? Be convinced that honour and effectiveness in negotiating with opponents are not measured by the degree of inflexibility in defending one's interests, but by the participants' capacity for respect, truth, benevolence and brotherhood or, let us say, by their humanity. Make gestures of peace, even audacious ones, to break free from vicious circles and from the deadweight of passions inherited from history. Then patiently weave the political, economic and cultural fabric of peace. Create – the hour is ripe and time presses – ever wider areas of disarmament. Have the courage to re-examine in depth the disquieting question of the arms trade. Learn to detect latent conflicts in time and settle them calmly before they arouse passions. Give appropriate institutional frameworks to regional groups and the world community. Renounce the utilization of legitimate and even spiritual values at the service of conflicts of interests, values which are then brought down to the level of these conflicts and make them more unyielding. Take care that the legitimate desire to communicate ideas is exercised through persuasion and not through the pressure of threats and arms.

By making resolute gestures of peace you will release the true aspirations of the peoples and will find in them powerful allies in working for the peaceful development of all. You will educate yourselves for peace, you will awaken in yourselves firm convictions and a new capacity for taking initiatives at the service of the great cause of peace.

III. THE SPECIFIC CONTRIBUTION BY CHRISTIANS

The importance of faith

All this education for peace – peace between peoples, in one's own country, in one's neighbourhood, and within oneself – is intended for all men and women of good will, as we are reminded by Pope John XXIII's Encyclical Letter *Pacem in Terris*. Peace is, at different degrees, within their capacities. And since 'Peace on earth... can never be established, never guaranteed, except by the diligent observance of the divinely established order' (*Pacem in Terris*, 1; AAS 55, 1963, p. 257), believers find in their religion light, motivation and strength in order to work for education to peace. True religious feeling cannot fail to promote true peace. The public authorities, by recognizing – as they should – religious liberty, favour the development of the spirit of peace at the deepest level of people's hearts and in the educational institutions fostered by believers. Christians, for their part, are especially educated by Christ and led by him to be builders of peace: 'Blessed are the peacemakers, for they shall be called children of God' (*Mt* 5: 9; cf. *Lk* 10:5, etc.). The reader will understand that I am devoting special attention at the end of this Message to the sons and daughters of the Church, in order to encourage their contribution to peace and to place it within the context of the great Plan of Peace revealed by God in Jesus Christ. The special contribution made by Christians and the Church to the work done by all will be all the better assured if it draws its nourishment from its own special sources, from its own special hope.

The Christian vision of peace

Dear Brothers and Sisters in Christ, the aspiration for peace that you share with all men and women corresponds to an initial call by God to form a single family of brothers and sisters, created in the image of the same Father. Revelation insists upon our freedom and our solidarity. The difficulties that we encounter in our journey towards peace are linked partly to our weakness as creatures, who must necessarily advance by slow and progressive steps. These difficulties are aggravated by our selfishness, by our sins of every sort, beginning with the original sin that marked a break with God, entailing a break between brothers and sisters. The image of the Tower of Babel well describes the situation. But we believe that Jesus Christ, by giving his life on the Cross, became our Peace: he broke down the wall of hate that divided the hostile brothers (cf. *Eph* 4:14). Having risen and entered into the glory of the Father, he mysteriously associates us with his Life: by reconciling us with God, he heals the wounds of sin and division and enables us to produce in our societies a rough outline of the unity that he is reestablishing in us. The most faithful disciples of Christ have been builders of peace, to the point of forgiving their enemies, sometimes even to the point of giving their lives for them. Their example marks the path for a new humanity no longer content with provisional compromises but instead achieving the deepest sort of brotherhood. We know that, without losing its natural consistency or its peculiar difficulties, our journey towards peace on earth is comprised within another journey, that of salvation, which reaches fulfilment in an eternal plenitude of grace, in total communion with God. Thus, the Kingdom of God, the Kingdom of Peace, with its own source, means and end, already permeates, without dilution, the whole of earthly activity. This vision of faith has a deep impact on the everyday action of Christians.

Christian dynamism for peace

It is true that we are advancing along the paths of peace with the weaknesses and the gropings of all those making the journey with us. With the latter we suffer from the tragic deficiencies of peace. We feel ourselves constrained to remedy them with even greater resolution, for the honour of God and for the honour of man. We do not claim to find in the Gospel text ready-made formulas for making today this or that advance towards peace. But on almost every page of the Gospel and of the history of the Church we find a spirit, that of brotherly love, powerfully teaching peace. We find, in the gifts of the Holy Spirit and in the sacraments, a strength drawn from the divine source. We find, in Christ, a hope. Setbacks cannot render vain the work of peace, even if the immediate results prove to be fragile, even if we are persecuted for our witness in favour of peace. Christ the Saviour associates with his destiny all those who work with love for peace.

Prayer for peace

Peace is our work: it calls for our courageous and united action. But it is inseparably and above all a gift of God: it requires our prayer. Christians must be in the first rank of those who pray daily for peace. They must also teach others *to pray for peace*. It will be their joy to pray with Mary, the Queen of Peace.

To everyone, Christians, believers, and men and women of good will, I say: Do not be afraid to take a chance on peace, to teach peace. The aspiration for peace will not be disappointed forever. Work for peace, inspired by charity which does not pass away, will produce its fruits. Peace will be the last word of History.

1 January 1980

TRUTH, THE POWER OF PEACE

In this message the Pope meditates on the theme of truth as a primary resource of peace because often violence is caused by various forms of non-truth. He comments on non-truths such as lies, partial or slanted information, sectarian propaganda, selective indignation, sly insinuations, manipulation of information as well as an ideological refusal of legitimate rights. He notes how blackmail and intimidation often result in individuals and groups, as well as governments and international organizations, keeping silent in helplessness and complicity in the face of violence. Above all, however, he comments: 'The first lie, the basic falsehood, is to refuse to believe in man.' In order to give peace a chance, it is necessary to help people change behaviour and attitudes by promoting sincerity and truth, calling things by their proper names: murder, torture and all forms of oppression and exploitation. It is attentiveness to the objective universal truth about man that develops men and women of peace and dialogue. Truth encourages us to count on the forces for peace that individuals and peoples have within them. Truth requires dialogue and honourable agreements. The Pope quotes his talk in Drogheda, Ireland, where he pleaded for an end to violence: 'Violence is a life...It is not the Christian way...Believe in peace and forgiveness and love; for they are of Christ'. And he ends with an invitation to 'do the truth' in gestures of forgiveness and reconciliation.

✳ ✳ ✳

To all of you who want to strengthen peace on earth,
To you, men and women of good will,
To you, citizens and leaders of the peoples,
To you, the young people of every land:

To all of you I address my message and invite you to celebrate the thirteenth World Day of Peace with a resolute effort of mind and action so as to stabilize from within the tottering and ever threatened edifice of peace by putting its content of truth back into it. Truth, the power of peace! Let us join together to strengthen peace through the resources of peace itself. The foremost resource is truth, for it is preeminently truth that is the serene and powerful driving force of peace, radiating unimpededly by its own power.

A diagnosis: non-truth serves the cause of war

1.   It is a fact, and no-one doubts it, that truth serves the cause of peace; it is also beyond discussion that non-truth in all its forms and at all levels (lies, partial or slanted information, sectarian propaganda, manipulation of the communications media, and so on) goes hand in hand with the cause of war.

Is there any need here to list all the different forms that non-truth takes? Let it suffice to give just a few examples. For, although there is justifiable disquiet at the increase of violence in national and international society and at open threats to peace, public opinion is often less sensitive to the various forms of non-truth that underlie violence and that create a fertile soil for it.

Violence flourishes in lies, and needs lies. It seeks to gain respectability in the eyes of the world by pretexts that have nothing to do with its reality and are often contradictory. What should one say of the practice of combatting or silencing those who do not share the same views by labelling them as enemies, attributing to them hostile intentions and using skilful and constant propaganda to brand them as aggressors?

Another form of non-truth consists in refusing to recognize and respect the objectively legitimate and inalienable rights of those who refuse to accept a particular ideology, or who appeal to freedom of thought. Non-truth is at work when oppressive intentions are attributed to those who clearly show that their one concern is to protect and defend themselves against real threats, threats which, alas, are still to be found both within a country and between countries.

Selective indignation, sly insinuations, the manipulation of information, the systematic discrediting of opponents – their persons, intentions and actions – blackmail and intimidation: these are forms of non-truth working to develop a climate of uncertainty aimed at forcing individuals, groups, governments, and even international organizations to keep silence in helplessness and complicity, to surrender their principles in part or to react in an irrational way. All these attitudes are equally capable of favouring the murderous game of violence and of attacking the cause of peace.

2.   Underlying all these forms of non-truth, and fostering and feeding upon them, is a mistaken ideal of man and of the driving forces within him. The first lie, the basic falsehood, is to refuse to believe in man, with all his capacity for greatness but at the same time with his need to be redeemed from the evil and sin within him.

Encouraged by differing and often contradictory ideologies, the idea is spreading that the individual and all humanity achieve progress principally through violent struggle. It has been thought that this could be demonstrated historically. Ingenious efforts have been made to build it into a theory. It has become more and more the custom to analyse everything in social and international life exclusively in terms of relationships of power and to organize accordingly in order to impose one's own interests. Of course, this widespread tendency to have recourse to trials of strength in order to make justice is often held in check by tactical or strategic pauses. But, as long as threats are permitted to remain, as long as selective support is given to certain forms of violence in line with interests or ideologies, as long as support is given to the claim that the advance of justice comes, in the final analysis, through violent struggle – as long as these things happen, then niceties, restraint and selectivity will periodically give way in the face of the simple and brutal logic of violence, a logic which can go as far as the suicidal exaltation of violence for its own sake.

Peace needs sincerity and truth

3.   With minds so confused, building up peace by works of peace is difficult. It demands that truth be restored, in order to keep individuals, groups and nations from losing confidence in peace and from consenting to new forms of violence.

Restoring peace means in the first place calling by their proper names acts of violence in all their forms. Murder must be called by its proper name: murder is murder; political or ideological motives do not change its nature, but are on the contrary degraded by it. The massacre of men and women, whatever their race, age or position, must be called by its proper name. Torture must be called by its proper name; and, with the appropriate qualifications, so must all forms of oppression and exploitation of man by man, of man by the State, of one people by another people. The purpose of doing so is not to give oneself a clear conscience by means of loud all-embracing denunciations – this would no longer be calling things by their proper names – nor to brand and condemn individuals and peoples, but to help to change people's behaviour and attitudes, and in order to give peace a chance again.

4.   To promote truth as the power of peace means that we ourselves must make a constant effort not to use the weapons of falsehood, even for a good purpose. Falsehood can cunningly creep in anywhere. If sincerity – truth with ourselves – is to be securely maintained, we must make a patient and courageous effort to seek and find the higher and universal truth about man, in the light of which we shall be able to evaluate different situations, and in the light of which we will first judge ourselves and our own sincerity. It is impossible to take up an attitude of doubt, suspicion and sceptical relativism

without very quickly slipping into insincerity and falsehood. Peace, as I said earlier, is threatened when uncertainty, doubt and suspicion reign, and violence makes good use of this. Do we really want peace? Then we must dig deep within ourselves and, going beyond the divisions we find within us and between us, we must find the areas in which we can strengthen our conviction that man's basic driving forces and the recognition of his real nature carry him towards openness to others, mutual respect, brotherhood and peace. The course of this laborious search for the objective and universal truth about man and the result of the search will develop men and women of peace and dialogue, people who draw both strength and humility from a truth that they realize they must serve, and not make use of for partisan interests.

Truth illumines the ways of peace

5.   One of violence's lies is to try to justify itself by systematically and radically discrediting opponents, their actions, and the social and ideological structures within which they act and think. But the man of peace is able to detect the portion of truth existing in every human undertaking, and moreover to discern the capacity for truth to be found within every human being.

The desire for peace does not cause the man of peace to shut his eyes to the tension, injustice and strife that are part of our world. He looks at them squarely. He calls them by their proper name, out of respect for truth. And since he is closely attuned to the things of peace, he is necessarily all the more sensitive to whatever is inconsistent with peace. This impels him to push courageously ahead and investigate the real causes of evil and injustice, in order to look for appropriate remedies. Truth is a force for peace because it sees the factors of truth that the other has – factors that share the nature of truth – and tries to link up with them.

6.   Truth does not allow us to despair of our opponents. The man of peace inspired by truth does not equate his opponent

with the error into which he sees him fall. Instead he reduces the error to its real proportions and appeals from it to man's reason, heart and conscience, in order to help him to recognize and accept truth. This gives the denunciation of injustice a specific tone: such denunciation cannot always prevent those responsible for injustice from stubbornly disregarding the obvious truth, but at least it does not set out to provoke such stubbornness, the cost of which is often paid by the victims of the injustice. One of the big lies that poison relations between individuals and groups consists in ignoring all aspects of an opponent's action, even the good and just ones, for the sake of condemning him more completely. Truth follows a different path; that is why truth does not throw away any of the chances for peace.

7.   Above all, truth gives us all the more reason not to despair of the victims of injustice. It does not allow us to drive them to the despair of resignation or violence.

It encourages us to count on the forces for peace that suffering individuals or peoples have deep within them. It believes that by confirming them in awareness of their dignity and inalienable rights it gives them the strength to exercise upon the forces of oppression effective pressure for transformation, pressure more effective than acts of violence, which generally lack any future prospect – except one of greater suffering. It is because I am convinced of this that I keep proclaiming the dignity and the rights of the person. Moreover, as I wrote in my Encyclical *Redemptor Hominis*, the logic behind the Universal Declaration of Human Rights and the very establishment of the United Nations Organization was aimed at creating 'the basis for continual revision of programmes, systems and regimes precisely from this single fundamental point of view, namely the welfare of man – or, let us say, of the person in the community' (no. 17, § 4). Since the man of peace draws from the light of truth and sincerity, he has clear ideas about existing injustices, tensions and conflicts. But instead of exacerbating frustration and strife he places his trust in man's higher faculties, his reason and his heart, in order to devise peaceful ways to a truly human and lasting result.

Truth strengthens the means of peace

8.   The path from a less human to a more human situation, both in national and in international life, is a long one, and it has to be travelled in stages. The man of peace knows this, he says so and he finds in the efforts for truth that I have just described the light he needs to keep his course set correctly. The man of violence knows it also, but he does not say so, and he deceives public opinion by holding up the glittering prospect of a radical and speedy solution, and then settles into his lie and explains away the constantly repeated delays in the arrival of the freedom that had been promised and the abundance that had been assured.

There is no peace without readiness for sincere and continual dialogue. Truth too requires dialogue, and therefore reinforces this indispensable means for attaining peace. Truth has no fear, either, of honourable agreements, because truth brings with it the light that enables it to enter into such an agreement without sacrificing essential convictions and values. Truth causes minds to come together; it shows what already unites the parties that were previously opposed; it causes the mistrust of yesterday to decrease, and prepares the ground for fresh advances in justice and brotherhood and in the peaceful co-existence of all human beings.

In this context I cannot fail to say a word about the arms race. The situation in which humanity is living today seems to include a tragic contradiction between the many fervent declarations in favour of peace and the no less real vertiginous escalation in weaponry. The very existence of the arms race can even cast a suspicion of falsehood and hypocrisy on certain declarations of the desire for peaceful coexistence. What is worse, it can often even justify the impression that such declarations serve only as a cloak for opposite intentions.

9.   We cannot sincerely condemn recourse to violence unless we engage in a corresponding effort to replace it by courageous political initiatives which aim at eliminating threats to peace by attacking the roots of injustice.

The profound truth of politics is contradicted just as much when it settles into passivity as when it hardens and degenerates into violence. Promoting the truth that gives strength to peace in politics means having the courage to detect in good time latent conflicts and to reexamine at suitable moments problems that have been temporarily defused by laws or agreements that have prevented them from getting worse. Promoting truth also means having the courage to foresee the future: to take into account the new aspirations, compatible with what is good, that individuals and peoples begin to experience as culture progresses, in order to adjust national and international institutions to the reality of humanity on the march.

Statesmen and international institutions therefore have an immense field for building a new and more just world order, based on the truth about man and established upon a just distribution not only of wealth but also of power and responsibility.

Yes, I am convinced of this: truth gives strength to peace within, and an atmosphere of greater sincerity makes it possible to mobilize human energies for the one cause that is worthy of them: full respect for the truth about man's nature and destiny, the source of true peace in justice and friendship.

For Christians: the truth of the Gospel

10.   To work for peace is the concern of all individuals and of all peoples. And because everyone is endowed with a heart and with reason and has been made in the image of God, he or she is capable of the effort of truth and sincerity which strengthens peace. I invite all Christians to bring to the common task the specific contribution of the Gospel which leads to the ultimate source of truth, to the Incarnate Word of God.

The Gospel places in striking relief the bond between falsehood and murderous violence, in the words of Christ: 'As it is, you want to kill me when I tell you the truth as I have learnt it from God ... What you are doing is what your father does ... The devil is your father, and you prefer to do what your father wants. He was a murderer from the start; he was never grounded in the truth; there is no truth in him at all; when he lies he is drawing on his own store, because he is a liar, and the father of lies' (*Jn* 8:40, 41, 44). This is why I was able to say with such conviction at Drogheda in Ireland and why I now repeat: 'Violence is a lie, for it goes against the truth of our faith, the truth of our humanity ... do not believe in violence; do not support violence. It is not the Christian way. It is not the way of the Catholic Church. Believe in peace and forgiveness and love; for they are of Christ' (nos. 9–10).

Yes, the Gospel of Christ is a Gospel of peace: 'Blessed are the peacemakers; they shall be called children of God' (*Mt* 5: 9). And the driving force of evangelical peace is truth. Jesus revealed to man the full truth about man; he restores man in the truth about himself by reconciling him with God, by reconciling him with himself and by reconciling him with others. Truth is the driving power of peace because it reveals and brings about the unity of man with God, with himself and with others. Forgiveness and reconciliation are constitutive elements of the truth which strengthens peace and which builds up peace. To refuse forgiveness and reconciliation is for us to lie and to enter into the murderous logic of falsehood.

Final appeal

11. I know that all men and women of good will can understand all this from personal experience, when they listen to the profound voice of their hearts. For this reason I invite you all, all of you who wish to strengthen peace by putting back into it its content of truth which dispels all falsehoods: join in the effort of reflection and of action which I propose to you for this thirteenth World Day of Peace by examining your own readiness to forgive and be reconciled, and by making gestures of forgiveness and reconciliation in the domain of your own family, social and political responsibilities. You will be doing the truth and the truth will make you free.

The truth will release unsuspected light and energy and give a new opportunity for peace in the world.

1 January 1981

TO SERVE PEACE, RESPECT FREEDOM

In highlighting freedom as a major way to serve peace, John Paul II is underlining one of the 'four pillars that support the house of peace' outlined by Pope John XXIII in his Encyclical, Pacem in Terris: 'Peace must be realized in truth; it must be built upon justice; it must be animated by love; it must be brought to being in freedom'. Freedom gives man his full humanity. But we need to respect true freedom. In his message the Pope outlines both the ways freedom is wounded, reduced or absent today and also the positive ways people are working to provide freedoms. Returning to what was to become a leitmotif of his pontificate, the Pope underlines how freedom is rooted in the transcendent dignity of each human being who has been endowed by God with the faculty of self-determination with regard to what is true and good. On this basis, the Pope advocates promoting free individuals in a free society, respecting the freedoms and rights of other individuals and communities. Freedom is the measure of the maturity of man and of nations. The message also reminds us of the 'counterfeits' of freedom. Opening up a universal perspective, the message affirms that the freedom of every people, nation and culture needs a worldwide consensus on this subject. He makes a plea in particular for rich countries to direct their aid towards actively eliminating absolute poverty. All of this calls for a climate of trust and responsibility, especially among Christians.

* * *

To all of you who are building peace,
To all of you who are the leaders of the nations,
To you, brothers and sisters, citizens of the world,
To you young people, who dare to dream of a better world:

It is to all of you, men and women of good will, that I address myself today, in order to invite you, on the occasion of the Fourteenth World Day of Peace (1 January 1981), to think about the state of the world and about the great cause of peace. I do this from a powerful conviction: that peace is possible, but that it is also something that has to be continually won, a good thing that has to be attained through ever renewed efforts. Each generation feels in a new way the permanent need for peace in the face of the daily problems of life. Yes, it is every day that the ideal of peace has to be made into a concrete reality by each one of us.

To serve peace, respect freedom

1. In presenting to you today the theme of freedom as the subject of your thoughts, I am following the line of Pope John XXIII in his Encyclical *Pacem in Terris*, when he put forward freedom as one of the 'four pillars that support the house of peace'. Freedom responds to a deep and widespread aspiration of the modern world, and this is shown for example by the frequency with which the term 'freedom' is used, even though not always in the same sense, by believers and non-believers, scientists and economists, those who live in democratic societies and those who live under totalitarian regimes. Each one gives the term a special nuance, and even a profoundly different meaning. As we seek to develop our service of peace, we must therefore understand clearly the real nature of this true freedom that is at one and the same time the root of peace and its fruit.

Conditions that call for a fresh examination today

2. Peace must be realized in truth; it must be built upon justice; it must be animated by love; it must be brought to

being in freedom (cf. *Pacem in Terris*). Without a deep and universal respect for freedom, peace will elude man. We have only to look around us to be convinced of this. For the spectacle that meets our eyes at the beginning of the Eighties seems hardly reassuring, although large numbers of men and women, whether ordinary citizens or leaders of society, are very worried about peace, often to the point of desperation. Their aspirations do not find realization in true peace, because of the absence of freedom, or the violation of freedom, or again because of the ambiguous or mistaken way in which freedom is exercised.

For what can be the freedom of nations, whose existence, aspirations and reactions are conditioned by fear instead of mutual trust, by oppression instead of the free pursuit of their common good? Freedom is wounded when the relationships between peoples are based not upon respect for the equal dignity of each but upon the right of the most powerful, upon the attitude of dominant blocs and upon military or political imperialism. The freedom of nations is wounded when small nations are forced to align themselves with large ones, in order to ensure their right to independent existence or to survival. Freedom is wounded when dialogue between equal partners is no longer possible, by reason of economic or financial domination exercised by privileged and powerful nations.

And within a nation, on the political level, does peace have a real chance when the free sharing in collective decisions or the free enjoyment of individual liberties is not guaranteed? There is no true freedom – which is the foundation of peace – when all powers are concentrated in the hands of a single social class, a single race or a single group, or when the common good is merged with the interests of a single party that is identified with the State. There is no true freedom when the freedoms of individuals are absorbed by a collective group 'denying all transcendence to man and his personal and collective history' (*Octogesima Adveniens*, 26). True freedom is also absent when various forms of anarchy, set up as a theory, lead to the systematic denial or challenging of all authority, leading in extreme cases to political terrorism or to blind acts of violence, whether spontaneous or organized. Nor is there any true freedom when internal security is set up as the single and supreme norm regulating relationships between authority and the citizens, as if it were the only means – or the main one – of maintaining peace. In this context, one cannot ignore the problem of systematic or selective repression – accompanied by assassination and torture, cases of disappearance or banishment – suffered by so many people, including bishops, priests, religious and Christian lay people working in the service of their neighbour.

3.   On the social level, it is hard to describe as truly free those men and women who lack the guarantee of honest and adequate employment, or all those people in country villages who are still the victims of regrettable servitude, often the heritage of a dependent past or colonial mentality. Nor is there enough freedom for those who, as the result of uncontrolled industrial, urban or bureaucratic development, find themselves caught up in a gigantic machine, in a tangle of unwanted or unmanageable procedures that leave no room for a social development worthy of man. Freedom is also reduced – and more than appears at first sight – in a society that lets itself be guided by the dogma of indefinite material growth, by the pursuit of wealth or by the arms race. The economic crisis now affecting all societies, if it is not faced with principles of another order, could easily lead to the adoption of measures that would reduce still further the measure of freedom that peace needs if it is to blossom and flourish.

At the level of the mind, freedom can also suffer from manipulation of various kinds. This is the case when the social communications media misuse their power and disregard strict objectivity. It is also the case when psychological procedures are used without regard for the dignity of the person. Moreover, freedom will always remain very incomplete, or at least hard to exercise, in the case of men, women and children for whom illiteracy constitutes a kind of daily slavery in a world that presupposes education.

At the beginning of 1981, which has been declared by the United Nations the Year of the Disabled, it is also fitting to include in this picture those of our brothers and sisters who have suffered damage to their physical or mental completeness. Is our society sufficiently aware of its duty to set in motion all means that will enable them to share more freely in life with others, to have access to the human advancement that corresponds to their rights as human beings and to their abilities, in accordance with their dignity?

Encouraging efforts already being made and praiseworthy accomplishments

4.   However, side by side with these typical examples in which more or less serious conditioning obstructs the proper exercise of freedom and could be changed, there is also another side to the picture of the modern world seeking peace in freedom, and it is a positive one. It is the image of a multitude of men and women who believe in this ideal, who are committed to placing freedom at the service of peace, to respecting it, to promoting it, to upholding and defending it, and who are ready to make the efforts and even sacrifices that this commitment demands. I am thinking of all the Heads of State, Heads of Government, politicians, international officials and civil leaders at all levels who are trying to make available to everyone the freedoms that have been solemnly proclaimed. My thoughts also go to those who know that freedom cannot be divided, and who as a result seek out, with full objectivity, in situations as they change, fresh attacks on freedom in the sphere of personal life, family life, cultural life, social and economic development and political life. I am thinking of men and women throughout the world, fired by a solidarity that knows no frontiers, for whom it is impossible, in a civilization that has become worldwide, to isolate their own freedom from the freedom that their brothers and sisters in other continents are struggling to gain and safeguard. I am thinking especially of the young people who believe that one only becomes really free by striving to obtain for others that same freedom.

Freedom is rooted in man

5.   Freedom in its essence is within man, is connatural to the human person and is the distinctive sign of man's nature. The freedom of the individual finds its basis in man's transcendent dignity: a dignity given to him by God, his Creator, and which directs him towards God. Because he has been created in God's image (cf. *Gen* 1:27), man is inseparable from freedom, that freedom which no external force or constraint can ever take away, and which constitutes his fundamental right, both as an individual and as a member of society. Man is free because he possesses the faculty of self-determination with regard to what is true and what is good. He is free because he possesses the faculty of choice, 'as moved and drawn in a personal way from within, and not by blind impulses in himself or by mere external constraint' (Constitution *Gaudium et Spes*, 17). To be free is to be able to choose and to want to choose; it is to live according to one's conscience.

[handwritten margin note: Freedom from a movement within — to live according to conscience]

Promoting free individuals in a free society

6.   Man must therefore be able to make his choices in accordance with values to which he gives his support; this is the way in which he will show his responsibility, and it is up to society to favour this freedom, while taking into account the common good.

The first and the most fundamental of these values is always man's relationship to God as expressed in his religious convictions. Religious freedom thus becomes the basis of the other freedoms. On the eve of the meeting in Madrid on European security and cooperation, I had the occasion to repeat what I have not ceased to state since the beginning of my ministry: 'Freedom of conscience and religion ... is ... a primary and inalienable right of the person; far more, to the extent that it touches upon the most intimate sphere of the spirit, one can even say that it underlies the raison d'etre, intimately anchored in each person, of the other freedoms' (Religious freedom and the final Document of Helsinki, 5: cf. *L'Osservatore Romano*, 15 November 1980).

The various authorities in society must make possible the exercise of true freedom in all its manifestations. They must endeavour to guarantee each individual's possibility of realizing his or her human potential to the full. They must allow each person a juridically protected domain of independence, so that every human being can live, individually and collectively, in accordance with the demands of his or her conscience. Moreover, this freedom is called for in the major international pacts and other documents, such as the Universal Declaration of Human Rights and the International Conventions on the same subject, as also in the vast majority of national Constitutions. This is only right, since the State, as the recipient of a mandate given by its citizens, must not only recognize the basic freedoms of individuals but also protect and foster them. The State will play this positive role by respecting the rule of law and seeking the common good in accordance with the demands of the moral law. Similarly, the freely constituted intermediate groups will make their own contribution to safeguarding and advancing these freedoms. This noble task concerns all living forces in society.

7.   But freedom is not merely a right that one claims for oneself. It is also a duty that one undertakes with regard to others. If it is really to serve peace, the freedom of each human individual and each community must respect the freedoms and rights of other individuals and communities. This respect sets a limit to freedom, but it also gives it its logic and its dignity, since we are by nature social beings.

Some kinds of 'freedom' do not really deserve the name, and we must take care to defend true freedom against various counterfeits. For example, the consumer society – that excess of goods not needed by man – can in a way constitute an abuse of freedom, when the more and more insatiable pursuit of goods is not subjected to the law of justice and of social love. Such consumerism involves a limitation of the freedom of others; and from the viewpoint of international solidarity it even affects whole societies which are unable to obtain the minimum of goods required for their essential needs. The existence of areas of absolute poverty in the world and the existence of hunger and malnutrition pose a serious question to the countries that have developed freely, without regard for those countries lacking even the minimum and perhaps at times at their expense. It could even be said that within the rich countries the uncontrolled pursuit of material goods and all kinds of services offers only an apparent increase of freedom to those who benefit from them, since it sets up as a basic human value the possession of things, instead of aiming at a certain material prosperity as the condition and means for the full development of the talents of the individual in collaboration with and in harmony with his fellowmen.

Likewise, a society built on a purely materialistic basis denies people their freedom when it submits individual freedoms to economic domination, when it represses man's spiritual creativity in the name of a false ideological harmony, when it denies people the exercise of their right of association, when in practice it reduces to nothing the power to participate in public affairs or acts in such a way that in this field individualism and civic and social non-participation become the general attitude.

Finally, true freedom is not advanced in the permissive society, which confuses freedom with licence to do anything whatever and which in the name of freedom proclaims a kind of general amorality. It is a caricature of freedom to claim that people are free to organize their lives with no reference to moral values, and to say that society does not have to ensure the protection and advancement of ethical values. Such an attitude is destructive of freedom and peace. There are many examples of this mistaken idea of freedom, such as the elimination of human life by legalized or generally accepted abortion.

Promoting free peoples in a free world

8.   Respect for the freedom of peoples and nations is an integral part of peace. Wars continue to break out and

destruction has fallen upon peoples and whole cultures because the sovereignty of a people or a nation was not respected. Every continent has seen and suffered from fratricidal wars and struggles caused by one nation's attempts to limit another's autonomy. One can even wonder if war may not become – or remain – a normal fact of our civilization, with 'limited' armed conflicts going on for long periods without exciting public concern, or with a succession of civil wars. The direct causes are many and complex: territorial expansionism, ideological imperialism for the triumph of which weapons of total annihilation are stockpiled, economic exploitation deliberately perpetuated, obsession with territorial security, ethnic differences exploited by arms dealers, and many other causes as well. Whatever their reason, these wars contain elements of injustice, contempt or hatred, and attacks on freedom. I stressed this when speaking last year to the General Assembly of the United Nations: 'The spirit of war, in its basic primordial meaning, springs up and grows to maturity where the inalienable rights of man are violated. This is a new and deeply relevant vision of the cause of peace, one that goes deeper and is more radical. It is a vision that sees the genesis, and in a sense the substance, of war in the more complex forms emanating from injustice viewed in all its various aspects: this injustice first attacks human rights and thereby destroys the organic unity of the social order and it then affects the whole system of international relations' ('Address to the United Nations', n.11 in *Insegnamenti di Giovanni Paolo II*, II.2 (1979), 530).

9.   Without a willingness to respect the freedom of every people, nation and culture, and without a worldwide consensus on this subject, it will be difficult to create the conditions for peace. But we must have the courage to believe they are possible. This presupposes a conscious public commitment on the part of each nation and its government to renounce claims and designs injurious to other nations. In

other words, it presupposes a refusal to accept any doctrine of national or cultural supremacy. There must also be a willingness to respect the internal processes of other nations, to recognize their personality within the human family, and therefore to be ready to question and correct any policy that would in fact be an interference or an exploitation in the economic, social or cultural spheres. In this context I would plead for a greater effort by the community of nations to aid young or developing nations to attain true control of their resources and self-sufficiency in food and the essential needs of life. I beg the rich countries to direct their aid with the primary aim of actively eliminating absolute poverty.

The preparation of juridical documents has its place in improving relations between nations. In order that freedom may be respected, it is also necessary to contribute to the progressive codification of the applications that flow from the Universal Declaration of Human Rights. In this matter of respecting the identity of each people, I would like to include particularly the right to see its religious traditions respected both internally and by other nations, and the right to participate in free exchanges in the religious, cultural, scientific and educational spheres.

A climate of trust and responsibility

10. The best guarantee of freedom and its real attainment depends upon the responsibility of individuals and peoples, upon the concrete efforts of each person at his own level, in his immediate environment, nationally and internationally. For freedom is not something that is given. It is something to be constantly won. It goes hand in hand with the sense of responsibility that everyone must have. One does not make people free without at the same time making them more aware of the demands of the common good and making them more responsible.

For this purpose, a climate of mutual trust must be established and strengthened. Without it freedom cannot develop. Everyone can see that this is an indispensable condition for true peace and the primary expression thereof. But, like freedom and peace, this trust is not something that is given: it is something that has to be gained, something that has to be deserved. When an individual does not accept his responsibility for the common good, when a nation does not feel that it has a share of responsibility for the destiny of the world, trust is jeopardized. This is even more so if one uses others for one's own selfish purposes, or simply indulges in manoeuvres aimed at making one's own interests prevail over the legitimate interests of others. Only trust merited by concrete action in favour of the common good will make possible, between individuals and nations, the respect for freedom which is a service to peace.

The freedom of the children of God

11.   Let me in conclusion address more especially those who are united with me in belief in Christ. Man cannot be genuinely free or foster true freedom unless he recognizes and lives the transcendence of his being over the world and his relationship with God; for freedom is always the freedom of man made in the image of his Creator. The Christian finds in the Gospel support for this conviction and a deeper understanding of it. Christ, the Redeemer of man, makes us free. The Apostle John records the words: 'if the Son makes you free, you will be free indeed' (*Jn* 8: 36). And the Apostle Paul adds: 'Where the Spirit of the Lord is, there is freedom' (2 *Cor* 3:1). To be set free from injustice, fear, constraint and suffering would be useless, if we were to remain slaves in the depths of our hearts, slaves of sin. To be truly free, man must be set free from this slavery and transformed into a new creature. The radical freedom of man thus lies at the deepest level: the level of openness to God by conversion of heart, for it is in man's heart that the roots of every form of subjection, every violation of freedom, are found. Finally for the Christian, freedom does not come from man himself: it is manifested in obedience to the will of God and in fidelity to his love. It is then that the disciple of Christ finds the strength to fight for freedom in this world. Faced by

the difficulties of this task, he will not allow himself to be driven to inertia and discouragement, for he places his hope in God, who supports and makes fruitful what is done in accordance with his Spirit.

Freedom is the measure of the maturity of man and of the nation. So I cannot end this message without renewing the urgent appeal that I made to you at the beginning: like peace, freedom is an effort to be ceaselessly renewed in order to give man his full humanity. Let us not await the peace of the balance of terror. Let us not accept violence as the way to peace. Let us instead begin by respecting true freedom: the resulting peace will be able to satisfy the world's expectations; for it will be a peace built on justice, a peace founded on the incomparable dignity of the free human being.

1 January 1982

PEACE: A GIFT OF GOD
ENTRUSTED TO US!

In the message for 1982, the year after the assassination attempt on his life, the Pope reviews the political and ideological threats to peace. He addresses the deepest threat to peace – the ignoring of God: 'Peace comes from God as its foundation.' Human responsibility is vital, and to this end the Pope notes the need for good information to ensure better self-knowledge on the part of both individuals and societies as a way towards peace. In this he sees the positive role of the media. He also commends the positive contribution of education programmes, scientific studies, the work of jurists, as well as research undertaken by psychologists and philosophers. He refers positively to cultural exchanges and initiatives in economics. He affirms the potential of political leaders for peace-building both within their own countries and on a world scale between nations. He encourages international organizations because they give experimental proof that even on a world level people are able to combine their efforts and seek peace together. While recognising the right to protect their existence and freedom by proportionate means against an unjust aggressor, the Pope refers to the issue of nuclear terror and other serious contemporary concerns, and comments that more than ever before human society is forced to provide itself with the means of consultation and dialogue needed in order to survive. In referring to Francis of Assisi he appeals to us to pray for the gift of peace.

✳ ✳ ✳

*To the young who in the world of tomorrow will make the
great decisions,*
*To the men and women who today bear responsibility for life
in society,*
To families and teachers,
To individuals and communities,
To Heads of State and Government leaders:

It is to all of you that I address this message at the dawn of the
year 1982. I invite you to reflect with me on the theme of the
new World Day: peace is a gift of God entrusted to us.

1.   This truth faces us when we come to decide our
commitments and make our choices. It challenges the whole of
humanity, all men and women who know that they are
individually responsible for one another, and together
responsible for the world.

At the end of the First World War my predecessor Pope
Benedict XV devoted an Encyclical to this theme. Rejoicing at
the cessation of hostilities and insisting on the need to remove
hatred and enmity through reconciliation inspired by mutual
charity, he began his Encyclical with a reference to 'peace, *that
magnificent gift from God*: as Augustine says, "even understood
as one of the fleeting things of earth, no sweeter word is heard,
no more desirable wish is longed for, and no better discovery can
be made than this gift" (*De Civitate Dei*, lib. XIX, c. x1)'
(Encyclical *Pacem Dei Munus: AAS* 12 [1920], p. 209).

Efforts for peace in a divided world

2.   Since then my predecessors have often had to recall this
truth in their constant endeavours to educate for peace and to
encourage work for a lasting peace. Today peace has become,
throughout the world, a major preoccupation not only for
those responsible for the destiny of nations but even more so
for broad sections of the population and numberless
individuals who generously and tenaciously dedicate
themselves to creating an outlook of peace and to establishing

genuine peace between peoples and nations. This is comforting. But there is no hiding the fact that, in spite of the efforts of all men and women of good will *there are still serious threats to peace in the world*. Some of these threats take the form of divisions within various nations; others stem from deep-rooted and acute tensions between opposing nations and blocs within the world community.

In reality, the confrontations that we witness today are distinguished from those of past history by certain new characteristics. In the first place, they are *worldwide*: even a local conflict is often an expression of tensions originating elsewhere in the world. In the same way, it often happens that a conflict has profound effects far from where it broke out. Another characteristic is *totality*: present-day tensions mobilize all the forces of the nations involved; moreover, selfish monopolization and even hostility are to be found today as much in the way economic life is run and in the technological application of science as in the way that the mass media or military resources are utilized. Thirdly, we must stress the *radical* character of modern conflicts: it is the survival of the whole human race that is at stake in them, given the destructive capacity of present-day military stockpiles.

In short, while many factors could contribute to uniting it, human society appears as a divided world: the forces for unity give way before the divisions between East and West, North and South, friend and enemy.

An essential problem

3.   The causes of this situation are of course complex and of various orders. *Political reasons* are naturally the easiest to distinguish. Particular groups abuse their power in order to impose their yoke on whole societies. An excessive desire for expansion impels some nations to build their prosperity with a disregard for – indeed at the expense of – others' happiness. Unbridled nationalism thus fosters plans for domination, which leave other nations with the pitiless dilemma of having to make the choice: either accepting satellite status and dependence or

adopting an attitude of competition and hostility. Deeper analysis shows that the cause of this situation is the application of certain concepts and *ideologies* that claim to offer the only foundation of the truth about man, society and history.

When we come up against the choice between peace and war, we find ourselves face to face with ourselves, with our nature, with our plans for our personal and community lives, with the use we are to make of our freedom. Are relationships between people to continue inexorably along lines of incomprehension and merciless confrontation, because of a relentless law of human life? Or are human beings – by comparison with the animal species which fight one another according to the 'law' of the jungle – specifically called upon and given the fundamental capability to live in peace with their fellows and to share with them in the creation of culture, society and history? In the final analysis, when we consider the question of peace, we are led to consider the meaning and conditions of our own personal and community lives.

Peace, a gift of God

4. Peace is not so much a superficial balance between diverging material interests – a balance pertaining to the order of quantity, of things. Rather it is, in its inmost reality, something that belongs to the essentially human order, the order of human subjects; it is thus of a rational and moral nature, the fruit of truth and virtue. It springs from the dynamism of free wills guided by reason towards the common good that is to be attained in truth, justice and love. This *rational and moral order* is based on a decision by the consciences of human beings seeking harmony in their mutual relationships, with respect for justice for everybody, and therefore with respect for the fundamental human rights inherent in every person. One cannot see how this moral order could ignore God, the first source of being, the essential truth and the supreme good.

In this very sense peace comes from God as its *foundation*: it is a gift of God. When claiming the wealth and resources of the universe worked on by the human mind – and it is often on their account that conflicts and wars have sprung up – 'man comes up against the leading role of the gift made by "nature", that is to say, in the final analysis, by the Creator' (Encyclical *Laborem Exercens*, 12). And God does more than *give creation* to humanity to administer and develop jointly at the service of all human beings without any discrimination: he also *inscribes in the human conscience* the laws obliging us to respect in numerous ways the life and the whole person of our fellow human beings, created like us in the image and after the likeness of God. God is thus *the guarantor* of all these fundamental human rights. Yes indeed, God is the source of peace: he calls to peace, he safeguards it, and he grants it as the fruit of 'justice'.

Moreover, God *helps* us interiorly to achieve peace or to recover it. In our limited life, which is subject to error and evil, we human beings go gropingly in search of peace, amid many difficulties. Our faculties are darkened by mere appearances of truth, attracted by false goods and led astray by irrational and selfish instincts. Hence we need to open ourselves to the transcendent light of God that illuminates our lives, purifies them from error and frees them from aggressive passion. God is not far from the heart of those who pray to him and try to fulfil his justice: when they are in continual dialogue with him, in freedom, God offers them peace as the fullness of the communion of life with God and with their brothers and sisters. In the Bible the word 'peace' recurs again and again in association with the idea of happiness, harmony, well-being, security, concord, salvation and justice, as the outstanding blessing that God, 'the Lord of peace' (2 *Thess* 3:16), already gives and promises in abundance: 'Now towards her I send flowing peace, like a river' (*Is* 66:12).

A gift of God, entrusted to us

5.   While peace is a gift, man is never dispensed from responsibility for seeking it and endeavouring to establish it by individual and community effort, throughout history. God's

gift of peace is therefore also at all times a human conquest and achievement, since it is offered to us in order that we may accept it freely and put it progressively into operation by our creative will. Furthermore, in his love for man, God never abandons us but even in the darkest moments of history drives us forward or leads us back mysteriously along the path of peace. Even the difficulties, failures and tragedies of the past and the present must be studied as providential lessons from which we may draw the wisdom we need in order to find new ways, more rational and courageous ways, for building peace. It is by drawing inspiration from the truth of God that we are given the ideal and the energy we require in order to overcome situations of injustice, to free ourselves from ideologies of power and domination, and to make our way towards true universal fraternity.

Christians, faithful to Christ who proclaimed 'the Good News of peace' and established peace within hearts by reconciling them with God, have still more decisive reasons – as I shall stress at the end of this message – for looking on peace as a gift of God, and for courageously helping to establish it in this world, in accordance with this longing for its complete fulfilment in the Kingdom of God. They also know that they are called upon to join their efforts with those of *believers in other religions* who tirelessly condemn hatred and war and who devote themselves, using different approaches, to the advancement of justice and peace.

We should first consider in its natural basis this deeply hopeful view of humanity as directed towards peace, and stress moral responsibility in response to God's gift. This illuminates and stimulates man's activity on the level of information, study and commitment for peace, three sectors that I would now like to illustrate with some examples.

Information

6. At a certain level, world peace depends on better self-knowledge on the part of both individuals and societies. This self-knowledge is naturally conditioned by information and by

the quality of the information. Those who seek and proclaim the truth with respect for others and with charity are working for peace. Those who devote themselves to pointing out the values in the various cultures, the individuality of each society and the human riches of individual peoples, are working for peace. Those who by providing information remove the barrier of distance, so that we feel truly concerned at the fate of faraway men and women who are victims of war or injustice, are working for peace. Admittedly, the accumulation of such information, especially if it concerns catastrophes over which we have no control, can in the end produce indifference and surfeit in those who remain mere receivers of the information without ever doing whatever is within their power. But, in itself, the role of the mass media continues to be a positive one: each one of us is now called upon to be the neighbour of all his or her brothers and sisters of the human race (cf. *Lk* 10:29–37).

High-quality information even has a direct influence upon education and political decisions. If the young are to be made aware of the problems of peace, and if they are to prepare to become workers for peace, educational programmes must necessarily give a special place to information about actual situations in which peace is under threat, and about the conditions needed for its advancement. Peace cannot be built by the power of rulers alone. Peace can be firmly constructed only if it corresponds to the resolute determination of all people of good will. Rulers must be supported and enlightened by a public opinion that encourages them or, where necessary, expresses disapproval. Consequently, it is also right that rulers should explain to the public those matters that concern the problems of peace.

Studies that help to build peace

7.   Building peace also depends upon the progress of research about it. Scientific studies on war, its nature, causes, means, objectives and risks have much to teach us on the conditions for peace. Since they throw light on the relationships between war and politics, such studies show that

there is a greater future in negotiation than in arms for settling conflicts.

It follows that the role of law in preserving peace is called upon to expand. It is well known that within individual States the work of *jurists* contributes greatly to the advancement of justice and respect for human rights. But their role is just as great for the pursuit of the same objectives on the international level and for refining the juridical instruments for building and preserving peace.

However, since concern for peace is inscribed in the inmost depths of our being, progress along the path of peace also benefits from the researches of *psychologists* and *philosophers*. Admittedly, the science of war has already been enriched by studies on human aggressiveness, death-impulses and the herd instinct that can suddenly take possession of whole societies. But much remains to be said about the fear we human beings have of taking possession of our freedom, and about our insecurity before ourselves and others. Better knowledge of life-impulses, of instinctive sympathy with other people, of readiness to love and share, undoubtedly helps us to grasp better the psychological mechanisms that favour peace.

By these researches psychology is thus called upon to throw light on and to complement the studies of the philosophers. Philosophers have always pondered the questions of war and peace. They have never been without responsibility in this matter. The memory is all too much alive of those famous philosophers who saw man as 'a wolf for his fellow man' and war as a historical necessity. However, it is also true that many of them wished to lay the foundation for a lasting or even everlasting peace by, for instance, setting forth a solid theoretical basis for international law.

All these efforts deserve to be resumed and intensified. The thinkers who devote themselves to such endeavours can benefit from the copious contribution of a present-day philosophical current that gives unique prominence to the theme of the person and devotes itself in a singular manner to an examination of the themes of freedom and responsibility. This can provide light for reflection on human rights, justice and peace.

Indirect action

8.   While the advancement of peace in a sense depends on information and research, it rests above all on the action that people take in its favour. Some forms of action envisaged here have only an indirect relationship with peace. However, it would be wrong to think of them as unimportant: as we shall briefly indicate through some examples, almost every section of human activity offers unexpected occasions for advancing peace.

Such is the case of *cultural exchanges*, in the broadest sense. Anything that enables people to get to know each other better through artistic activity breaks down barriers. Where speech is unavailing and diplomacy is an uncertain aid, music, painting, drama and sport can bring people closer together. The same holds for *scientific research*: science, like art, creates and brings together a universal society which gathers all who love truth and beauty, without division. Thus science and art are, each at its own level, an anticipation of the emergence of a universal peaceful society.

Even *economic life* should bring people closer together, by making them aware of the extent to which they are interdependent and complementary. Undoubtedly, economic relationships often create a field of pitiless confrontation, merciless competition and even sometimes shameless exploitation. But could not these relationships become instead relationships of service and solidarity, and thereby defuse one of the most frequent causes of discord?

Justice and peace within nations

9.   While peace should be everyone's concern, the building of peace is a task that falls directly and principally to *political leaders*. From this point of view the chief setting for the building up of peace is always the nation as a politically

organized society. Since the purpose for which a political society is formed is the establishment of justice, the advancement of the common good and participation by all, that society will enjoy peace only to the extent that these three demands are respected. Peace can develop only where the elementary requirements of justice are safeguarded.

Unconditional and effective respect for each one's imprescriptible and inalienable rights is the necessary condition in order that peace may reign in a society. Vis-a-vis these basic rights all others are in a way derivatory and secondary. In a society in which these rights are not protected, the very idea of universality is dead, as soon as a small group of individuals set up for their own exclusive advantage a principle of discrimination whereby the rights and even the lives of others are made dependent on the whim of the stronger. Such a society cannot be at peace with itself: it has within it a principle leading to division. For the same reason, a political society can really collaborate in building international peace only if it is itself peaceful, that is to say if it takes seriously the advancement of human rights at home. To the extent that the rulers of a particular country apply themselves to building a fully just society, they are already contributing decisively to building an authentic, firmly based and lasting peace (cf. Encyclical *Pacem in Terris*, 11).

Justice and peace between nations

10.   While peace within individual nations is a necessary condition for the development of true peace, it is not enough in itself. The building of peace on a world scale cannot be the result of the separate desires of nations, for they are often ambiguous and sometimes contradictory. It was to make up for this lack that States provided themselves with appropriate *international organizations*, one of the chief aims of which is to harmonize the desires of different nations and cause them to converge for the safeguarding of peace and for an increase of justice between nations.

By the authority that they have gained and by their achievements, the great International Organizations have done remarkable work for peace. They have of course had failures; they have not been able to prevent all conflicts or put a speedy end to them. But they have helped to show the world that war, bloodshed and tears are not the way to end tensions. They have provided, so to speak, experimental proof that even on the world level people are able to combine their efforts and seek peace together.

The peace dynamism of Christianity

11.   At this point in my message I wish to address more especially my brothers and sisters in the Church. The Church supports and encourages all serious efforts for peace. She unhesitatingly proclaims that the activity of all those who devote the best of their energies to peace forms part of God's plan of salvation in Jesus Christ. But she reminds Christians that they have still greater reasons for being active witnesses of God's gift of peace.

In the first place, Christ's word and example have given rise to new attitudes in favour of peace. Christ has taken the ethics of peace far beyond the ordinary attitudes of justice and understanding. At the beginning of his ministry he proclaimed: 'Blessed are the peacemakers, for they shall be called children of God' (*Mt* 5:9). He sent his disciples to bring peace from house to house, from town to town (*Mt* 10:11–13). He exhorted them to prefer peace to vengeance of any kind and even to certain legitimate claims on others – so great was his desire to tear from the human heart the roots of aggressiveness (*Mt* 5:38–42). He asked them to love those whom barriers of any sort have turned into enemies (*Mt* 5:43–48). He set up as examples people who were habitually despised (*Lk* 10:33; 17:16). He exhorted people to be always humble and to forgive without any limit (cf. *Mt* 18:21–22). The attitude of sharing with those in utter want – on which he made the last judgment hinge (cf. *Mt* 25:31–46) – was to make a radical contribution to the establishment of relations of fraternity.

These appeals of Jesus and his example have had a widespread influence on the attitude of his disciples, as two millennia of history testify. But Christ's work belongs to a very deep level, of the order of a mysterious transformation of hearts. He really brought 'peace among men with whom God is pleased' in the words of the proclamation made at his birth (cf. *Lk* 2:14), and this not only by revealing to them the Father's love but above all by reconciling them with God through his sacrifice. For it was sin and hatred that were an obstacle to peace with God and with others: he destroyed them by the offering of his life on the Cross; he reconciled in one body those who were hostile (cf. *Eph* 2:16; *Rom* 12:5). His first words to his Apostles after he rose were: 'Peace be with you' (*Jn* 20:19). Those who accept the faith form in the Church a prophetic community: with the Holy Spirit communicated by Christ, after the Baptism that makes them part of the Body of Christ, they experience the peace given by God in the sacrament of Reconciliation and in Eucharistic communion; they proclaim 'the gospel of peace' (*Eph* 6:15); they try to live it from day to day, in actual practice; and they long for the time of total reconciliation when, by a new intervention of the living God who raises the dead, we shall be wholly open to God and our brothers and sisters. Such is the vision of faith which supports the activity of Christians on behalf of peace.

Thus, by her very existence, the Church exists within the world as a society of people who are reconciled and at peace through the grace of Christ, in a communion of love and life with God and with all their brothers and sisters, beyond human barriers of every sort; in herself she is already, and she seeks to become ever more so in practice, a gift and leaven of peace offered by God to the whole of the human race. Certainly, the members of the Church are well aware that they are often still sinners, in this sphere too; at least they feel the grave responsibility of putting into practice this gift of peace. For this they must first overcome their own divisions, in order to set out without delay towards the fullness of unity in Christ; thus they collaborate with God in order to offer his peace to

65

the world. They must also of course combine their efforts with the efforts of all men and women of good will working for peace in the different spheres of society and international life. The Church wishes her children to join, through their witness and their initiatives, the first rank of those preparing peace and causing it to reign. At the same time, she is very aware that, on the spot, it is a difficult task, one that calls for much generosity, discernment and hope, as a real challenge.

Peace as a constant challenge to Christians

12.   Christian optimism, based on the glorious Cross of Christ and the outpouring of the Holy Spirit, is no excuse for self-deception. For Christians, peace on earth is always a challenge, because of the presence of sin in man's heart. Motivated by their faith and hope, Christians therefore apply themselves to promoting a more just society; they fight hunger, deprivation and disease; they are concerned about what happens to migrants, prisoners and outcasts (cf. *Mt* 25:35–36). But they know that, while all these undertakings express something of the mercy and perfection of God (cf. *Lk* 6:36; *Mt* 4:48), they are always limited in their range, precarious in their results and ambiguous in their inspiration. Only God the giver of life, when he unites all things in Christ (cf. *Eph* 1:10), will fulfil our ardent hope by himself bringing to accomplishment everything that he has undertaken in history according to his Spirit in the matter of justice and peace.

Although Christians put all their best energies into preventing war or stopping it, they do not deceive themselves about their ability to cause peace to triumph, nor about the effect of their efforts to this end. They therefore concern themselves with all human initiatives in favour of peace and very often take part in them; but they regard them with realism and humility. One could almost say that they 'relativize' them in two senses: they relate them both to the sinful condition of humanity and to God's saving plan. In the first place, Christians are aware that plans based on aggression, domination and the manipulation of others lurk in human hearts, and sometimes even secretly nourish human intentions, in spite of certain declarations or manifestations of a pacifist nature. For Christians know that in this world a totally and permanently peaceful human society is unfortunately a utopia, and that ideologies that hold up that prospect as easily attainable are based on hopes that cannot be realized, whatever the reason behind them. It is a question of a mistaken view of the human condition, a lack of application in considering the question as a whole; or it may be a case of evasion in order to calm fear, or in still other cases a matter of calculated self-interest. Christians are convinced, if only because they have learned from personal experience, that these deceptive hopes lead straight to the false peace of totalitarian regimes. But this realistic view in no way prevents Christians from working for peace; instead, it stirs up their ardour, for they also know that Christ's victory over deception, hate and death gives those in love with peace a more decisive motive for action than what the most generous theories about man have to offer; Christ's victory likewise gives a hope more surely based than any hope held out by the most audacious dreams.

This is why Christians, even as they strive to resist and prevent every form of warfare, have no hesitation in recalling that, in the name of an elementary requirement of justice, peoples have a right and even a duty to protect their existence and freedom by proportionate means against an unjust aggressor (cf. Constitution *Gaudium et Spes*, 79). However, in view of the difference between classical warfare and nuclear or bacteriological war a difference so to speak of nature and in view of the scandal of the arms race seen against the background of the needs of the Third World, this right, which is very real in principle, only underlines the urgency for world society to equip itself with effective means of negotiation. In this way the nuclear terror that haunts our time can encourage us to enrich our common heritage with a very simple discovery that is within our reach, namely that war is the most barbarous and least effective way of resolving conflicts. More than ever before, human society is forced to provide itself with the means of consultation and dialogue which it needs in order to survive, and therefore with the institutions necessary for building up justice and peace.

May it also realize that this work is something beyond human powers!

Prayer for peace

13.　Throughout this message, I have appealed to the responsibility of people of good will, especially Christians, because *God has indeed entrusted peace to men and women.* With the realism and hope that faith makes possible, I have tried to draw the attention of citizens and leaders to a certain number of achievements or attitudes that are already feasible and capable of giving a solid foundation to peace. But, over and above or even in the midst of this necessary activity, which might seem to depend primarily on people, *peace is above all a gift of God* – something that must never be forgotten – and must always be implored from his mercy.

This conviction is certainly seen to have animated people of all civilizations who have given peace the first place in their prayers. Its expression is found in all religions. How many men, having experienced murderous conflicts and concentration camps, how many women and children, distressed by wars, have in times past turned to the God of peace! Today, when the perils have taken on a seriousness all their own by reason of their extent and radical nature, and when the difficulties of building peace have taken on a new nature and seem often insoluble, many individuals may spontaneously find themselves resorting to prayer, even though prayer may be something unfamiliar.

Yes, our future is in the hands of God, who alone gives true peace. And when human hearts sincerely think of work for peace it is still God's grace that inspires and strengthens those thoughts. All people are in this sense invited to echo the sentiments of Saint Francis of Assisi, the eighth-century saint whose birth we are celebrating: Lord, make us instruments of your peace: where there is hatred, let us sow love; where there is injury, pardon; when discord rages, let us build peace.

Christians love to pray for peace, as they make their own the prayer of so many psalms punctuated by supplications for peace and repeated with the universal love of Jesus. We have here a shared and very profound element for all ecumenical activities. Other believers all over the world are also awaiting from Almighty God the gift of peace, and, more or less consciously, many other people of good will are ready to make the same prayer in the secret of their hearts. May fervent supplications thus rise to God from the four corners of the earth! This will already create a fine unanimity on the road to peace. And who could doubt that God will hear and grant this cry of his children: Lord, grant us peace! Grant us your peace!

1 January 1983

DIALOGUE FOR PEACE:
A CHALLENGE FOR OUR TIME

Taking people's aspiration for peace and dialogue ('What political party will not include in its programme the quest for peace?') as his starting point, the Pope encourages the introduction of mechanisms and phases of dialogue wherever peace is threatened in families, society, between countries and between blocs of countries. He tells us there have been 150 armed conflicts since World War II. Despite other views to the contrary, the Pope reaffirms his belief that, through constantly renewed confidence in the human person's social nature and human dignity, as well as by constantly beginning again, true dialogue is possible. He provides a stimulating list of the qualities of true dialogue and urges 'a wager upon the social nature of people.' He examines obstacles to the dialogue for peace. Since dialogue on the national level is now achieving positive results in many countries, he proposes applying dialogue also on the international level. Human rights, justice between peoples, economics, disarmament and the common international good are listed as the object of international dialogue. He hopes for an international juridical system. In reaffirming his confidence in the leaders and members of international organizations he asserts his belief that these organizations can become places and instruments par excellence for true dialogue. Finally, he explains how Christians are particularly called to take up the challenges of dialogue.

* * *

1.　In the threshold of the New Year 1983, for the sixteenth World Day of Peace, I present to you this message on the theme *Dialogue for Peace, a challenge for our time*. I am addressing it to all those who are, on the one hand, a people responsible for peace: those who preside over the destiny of peoples, international officials, politicians, diplomats. But I am also addressing it to the citizens of each country. All are in fact called by the need to prepare true peace, to maintain it or to reestablish it, on solid and just foundations. Now I am deeply convinced that dialogue – true dialogue – is an essential condition for such peace. Yes, this dialogue is necessary, not only opportune. It is difficult, but it is possible, in spite of the obstacles that realism obliges us to consider. It therefore represents a true challenge, which I invite you to take up. And I do this without any other purpose than that of contributing, myself and the Holy See, to peace, by taking very much to heart the destiny of humanity, as the heir of the message of Christ and as the first one responsible for that message, which is above all a message of Peace for all men.

People's aspiration for peace and dialogue

2.　I am sure that in this I am voicing *the basic aspiration* of the men and women of our time. Is not this desire for peace affirmed by all leaders in their good wishes to their nations or in the declarations which they address to other countries? What political party will abstain from including in its programme the quest for peace? As for the International Organizations, they were created to promote and guarantee peace, and they maintain this objective in spite of setbacks. Public opinion itself, when it is not artificially aroused by some passionate feeling of pride or unjust frustration, opts for peaceful solutions. In addition, more and more movements work, even with a lucidity or sincerity that can sometimes leave much to be desired, in order to cause people to realize the need to eliminate, not only all war, but everything which can lead to war. Citizens, in general, wish there to be a climate of peace which will guarantee their search for well-being, particularly when they find themselves faced – as in our own days – by an economic crisis which threatens all workers.

But it would be necessary to go to the logical conclusion of this aspiration, which is happily very widespread: peace will not be established, nor will it be maintained, unless one takes the means. And the means par excellence is adopting an attitude of dialogue, that is of patiently introducing the mechanisms and phases of dialogue wherever peace is threatened or already compromised, in families, in society, between countries or between blocs of countries.

Past experience shows the importance of dialogue

3.   *The experience of history*, even recent history, shows in fact that dialogue is necessary for true peace. It would be easy to find cases where the conflict seemed fatal, but where war was avoided or abandoned, because the parties believed in the value of dialogue and practised this dialogue, in the course of long and honest discussions. On the contrary, where there have been conflicts – and, contrary to a widespread opinion, one can, alas, number more than a hundred and fifty armed conflicts since the Second World War – it was that dialogue did not really take place, or that it was falsified, made into a snare, or deliberately reduced. The year which has just ended has once more offered the spectacle of violence and war. People have shown that they preferred to use their arms rather than to try to understand one another. Yes, side by side with signs of hope, the year 1982 will leave in many human families a memory of desolation and ruin, a bitter taste of tears and death.

Dialogue for peace is necessary

4.   Now, who then would dare to make light of such wars, some of which are still going on, or of states of war, or of the deep frustrations that wars leave behind? Who would dare to envisage, without trembling, yet more extensive and much more terrible wars, which still threaten? Is it not necessary *to give everything in order to avoid war*, even the 'limited war'

thus euphemistically called by those who are not directly concerned in it, given the evil that every war represents its price that has to be paid in human lives, in suffering, in the devastation of what would be necessary for human life and development, without counting the upset of necessary tranquillity, the deterioration of the social fabric, the hardening of mistrust and hatred which wars maintain towards one's neighbour?

And today when even conventional wars become so murderous, when one knows the tragic consequences that nuclear war would have, the need to stop war or to turn aside its threat is all the more imperious. And thus we see as more fundamental the *need to have recourse to dialogue*, to its political strength, which must avoid recourse to arms.

Dialogue for peace is possible

5.   But some people today, who consider themselves realists, are doubtful about the possibility of dialogue and its effectiveness, not least when the positions are so tense and irreconcilable that they seem to allow no space for any agreement. How many negative experiences, how many repeated setbacks, would seem to support this disillusioned viewpoint!

And yet, *dialogue for peace is possible*, always possible. It is not a utopia. Moreover, even when dialogue has not seemed possible, and when one has come to the point of armed confrontation, has it not been necessary, after all, after the devastation of war, which has shown the power of the conqueror, but has resolved nothing regarding the rights which were contested, has it not been necessary to seek for dialogue? To tell the truth the conviction which I am affirming here does not repose upon this fatality, but upon a reality: on a consideration of *the profound nature of the human person*. Those who share the Christian faith will be more easily persuaded of this, even if they also believe in the congenital weakness and sin which mocks the human heart since the beginning. But every person, whether a believer or not, while

73

remaining prudent and clearsighted concerning the possible hardening of his brother's heart, can and must preserve enough confidence in man, in his capacity of being reasonable, in his sense of what is good, of justice, of fairness, in his possibility of brotherly love and hope, which are never totally perverted, in order to aim at recourse to dialogue and to the possible resumption of dialogue. Yes, people are finally capable of overcoming divisions, conflicts of interests, even if the oppositions would seem radical ones – especially when each party is convinced that it is defending a just cause – if they believe in the virtue of dialogue, if they accept to meet face to face to seek a peaceful and reasonable solution for conflicts. It is even more necessary that they should not allow themselves to be discouraged by real or apparent failures. It is all the more necessary that they should consent to begin again ceaselessly to propose true dialogue – by removing obstacles and by eliminating the defects of dialogue which I shall speak about later – and to travel to the end this single road which leads to peace, with all its demands and conditions.

The virtues of true dialogue

6.   I therefore consider it useful to recall at this point the *qualities of true dialogue*. They apply in the first place to dialogue between individuals. But I am thinking also and especially of dialogue between social groups, between political forces in a nation, between States within the international community. They also apply to dialogue between the vast human groupings which are distinguished from one another and which face one another on the levels of race, culture, ideology or religion. So the students of warfare recognize that most conflicts find their roots here, at the same time as being connected with the great present day antagonisms of East–West on the one hand, North–South on the other.

Dialogue is a central and essential element of ethical thinking among people, whoever they may be. Under the aspect of an exchange, of communication between human beings that language makes possible, it is in fact a common quest.

Basically, it presupposes the *search for what is true, good and just* for every person, for every group and every society, in the grouping which one is a member of or in the grouping which presents itself as the opposing one.

It therefore demands first of all *openness and welcome*: that each party should explain its thoughts, but should also *listen* to the explanation of the situation such as the other party describes it, sincerely feels it, with the real problems which are proper to the party, its rights, the injustices of which it is aware, the reasonable solutions which it suggests. How could peace become established while one party has not even taken the trouble to consider the conditions of the other party's existence!

To engage in dialogue thus presupposes that each party should accept the *difference* and the *specific nature* of the other party. It also presupposes that each party should become really aware of what separates it from the other, and that it should assume it, with a risk of tension that comes from it, without renouncing through cowardice or constraint what it knows to be true and just, for this would result in a shaky compromise. And, on the other hand, one should not attempt to reduce the other party to a mere object, but one should consider the party to be an intelligent, free and responsible subject.

Dialogue is at the same time the search for what is and *which remains common to people*, even in the midst of tensions, opposition and conflicts. In this sense, it is to make the other party a neighbour. It is to accept its contribution, it is to share with it responsibility before truth and justice. It is to suggest and to study all the possible formulas for honest reconciliation, while being able to link to the just defence of the interests and honour of the party which one represents the no less just understanding and respect for the reasons of the other party, as well as the demands of the general good which is common to both.

Furthermore, is it not more and more obvious that all the peoples of the earth find themselves in a situation of mutual interdependence on the economic, political and cultural levels?

Anyone who attempted to free himself from this solidarity would soon suffer from it: himself.

Finally, true dialogue is the search for what is good by peaceful means. It is the persistent determination to have recourse to all the possible formulas of negotiation, mediation and arbitration, to act in such a way that the factors which bring people together will be victorious over the factors of division and hate. It is a recognition of the inalienable dignity of human beings. It rests upon respect for human life. It is a *wager upon the social nature of people*, upon their calling to go forward together, with continuity, by a converging meeting of minds, wills, hearts, towards the goal that the Creator has fixed for them. This goal is to make the world a place for everybody to live in and worthy of everybody.

The political virtue of such a dialogue could not fail to bear fruit for peace. My esteemed predecessor Paul VI devoted to dialogue a large part of his first Encyclical *Ecclesiam Suam*. He wrote: 'Openness to dialogue which is disinterested, objective and frank, is in itself a declaration in favour of free and honest peace. It excludes pretense, rivalry, deceit and betrayal' (*AAS* 56, 1964, p. 654). This virtue of dialogue demands of the political leaders of today much clearsightedness, honesty and courage, not only with regard to other peoples, but with regard to the public opinion of their own people. It presupposes often a true conversion. But there is no other possibility in the face of the threat of war. And once again, it is not an illusion. It would be easy to quote those of our contemporaries who have gained honour by practising it thus.

Obstacles to dialogue, false forms of dialogue

7.   On the other hand, it seems to me salutary also to condemn *particular obstacles to the dialogue for peace*.

I am not speaking about the difficulties inherent in political dialogue such as the frequent difficulty of reconciling concrete interests which oppose one another; there is also the frequent difficulty of emphasizing too precarious conditions of existence without being able to point to injustice properly speaking on the part of others.

I am thinking of what *damages or prevents the normal process of dialogue*. I have already let it be understood that dialogue is blocked by an a priori decision to concede nothing, by a *refusal to listen,* by a claim to be – oneself and only oneself – the measure of justice. This attitude can coneeal quite simply the blind and deaf *selfishness* of a people, or more often the *will to power* of its leaders. It also happens that this attitude coincides with an exaggerated and out-of-date concept of the *sovereignty and security* of the State. The State then runs the risk of becoming the object of a so to speak unquestionable worship. It runs the risk of justifying the most questionable undertaking. Orchestrated by the powerful means at the disposal of propaganda, such worship – which is not to be confused with properly understood patriotric attachment to one's own nation – can inhibit the critical sense and moral sense of the more aware citizens and can encourage them to go to war.

For all the more reason one must mention the tactical and deliberate *lie,* which misuses language, which has recourse to the most sophisticated techniques of propaganda, which deceives and distorts dialogue and incites to aggression.

Finally, while certain parties are fostered *by ideologies* which, inspite of their declarations, are opposed to the dignity of the human person, to his or her just aspirations according to the healthy principles of reason, of the natural and eternal law (cf. *Pacem in Terris,* AAS 55, 1963, p. 300), ideologies which see in struggle the motive force of history, that see in force the source of rights, that see in the discernment of the enemy the ABC of politics, dialogue is fixed and sterile. Or, if it still exists, it is a superficial and falsified reality. It becomes very difficult, not to say impossible, therefore. There follows almost a complete lack of communication between countries and blocs. Even the international institutions are paralyzed. And the setback to dialogue then runs the risk of serving the arms race.

However, even in what can be considered as an impasse to the extent that individuals support such ideologies, the attempt to have a lucid dialogue seems still necessary in order to unblock the situation and to work for the possible establishment of peace on particular points. This is to be done by counting upon common sense, on the possibilities of danger for everyone and on the just aspirations to which the peoples themselves largely adhere.

Dialogue on the national level

8.   Dialogue for peace must be established in the first place *on the national level* in order to resolve social conflicts, in order to seek the common good. While bearing in mind the interests of different groups, the common effort for peace must be made ceaselessly, in the exercise of freedoms and duties which are democratic for all, thanks to the structures of participation and thanks to the many means of reconciliation between employers and workers, in the manner of respecting and associating the cultural, ethnic and religious groups which make up a nation. When unfortunately dialogue between government and people is absent, social peace is threatened or absent; it is like a state of war. But history and present day observation show that many countries have succeeded or are succeeding in establishing a true working together, to resolve the conflicts which arise within them, or even to prevent them, by acquiring means of dialogue which are truly effective. They also give themselves a legislation which is in constant evolution, which appropriate jurisdictions cause to be respected in order to correspond to the common good.

Dialogue for peace on the international level

9.   If dialogue has shown itself to be producing results on the national level why should it not be so on *the international level*. It is true that the problems are more complicated, the parties and interests in question are more numerous and less homogeneous. But the means par excellence always remains honest and patient dialogue. Where this is missing between nations, every effort must be made to restore it. Where it is

insufficient, it must be perfected, dialogue should never be set aside by having recourse to the force of arms in order to resolve conflicts. And the great responsibility which is here engaged is not only that of the opposing parties, whose passion it is difficult to dominate. It is also and much more the responsibility of more powerful countries which fail to help them to restore dialogue, which push them into war, or which tempt them by arms trading.

Dialogue between nations must be based upon the strong conviction that the good of the people cannot be finally accomplished against the good of another people: all have the same rights, the same claims to a worthy life for their citizens. It is also essential to make progress in overcoming artificial divisions, inherited from the past, and the antagonism of blocs. Greater recognition must be given to the increasing interdependence between the nations.

The object of international dialogue

10.   If one wishes to state exactly *the object of international dialogue*, one can say that it must be notably concerned with the rights of man, with justice between peoples, with economics, with disarmament, and with the common international good.

Yes, it must be directed towards the recognition of individuals and human groups in their specific nature; in their original character, with the area of freedom which they need, and notably in the exercise of their basic rights. On this subject, one can hope for an international juridical system which is more receptive to the appeals of those whose rights are violated and one can hope for jurisdictions which have effective means capable of making their authority respected.

If injustice in all its forms is the first source of violence and war it goes without saying that, in a general way, dialogue for peace cannot be dissociated from *dialogue for justice*, on behalf of peoples who suffer frustration and domination by others.

Dialogue for peace will also necessarily involve a discussion of the rules which govern *economic life*. For the temptation to violence and war will always be present in societies where greed and the search for material goods impels a wealthy minority to refuse the mass of people the satisfaction of the most elementary rights to food, education, health and life (cf. *Gaudium et Spes*, 69). This is true at the level of every country; but also in the relationships between countries, especially if bilateral relations continue to be prevalent. It is here that openness to multilateral relationships, notably in the framework of the International Organizations, brings an opportunity for dialogue which is less burdened by inequalities and therefore more favourable to justice.

Obviously the object of international dialogue will also concern itself with the dangerous *arms race* in such a way as to reduce it progressively, as I suggested in the message I sent to the United Nations Organization last June, and in conformity with the message that the learned members of the Pontifical Academy of Sciences took on my behalf to the leaders of the nuclear powers. Instead of being at the service of people, the economy is becoming militarized. Development and well-being are subordinated to security. Science and technology are being degraded into the auxiliaries of war. The Holy See will not grow weary in insisting upon the need to put a stop to the arms race through progressive negotiations, by appealing for a reciprocity. The Holy See will continue to encourage all steps, even the smallest one, of reasonable dialogue in this very important sphere.

But the object of dialogue for peace cannot be reduced to a condemnation of the arms race; it is a question of searching for a whole more just *international order*, consensus on the more equitable sharing of goods, services, knowledge, information, and a firm determination to order these latter to the common good. I know that such a dialogue, of which the North–South dialogue forms a part, is very complex; it must be resolutely pursued, in order to prepare the conditions for true peace as we approach the third millennium.

Appeals to leaders

11.   After these considerations my message is intended to be above all an appeal to take up the challenge to dialogue for peace.

I address it in the first place to you, the *Heads of State and Government*! May you be able, in order that your people may know real social peace, to permit all the conditions for dialogue and common effort which, when justly established, would not compromise but would favour, in the long term, the common good of the nation, in freedom and independence! May you be able to conduct this dialogue on equal terms with the other countries, and assist the parties in conflict to find the paths of dialogue, of reasonable reconciliation and of just peace!

I also appeal to you, *the diplomats*, whose noble profession it is, among other things, to deal with disputed points and to seek to resolve them through dialogue and negotiation, in order to avoid recourse to arms, or to take the place of the belligerents. It is a work of patience and perseverance, which the Holy See values all the more in view of the fact that it itself is engaged in diplomatic relationships, in which it seeks to cause dialogue to be adopted as the most suitable means of overcoming differences.

I wish above all to repeat my confidence in you, the leaders and members of the *International Organizations*, and in you, the international officials! In the course of the last ten years, your Organizations have too often been the object of attempts at manipulation on the part of nations wishing to exploit such bodies. However, it remains true that the present multiplicity of violent clashes, divisions and blocks on which bilateral relations founder, offer the great International Organizations the opportunity to engage upon a qualitative change in their activities, even to reform on certain points their own structures in order to take into account new realities and to enjoy effective power. Whether they are regional or worldwide, your Organizations have an exceptional chance to seize: to regain, in all its fullness, the mission which is theirs by virtue of their origin, their charter and their mandate; *to become the places and instruments par excellence for true dialogue for peace.* Far from allowing themselves to be overcome by paralyzing pessimism and discouragement, they have the possibility of affirming themselves still more as centres of encounter, where one can envisage the most audacious questioning of the practices which today prevail in political, economic, monetary and cultural exchanges.

I also make a particular appeal to you who *work in the mass media!* The sad events which the world has experienced in recent times have confirmed the importance of enlightened opinion in order that a conflict might not degenerate into war. Public opinion, in fact, can put a brake on warlike tendencies or, on the contrary, support these same tendencies to the point of blindness. Now, as those responsible for radio and television broadcasts, and for the press, you have an ever more preponderant role in this sphere; I encourage you to weigh your responsibility and to show with the greatest objectivity, the rights, the problems and the attitudes of each of the parties in order to promote understanding and dialogue between groups, countries and civilizations.

Finally, I must address myself to every man and woman and also to you, the young; you have many opportunities to break down the barriers of selfishness, lack of understanding and aggression by your way of carrying on a dialogue, every day, in your family, your village, your neighbourhood, in the associations in your city, your region, without forgetting the Non-governmental Organizations. Dialogue for peace is the task of everyone.

Particular reasons for Christians to take up the challenge of dialogue

12.   And now, I exhort you especially, the *Christians*, to take your part in this dialogue in accordance with the responsibilities that are yours, to pursue them with that quality of openness, frankness and justice that is called for by the *charity* of Christ, to take them up again ceaselessly, with the

tenacity and *hope* which faith enables you to have. You also know the need for *conversion* and *prayer*, for the main obstacle to the establishment of justice and peace is to be found *in man's heart, in sin* (cf. *Gaudium et Spes*, 10), as it was in the heart of Cain when he refused dialogue with his brother Abel (cf. *Genesis* 4:6–9). Jesus has taught us how to listen, to share, to act towards other people as one would wish for oneself, to settle differences while one travels together (cf. *Mt* 5:25), to pardon. And above all, by his death and Resurrection, he came to deliver us from the sin which sets up one against the other, to give us his peace, to break down the wall which separates the peoples. This is why the Church does not cease to implore the Lord to grant people the gift of his Peace, as the Message of last year emphasized. People are no longer vowed to not understanding one another or to being divided from one another, as at Babel (cf. *Genesis* 11:7–9). In Jerusalem, on the day of Pentecost, the Holy Spirit caused the first disciples of the Lord to rediscover, beyond the diversity of languages, the royal road to peace in brotherhood. The Church remains the *witness of this great hope.*

* * *

May Christians be ever more aware of their vocation to be, against winds and tides, the humble shepherds of that peace which, on Christmas night, God entrusted to us!

And, with them, may all men and women of good will be enabled to take up *this challenge for our time*, even in the midst of the most difficult situations, that is to say, may they be enabled to do everything in order to avoid war and to commit themselves for this purpose, with increased conviction, to the path which removes the threat of war: *dialogue for peace!*

1 January 1984

'FROM A NEW HEART, PEACE IS BORN'

This is a message addressed primarily towards each individual person. It is an invitation to renewal of 'heart'. The context is a certain uneasiness that the Pope senses in public opinion due to the 'web of tensions' in the East–West and North–South divide of the contemporary world. War has its origins in the human 'heart' defined as 'the innermost depth of the human person, in his or her relationship to good, to others, to God and also to brotherhood and peace.' The Pope speaks of the 'psychoses of hatred' that can set in through ideological and systematic manipulation of passions. He refers to ephemeral liberations throughout history where no real change of heart occurred. In order to renew systems and institutions, however, the human 'heart' must be renewed and this means 'conversion': 'In a word, the new heart is the heart which allows itself to be inspired by love ... It is a question of ... becoming – in intentions, feelings and whole conduct – a fraternal being...'. A true and courageous freedom of spirit is needed to confront bad systems. All of us are called to be involved in promoting a new mentality of peace, solidarity, mutual trust and respect for human rights. Public leaders and those who form public opinion have special responsibilities. Christians are invited to let their lives be transformed by the Word who came to preach peace and reconcile us.

✳ ✳ ✳

To the political leaders of the nations,
To those active in economic, social and cultural life,
To the young, who hope for a world of fraternity and
solidarity,
To all of you, men and women, who desire peace!

I address myself to you at the dawn of the year 1984 which presents itself everywhere full of questions and anxiety, but at the same time rich in hope and prospects. My appeal on the occasion of the seventeenth World Day of Peace springs from the depths of my heart, and I know that I re-echo the desire of many men and women who yearn for fraternity in a divided world. The message that I send to you is both simple and demanding, for it concerns each of you personally. It invites each one to do his or her share in the establishment of peace in the world without passing this duty on to others. The theme that I propose today for your consideration and action is this: 'From a new heart, peace is born'.

A paradoxical situation

1.   Today, one cannot help being struck by shadows and threats, but at the same time without forgetting the lights and hopes.

Truly, *peace is fragile*, and injustice abounds. Implacable wars are being waged in several countries; and they continue despite the accumulation of death, grief and ruin; and without any apparent progress towards a solution. Violence and fanatical terrorism do not spare other countries, and it is the innocent who too often pay the price, while passions increase and fear risks leading to all sorts of extremism. In many regions human rights are violated, freedom is mocked, people are imprisoned unjustly, summary executions are perpetrated for partisan reasons and, in this twentieth century which has seen a multiplication of Declarations and of courts of appeal, humanity is ill-informed, or if it is informed, it remains almost helpless to stop these abuses. Numerous countries are engaged in the painful struggle to overcome hunger, disease and underdevelopment, while the rich countries reinforce their position and the arms race continues to absorb unjustifiably resources that could be better used. The build-up of conventional, chemical, bacteriological and, especially, nuclear weapons causes an oppressive threat to weigh upon the future of the nations, notably in Europe, and causes justifiable concern to their population. A new and grave uneasiness fills public opinion, and I understand it.

The contemporary world is, as it were, imprisoned in a web of tensions. The tension between what is commonly called East and West affects not only relations between the countries directly involved; it also affects and even aggravates many other difficult situations in other parts of the world. Faced with such a situation, we must take note of the formidable danger represented by this growing tension and large-scale polarization, especially when we consider the unprecedented means of massive and unheard-of destruction which are available. And yet, though fully aware of this danger, the protagonists experience great difficulty, not to say helplessness, in halting this process, in finding ways to reduce these tensions by means of concrete steps towards de-escalation, towards the reduction of the levels of armaments, towards agreements which would make it possible to devote more efforts to the priority aims of economic, social and cultural progress.

Although the tension between East and West, with its ideological background, monopolizes the attention and fuels the apprehension of a great number of countries, especially in the northern hemisphere, it should not overshadow another more fundamental tension *between North and South* which affects the very life of a great part of humanity. Here it is the question of the growing contrast between the countries that have had an opportunity to accelerate their development and increase their wealth, and the countries locked in a condition of underdevelopment. This is another gigantic source of opposition, bitterness, revolt or fear, especially as it is fed by many kinds of injustice.

It is in the face of these enormous problems that I propose the theme of a renewal of 'heart'. It may be thought that the proposal is too simple and the means disproportionate. And yet, if one reflects well on it, the analysis outlined here permits us to go to the very depths of the problem and is capable of calling into question the presuppositions that precisely constitute a threat to peace. Humanity's helplessness to resolve the existing tensions reveals that the obstacles, and likewise the hopes, come from something deeper than the systems themselves.

War springs from the human spirit

2.   It is my deep conviction, it is the leitmotiv of the Bible and of Christian thought, and is, I hope, the intuition of many men and women of good will, that war has its origins in the human heart. It is man who kills and not his sword, or in our day, his missiles.

The 'heart' in the biblical sense is the innermost depth of the human person, in his or her relationship to good, to others, to God. It is not primarily a question of affectivity, but of *conscience*, of convictions, of the system of thought to which one is bound, as also the passions which influence one. In his heart, man is sensitive to the absolute values of good, to justice, brotherhood and peace.

The disorder of the heart is notably the disorder of the conscience when the latter calls good or bad what it intends to choose for the satisfaction of its material interests or its desire for power. Even the complex nature of the exercise of power does not exclude that there exists always the responsibility of the individual conscience in the preparation, beginning or extension of a conflict. The fact that responsibility is shared by a group does not alter this principle.

But this conscience is often solicited, not to say subjugated, *by socio-political and ideological systems* that are themselves the work of the human spirit. To the extent to which people allow themselves to be seduced by systems that present a global vision of humanity that is exclusive and almost Manichean, to the extent that they make the struggle against others, their elimination or enslavement the condition of progress, they shut themselves up within a war mentality which aggravates tensions and they reach the point of being almost incapable of dialogue. Sometimes their unconditional attachment to these systems becomes a form of power-worship, the worship of strength and wealth, a form of slavery that takes away freedom from the leaders themselves.

Over and above ideological systems properly so-called, *the passions* that disturb the human heart and incline it to war are also of many kinds. People can allow themselves to be carried away by a sense of racial supremacy and by hatred of others for this reason, or by jealousy, envy of the land and resources of others, or in a general way, by the desire for power, by pride, by a desire to extend their control over other peoples whom they despise.

Certainly, passions are often born of the *real frustrations* of individuals and peoples when others have refused to guarantee their existence or when social conditions are slow to adopt democracy or the sharing of wealth. *Injustice* is already a great vice in the heart of the exploiter. But passions are sometimes fed deliberately. It is difficult for wars to start if the people on both sides do not have powerful feelings of mutual hostility, or if they are not convinced that the claims of their opponents threaten their vital interests. This explains the ideological *manipulations* resorted to by those with aggressive intentions. Once fighting has begun, hostility is bound to increase, for it is nourished by the sufferings and atrocities experienced by each side. Psychoses of hatred can then result.

In the final analysis, therefore, the fact of recourse to violence and to war comes from man's sin, from his blindness of spirit and the disorder of his heart, which invoke the motive of injustice in order to spread or harden tension or conflict.

Yes, war is born *from the sinful heart of man*, ever since the jealousy and violence that filled the heart of Cain when he met his brother Abel, according to the ancient biblical narrative. Is it not a question really of an even more profound rupture, when people become incapable of agreeing on what is good

88

and evil, on the values of life of which God is the source and guarantor? Does not this explain the drifting of man's 'heart', when he fails to make peace with his fellowman on the basis of truth, with uprightness of spirit and goodness of heart?

The re-establishment of peace would itself be of short duration and quite illusory if there were not a true change of heart. History has taught us that, even in the case of countries that have been occupied or where rights have been suppressed, the 'liberation' for which people had yearned for so long has proved a disappointment, in that the leaders and the citizens have held on to their narrowness of spirit, their intolerance and their hardness, without overcoming their antagonisms. In the Bible itself, the Prophets denounced these ephemeral liberations when there was no real change of heart, no real 'conversion'.

Conversion essential

From a new heart, peace is born

3.   If the present systems generated by the 'heart' of man turn out to be incapable of ensuring peace, then it is the 'heart' of man that must be renewed, in order to renew systems, institutions and methods. Christian faith has a word for this fundamental change of heart: it is 'conversion'. Speaking generally, it is a matter of rediscovering clearsightedness and impartiality with freedom of spirit, the sense of justice with respect for the rights of man, the sense of equity with global solidarity between the rich and the poor, mutual trust and fraternal love.

NB

In the first place individuals and nations must acquire a true freedom of spirit in order to become conscious of the sterile attitudes of the past, of the biased and partial character of philosophical and social systems which begin from debatable premises and which reduce man and history to a closed system of materialistic forces, which rely on nothing but the force of arms and the power of the economy, which shut human beings into categories in opposition to each other, which present one-sided solutions, which ignore the complex reality of the life of nations and hinder their being treated as free. So a reexamination is needed of these systems that manifestly lead to deadlock, that freeze dialogue and understanding, develop mistrust, increase threats and dangers, without resolving the real problems, without offering true security, without making people truly happy, peaceful and free. This transformation in depth of the spirit and the heart certainly calls for great courage, the courage of humility and clearmindedness. It must influence the collective mind, by first touching the conscience of the individual. Is this an impossible hope? The impotence and danger in which our contemporaries find themselves urge them not to put off this return to the truth which alone will make them free and capable of better systems. This is the first condition for creating the 'new heart'.

The other positive elements are well known. It is enough to mention them. Peace is authentic if it is the fruit of justice, *Opus iustitiae pax*, as the Prophet Isaiah said (cf. *Is* 32:17): justice between social partners and between peoples. And a society is just and human if it respects the fundamental rights of the human person. Moreover, the spirit of war rises and grows strong where the inalienable rights of man are violated. Even if dictatorship and totalitarianism temporarily suppress the complaint of exploited and oppressed human beings, the just person clings to the conviction that nothing can justify this violation of the rights of man; he has the courage to intercede for others who suffer and he refuses to surrender in the face of injustice, to compromise with it; and likewise, however paradoxical it may appear, the person who deeply desires peace rejects any kind of pacifism which is cowardice or the simple preservation of tranquillity. In fact those who are tempted to impose their domination will always encounter the resistance of intelligent and courageous men and women, prepared to defend freedom in order to promote justice.

Equality also demands a strengthening of the relationships of justice and solidarity with poor countries, and especially those experiencing poverty and famine. The phrase of Paul VI has become henceforth the conviction of many: 'Development is the new name for peace'. The rich countries then emerge from their collective egoism in order to think in new terms about exchanges and mutual aid, opening themselves to a worldwide horizon.

Still more, the new heart seeks to banish the fear and psychosis of war. It replaces the axiom which holds that peace results from the balance of arms, with the principle that true peace can be built up only in mutual trust (cf. *Pacem in Terris*, 113). Certainly, it remains alert and clearsighted in order to detect lies and manipulation, and in order to go forward with prudence. But it dares to undertake and ceaselessly resume dialogue, which was the subject of my message last year.

In a word, the new heart is the heart which allows itself to be inspired by love. Already Pius XI stated that there cannot 'be true external peace between individuals and peoples where the spirit of peace does not possess minds and hearts..., minds, in order to recognize and respect the rights of justice; hearts, in order that justice be linked with charity and that charity may even prevail over justice, for if peace must be the work and fruit of justice..., it belongs rather to charity than to justice' (Discourse of 24 December 1930, AAS [1930], p. 535). It is a question of renouncing violence, falsehood and hatred, of becoming – in intentions, feelings and whole conduct – a fraternal being, one who recognizes the dignity and the needs of the other person, and seeks to cooperate with him or her in order to create a world of peace.

Appeal to political leaders and those who form public opinion

4.   As it is necessary to acquire a new heart, to promote a new mentality of peace, all men and women, whatever their place in society, truly can and must assume their share of responsibility in the construction of a true peace, in the circle where they live, in the family, at school, in business, in the city. In their cares, conversations and actions, they must feel concerned for all their brothers and sisters who are part of the same human family, even if they live at the other end of the world.

But obviously responsibility has various degrees. The responsibility of *Heads of State, of political leaders*, is primary for the establishment and development of peaceful relations between the different parts of the nation and between peoples. They more than others must be convinced that war is in itself irrational and that the ethical principle of the peaceful settlement of conflicts is the only way worthy of man. Of course, one is obliged to take into consideration the massive presence of violence in human history. It is the sense of reality in the service of the fundamental concern for justice which forces one to maintain the principle of legitimate defence in this history. But the dreadful risks of the arms of massive destruction must lead to the working out of processes of cooperation and disarmament which will make war in practice unthinkable. Peace must be won. All the more so, the conscience of political leaders must forbid them to allow themselves to be carried away in dangerous adventures in which passion overrides justice. They must not sacrifice uselessly the lives of their fellow-citizens in such adventures, or provoke conflicts among others, or use the pretext of the precariousness of peace in one region in order to extend their authority into new territories. These leaders must weigh all this in their minds and consciences, and exclude political opportunism; they will render account for this to their peoples and to God.

But I say again that peace is the duty of everyone. The *International Organizations* also have a large role to play in order to make universal solutions prevail, above partisan points of view. And my appeal is directed especially to all those who exercise through the media an influence on *public opinion*, all those who are *engaged in the education* of young people and adults: it is to them that is entrusted the formation of the spirit of peace. In society, can one not count especially on the young? In the face of the threatening future which they foresee, they certainly aspire more than others to peace, and many of them are prepared to devote their generosity and their energies to peace. Let them show inventiveness at its service, without abandoning clearsightedness, and so let them show the courage to weigh up all the aspects of long-term solutions! In short, everyone, all men and women, must contribute to peace, contributing their particular sensitivities and playing their particular roles. Thus *women*, who are intimately connected to the mystery of life, can do much to advance the spirit of peace, in their care to ensure the preservation of life and in their conviction that real love is the only power which can make the world liveable for everyone.

Appeal to Christians

5.   Christians, disciples of Jesus, caught up in the tensions of our age, we must recall that there is no happiness except for the 'peacemakers' (cf. *Mt* 5:9).

The Catholic Church is celebrating the Holy Year of the Redemption: the whole Church is invited to allow herself to be taken over by the Saviour who said to the people, as he went to the extreme of love: 'My peace I give you' (cf. *Jn* 14:27). In her, all must share with their brothers and sisters the proclamation of salvation and the vigour of hope.

The Synod of Bishops on Reconciliation and Penance recently recalled the first words of Christ: 'Repent, and believe in the gospel' (*Mk* 1:15). The message of the Synod Fathers shows us on which road we must go forward in order to be true peacemakers: 'The Word calls us to repent. "*Change your heart*, it tells us, seek pardon, and *be reconciled with the Father*". The plan of the Father for our society is that we live as one family in justice, truth, freedom and love' (cf *Nuntius Patrum Synoclalium ad Populum Dei*, 29 October 1983). This family will only be united in deep peace if we hear the call to return to the Father, to be reconciled with God himself.

Answering this call, cooperating with God's plan is to allow the Lord to convert us. Let us not count on our power alone, nor only on our so often failing will. Let us allow our lives to be transformed, for 'all this is from God, who through Christ reconciled us to himself and gave us the ministry of reconciliation' (2 *Cor* 5:18).

Let us rediscover the power of *prayer*: to pray is to be reconciled with him whom we invoke, whom we meet, who makes us live. To experience prayer is to accept the grace which changes us; the Spirit, united to our spirit, commits us to conform our life with the Word of God. To pray is to enter into the action of God upon history: he, the sovereign actor of history, has wished to make people his collaborators.

Paul says to us about Christ: 'For he is our peace, who has made us both one, and has broken down the dividing wall of hostility' (*Eph* 2:14). We know what a great power of mercy transforms us in the *Sacrament of Reconciliation*. This gift overwhelms us. In that case, in all loyalty, we cannot remain resigned to the divisions and confrontations which set us against one another even though we share the same faith; we cannot accept, without reacting, the fact that conflicts are dragging on which are destroying the unity of humanity, which is called to become one single body. If we celebrate forgiveness, can we fight one another endlessly? Can we remain enemies while we invoke the same living God? If Christ's law of love is our law, shall we remain silent and inert while the wounded world looks to us to join the front ranks of those who are building peace?

Humble and conscious of our weakness, let us come to the *Eucharistic table*, where he who gives his life for the multitude of his brethren gives us a new heart, where he puts into us a new spirit (cf. *Ezek* 36:26). In the depth of our poverty and disarray, through him let us give thanks, for he unites us by his presence and the gift of himself, he 'who came and preached peace to you who were far off and peace to those who were near' (*Eph* 2:17). And if it is given to us to welcome him, it is up to us to be his witnesses through our fraternal work in all the workshops of peace.

Conclusion

Peace has many different forms. There is peace between nations, peace in society, peace between citizens, peace between religious communities, peace within undertakings, neighbourhoods, villages and, especially, peace inside families. In addressing myself to Catholics, and also to other Christian brethren and to men and women of good will, I have deplored a certain number of obstacles to peace. They are grave, they present serious threats. But since they depend on the spirit, the will, the human 'heart', with the help of God people can overcome them. They must refuse to give in to fatalism and discouragement. Positive signs are already piercing the darkness. Humanity is becoming aware of the indispensable solidarity which links peoples and nations, for the solution of the majority of the great problems: employment, the use of terrestrial and cosmic resources, the advancement of less favoured nations, and security. The reduction of arms, controlled and worldwide, is considered by many a vital necessity. There are many calls to use every means in order to banish war from the horizon of humanity. There are also many new appeals for dialogue, cooperation and reconciliation, and numerous fresh initiatives. The Pope is anxious to encourage them. 'Blessed are the peacemakers!' Let us always unite clearsightedness with generosity! Let peace be more genuine and let it take root in man's very heart! Let the cry of the afflicted who await peace be heard! Let every individual commit all the energy of a renewed and fraternal heart to the building of peace throughout the universe!

1 January 1985
PEACE AND YOUTH
GO FORWARD TOGETHER

In the UN International Youth Year, Pope John Paul's message is an enthusiastic endorsement of young people's contribution to peace at all levels. Ideologies have dominated political, economic and social ways of thinking but by making fundamental moral choices the new generation of men and women can free history from false paths and build a new civilization of fraternal solidarity. He believes in young people and encourages them 'not to be afraid of your own youth'. How young people will respond to the challenges of peace and justice will depend on the answers they give to the many interconnected questions they ask in their pilgrimage of discovery. The inevitable question is how you understand what it is to be human: 'Ask yourselves what kind of people you want yourselves and your fellow human beings to be, what kind of culture you want to build...' It is not enough simply to see material goods as the answer. Obviously that will lead to the fundamental question: 'Who is your God?' because when God dies in the conscience of the human person, there follows inevitably the death of man, the image of God. In the midst of 'many siren calls of self-interest', the Pope invites young people to 'drink deeply at the sources of truth' and make choices that incorporate values. He directs their gaze beyond the East–West problem to the North–South tensions in the world.

✳ ✳ ✳

To all of you who believe in the urgency of peace,
To you, parents and educators, who want to be the promoters
of peace,
To you, political leaders, who bear direct responsibility for the
cause of peace,
To you, men and women of culture, who seek to build peace in
today's civilization,
To all of you who suffer for the sake of peace and justice,
And above all to you, the young people of the world, whose
decisions about yourselves and your vocation in society will
determine the prospects for peace today and tomorrow,
To all of you, and to all people of good will, I send my message
on the Eighteenth World Day of Peace because peace is an
overriding concern, an unavoidable challenge, an immense
hope.

The problems and the hopes of the world confront us every day

1.   It is true: the challenge of peace remains with us. We are living in a difficult time when the threats of destructive violence and war are many. Profound disagreements pit different social groups, peoples and nations one against the other. There are many situations of injustice that do not break forth into open conflicts solely because the violence of those who retain power is so great that it deprives the powerless of the energy and opportunity to claim their rights. Yes, there are people today who are prevented by totalitarian regimes and ideological systems from exercising their fundamental right to decide for themselves about their own future. Men and women today suffer insupportable insults to their human dignity through racial discrimination, forced exile and torture. They are victims of hunger and disease. They are prevented from practising their religious beliefs or from developing their own culture.

   It is important to discern the ultimate causes of this state of conflict that makes peace precarious and unstable. The effective promotion of peace demands that we should not limit

97

ourselves to deploring the negative effects of the present situation of crisis, conflict and injustice; what we are really required to do is to destroy the roots that cause these effects. Such ultimate causes are to be found especially in the ideologies that have dominated our century and continue to do so, manifesting themselves in political, economic and social systems and taking control of the way people think. These ideologies are marked by a totalitarian attitude that disregards and oppresses the dignity and transcendent values of the human person and his or her rights. Such an attitude seeks political, economic and social domination with a rigidity of purpose and method that is closed to any authentic dialogue or real sharing. Some of these ideologies have even become a sort of false secularistic religion, claiming to bring salvation to the whole of humanity but without providing any proof of its own truth.

But violence and injustice have deep roots in the heart of each individual, of each one of us, in people's everyday ways of thinking and behaving. We have only to think of the conflicts and divisions within families, between married couples, between parents and children, in the schools, in professional life, in the relationships between social groups and between the generations. We have only to think of the cases where the basic right to life of the weakest and most defenceless human beings is violated.

Faced with these, and many more evils, it is still not right to lose hope – so abundant are the energies that continually spring up in the hearts of people who believe in justice and peace. The present crisis can and must become the occasion for conversion and for the renewal of mentalities. The time we are living in is not just a period of danger and worry. It is an hour for hope.

Peace and youth go forward together

2.   The present difficulties are really a test of our humanity. They can be turning points on the road to lasting peace for they kindle the boldest dreams and unleash the best energies of

mind and heart. Difficulties are a challenge to all; hope is an imperative for all. But today I want to draw your attention to the role that youth is called upon to play in the endeavour to bring about peace. As we prepare to enter a new century and a new millennium, we must be aware that the future of peace and therefore the future of humanity have been entrusted, in a special way, to the fundamental moral choices that a new generation of men and women are being called upon to make. In a very few years, the young people of today will hold responsibility for family life and for the life of nations, for the common good of all and for peace. Young people have already begun to ask themselves all over the world: What can I do? What can we do? Where does our path take us? They want to make their contribution to the healing of a wounded and weakened society. They want to offer new solutions to old problems. They want to build a new civilization of fraternal solidarity. Taking inspiration from these young people, I wish to invite everyone to reflect on those realities. But I want to address myself in a special and direct way to the young people of today and tomorrow.

Young people, do not be afraid of your own youth

3.   The first appeal I want to address to you, young men and women of today, is this: Do not be afraid! Do not be afraid of your own youth, and of those deep desires you have for happiness, for truth, for beauty and for lasting love! Sometimes people say that society is afraid of these powerful desires of young people, and that you yourselves are afraid of them. Do not be afraid! When I look at you, the young people, I feel great gratitude and hope. The future far into the next century lies in your hands. The future of peace lies in your hearts. To construct history, as you can and must, you must free history from the false paths it is pursuing. To do this, you must be people with a deep trust in man and a deep trust in the grandeur of the human vocation – a vocation to be pursued with respect for truth and for the dignity and inviolable rights of the human person.

What I see arising in you is a new awareness of your responsibility and a fresh sensitivity to the needs of your fellow human beings. You are touched by the hunger for peace that so many share with you. You are troubled by so much injustice around you. You sense overwhelming danger in the gigantic stockpiles of arms and in the threats of nuclear war. You suffer when you see widespread hunger and malnutrition. You are concerned about the environment today and for the coming generations. You are threatened by unemployment, and many of you are already without work and without the prospect of meaningful employment. You are upset by the large number of people who are oppressed politically and spiritually and who cannot enjoy the exercise of their basic human rights as individuals or as a community. All this can give rise to a feeling that life has little meaning.

In this situation, some of you may be tempted to take flight from responsibility: in the fantasy worlds of alcohol and drugs, in shortlived sexual relationships without commitment to marriage and family, in indifference, in cynicism and even in violence. Put yourselves on guard against the fraud of a world that wants to exploit or misdirect your energetic and powerful search for happiness and meaning. But do not avoid the search for the true answers to the questions that confront you. Do not be afraid!

The inevitable question: What is your idea of man?

4.   Among the inevitable questions that you must ask yourselves, the first and foremost is this: What is your idea of man? What, to you, makes up the dignity and the greatness of a human being? This is a question that you young people have to ask yourselves but which you also put to the generation that has preceded you, to your parents and to all those who at various levels have had the responsibility of caring for the goods and values of the world. In the attempt to respond to this question honestly and openly, young and old can be led to reconsider their own actions and their own histories. Is it not true that very often, especially in the more developed and richer nations, people have given in to a

materialistic idea of life? Is it not true that parents sometimes feel that they have fulfilled their obligations to their children by offering them, beyond the satisfaction of basic necessities, more material goods as the answer for their lives? Is it not true that, by doing this, they are passing on to the younger generations a world that will be poor in essential spiritual values, poor in peace and poor in justice? Is it not equally true that in other nations, the fascination with certain ideologies has left to the younger generations a legacy of new forms of enslavement without the freedom to pursue the values that truly enhance life in all its aspects? Ask yourselves what kind of people you want yourselves and your fellow human beings to be, what kind of culture you want to build. Ask yourselves these questions and do not be afraid of the answers, even if they will require of you a change of direction in your thoughts and loyalties.

The fundamental question: Who is your God?

5.   The first question leads to an even more basic and fundamental one: Who is your God? We cannot define our notion of man without defining an Absolute, a fullness of truth, of beauty and of goodness by which we allow our lives to be guided. Thus it is true that a human being, 'the visible image of the invisible God', cannot answer the question about who he or she is without at the same time declaring who his or her God is. It is impossible to restrict this question to the sphere of people's private existence. It is impossible to separate this question from the history of nations. Today, a person is exposed to the temptation to refuse God in the name of his or her own humanity. Wherever this refusal exists, there the shadow of fear casts its ever darkening pall. Fear is born wherever God dies in the consciences of human beings. Everyone knows, albeit obscurely and with dread, that wherever God dies in the conscience of the human person, there follows inevitably the death of man, the image of God.

Your answer: Choices based on values

6.   Whatever answers you give to these two interconnected questions will set the direction for the rest of your lives. Each of us, during the years of our youth, has had to struggle with these questions and, at some point, has had to come to some conclusion that has shaped our future choices, our future paths, our future lives. The answers which you, young people, give to these questions will also determine how you respond to the great challenges of peace and justice. If you have decided that your God will be yourself with no regard for others, you will become instruments of division and enmity, even instruments of warfare and violence. In saying this, I wish to point out to you the importance of choices that incorporate values. Values are the underpinnings of the choices that determine not only your own lives but also the policies and strategies that build life in society. And remember that it is not possible to create a dichotomy between personal and social values. It is not possible to live in inconsistency: to be demanding of others and of society and then decide to live a personal life of permissiveness.

You must then decide what values you want to build society upon. Your choices now will decide whether in the future you will suffer the tyranny of ideological systems that reduce the dynamics of society to the logic of class struggle. The values that you choose today will decide whether relations between nations will continue to be overshadowed by tragic tensions that are the product of undeclared or openly touted designs to subdue all peoples to regimes where God does not count, and where the dignity of the human person is sacrificed to the demands of an ideology that attempts to deify the collectivity. The values that you commit yourselves to in your youth will determine whether you will be satisfied with the heritage of a past in which hatred and violence suffocate love and reconciliation. Upon the choices of each one of you today will depend the future of your brothers and sisters.

The value of peace

7.   The cause of peace, the constant and unavoidable challenge of our day, helps you to discover yourselves and your values. The realities are stark and frightening. Millions spent on weapons. Resources of material and intellectual talent devoted solely to the production of arms. Political stances that at times do not reconcile and bring peoples together, but rather erect barriers and isolate nation from nation. In such circumstances a just sense of patriotism can fall victim to overzealous partisanship, and honourable service in defence of one's country can become the subject of misinterpretation and even ridicule (cf. *Gaudium et Spes*, 79). In the midst of many siren calls of self-interest, the man and woman of peace must learn to heed first the values of life and then move with confidence to put those values into practice. The call to be peacemakers will then rest firmly on the call to conversion of heart, as I suggested in last year's World Day of Peace Message. It will then be strengthened by a commitment to honest dialogue and sincere negotiations based on mutual respect, coupled with a realistic assessment of the just demands and legitimate interests of all partners. It will seek to diminish the weapons whose existence in great numbers strikes fear into people's hearts. It will devote itself to building the bridges – cultural, economic, social, political – that will allow greater exchange among nations. It will promote the cause of peace as the cause of everyone, not by slogans that divide or by actions that needlessly arouse passions, but by the calm confidence that is the fruit of a commitment to true values and to the good of all humanity.

The value of justice

8.   The good of all humanity is ultimately the reason why you must make the cause of peace your own. In saying this, I invite you to direct your attention away from an exclusive concentration on the threat to peace usually referred to as the East–West problem and, instead, to think about the whole

world, and thus the socalled North–South tensions as well. As in the past, so today I wish to affirm that these two issues – peace and development – are interrelated and must be addressed together if the young people of today are to inherit a better world tomorrow.

One aspect of this relationship is the deployment of resources for one purpose (armaments), rather than for another (development). But the real connection is not simply the use of resources, important as that may be. It is between the values that commit one to peace and the values that commit one to development in the true sense. For as certainly as true peace demands more than just the absence of war or merely the dismantling of weapons systems, so too development, in its true and integral sense, can never be reduced solely to an economic plan or to a series of technological projects, no matter how good they may be. In the whole area of progress that we call peace and justice, the same values have to be applied that spring from the idea we have about who man is and who God is in relation to the whole human race. The same values that commit one to be a peacemaker will be the values that impel one to foster the integral development of every human being and of all peoples.

The value of participation

9.   A world of justice and peace cannot be created by words alone and it cannot be imposed by outside forces: it must be desired and must come about through the contribution of all. It is essential for every human being to have a sense of participating, of being a part of the decisions and endeavours that shape the destiny of the world. Violence and injustice have often in the past found their root causes in people's sense of being deprived of the right to shape their own lives. Future violence and injustice cannot be avoided when and where the basic right to participate in the choices of society is denied. But this right must be exercised with discernment. The complexity of life in modern society demands that people delegate the power

of decision-making to their leaders. They must be able to trust that their leaders will make decisions for the good of their own people and of all peoples. Participation is a right, but it carries with it obligations: to exercise it with respect for the dignity of the human person. The mutual trust between citizens and leaders is the fruit of the practice of participation, and participation is a cornerstone for building a world of peace.

Life: a pilgrimage of discovery

10.   I invite all of you, young people of the world; to take up your responsibility in this greatest of spiritual adventures that a person will face: to build human life, as individuals and in society, with respect for the vocation of man. For it is true to say that life is a pilgrimage of discovery: the discovery of who you are, the discovery of the values that shape your lives, the discovery of the peoples and nations to which all are bound in solidarity. While this voyage of discovery is most evident in the time of youth, it is a voyage that never ends. During your whole lifetime, you must affirm and reaffirm the values that form yourselves and that form the world: the values that favour life, that reflect the dignity and vocation of the human person, that build a world in peace and justice.

A remarkable worldwide consensus exists among young people about the necessity of peace, and this constitutes a tremendous potential force for the good of all. But young people must not be satisfied with an instinctive desire for peace: this desire must be transformed into a firm moral conviction that encompasses the full range of human problems and builds on deeply treasured values. The world needs young people who have drunk deeply at the sources of truth. You have to listen to the truth and for this you need purity of heart; you have to understand it, and for this you need deep humility; you have to surrender to it and share it, and for this you need the strength to resist the temptations of pride, selfishness and manipulation. You must form in yourselves a deep sense of responsibility.

The responsibility of Christian youth

11.   I wish earnestly to commend this sense of responsibility and commitment to moral values to you, the Christian youth, and together with you, to all our brothers and sisters who confess the Lord Jesus. As Christians you are conscious of being children of God, sharing in the divine nature, being enveloped in the fullness of God in Christ. The Risen Christ gives you peace and reconciliation as his first gift. God, who is eternal peace, has made peace with the world through Christ, the Prince of Peace. That peace has been poured into your hearts and it lies deeper than all the unrest of your minds, all the torments of your hearts. God's peace takes charge of your minds and hearts. God gives you his peace not as a possession which you can hoard, but as a treasure which you possess only when you share it with others.

In Christ, you can believe in the future even though you cannot discern its shape. You can hand yourselves over to the Lord of the future, and thus overcome your discouragement at the magnitude of the task and the price to be paid. To the dismayed disciples on the way to Emmaus, the Lord said: 'Was it not necessary that the Christ should suffer these things and enter into his glory?' (*Lk* 24:26). The Lord speaks those same words to each one of you. So do not be afraid to commit your lives to peace and justice, for you know that the Lord is with you in all your ways.

International Youth Year

12.   In this year which the United Nations Organization has declared International Youth Year, it has been my wish to address my annual message for the World Day of Peace to all of you, the young people around the world. May this Year be for everyone a year of deeper commitment to peace and justice. May you make every choice with courage and live it with fidelity and responsibility. Whatever paths you set out upon, do so with hope and trust: hope in the future that, with God's help, you can shape; trust in the God who watches over you in

all that you say and do. Those of us who have preceded you want to share with you a deep commitment to peace. Those who are your contemporaries will be united with you in your efforts. Those who come after you will be inspired by you so long as you seek the truth, and live by authentic moral values. The challenge of peace is great, but greater is the reward; for in committing yourselves to peace you will discover the best for yourselves as you seek the best for everyone else. You are growing, and with you peace is growing.

May this International Youth Year also be a time for parents and educators to take a new look at their responsibilities towards young people. Too often their guidance is refused and their achievements questioned. Yet they have so much to offer in wisdom, strength and experience. Their task of accompanying youth in the search for meaning cannot be assumed by anyone else. The values and models which they hold up to the young must, however, be clearly seen in their own lives, lest their words lack conviction and their lives be a contradiction which the young will rightly reject.

At the close of this Message I pledge my prayers every day of this International Youth Year that young people will respond to the call of peace. I urge all my brothers and sisters to join with me in this prayer to our Father in heaven that he may enlighten all of us who bear the responsibility for peace, but especially the young, so that youth and peace may indeed go forward together!

1 January 1986

PEACE IS A VALUE WITH NO FRONTIERS NORTH–SOUTH, EAST–WEST: ONLY ONE PEACE

This message for the UN International Year of Peace is a plea for a new international system based on recognition of the unity of the human family. Speaking out against a view of the world in terms of power blocs, the Pope widens the normal East–West perspective typical of the cold war to draw attention to the North–South tensions. He proposes a vision of the world as one human family that takes account of problems such as large debts in poorer countries, social injustices and ideological conflicts as well as resources being poured into arms. He advocates new types of society and international relations with resources directed to solidarity, dialogue and universal brotherhood. Reducing differences between North and South will mean: 'thinking of the prices of raw materials, the need for technological expertise, the training of the work force, the potential productivity of the millions of unemployed, the debts poor nations are carrying and a better and more responsible use of funds within developing countries.' In short, his appeal is for social solidarity between all, both in the East–West and the North–South relations. He encourages the Helsinki and other dialogues concerning limitations in armaments. Finally, he reminds Christians that the heart of the Church's mission is 'the promotion of unity'. He also praises international volunteer work aimed at sharing and fraternity.

* * *

Peace as a universal value

1.   At the beginning of the New Year, taking my inspiration from Christ, the Prince of Peace, I renew my commitment and that of the whole Catholic Church to the cause of peace. At the same time I extend to every individual and to all peoples of the earth my earnest greeting and my good wishes: Peace to all of you! Peace to all hearts! Peace is a value of such importance that it must be proclaimed anew and promoted by all. There is no human being who does not benefit from peace. There is no human heart that is not uplifted when peace prevails. All the nations of the world can fully realize their interlinked destinies only if, together, they pursue peace as a universal value.

On the occasion of this nineteenth World Day of Peace, in the International Year of Peace proclaimed by the United Nations Organization, I offer to everyone as a message of hope my profound conviction: 'Peace is a value with no frontiers'. It is *a value that responds to the hopes and aspirations of all people and all nations*, of young and old, and of all men and women of good will. This is what I proclaim to everyone, and especially to the leaders of the world.

The question of peace as a universal value needs to be faced with extreme intellectual honesty, sincerity of spirit and an acute sense of responsibility to oneself and to the nations of the earth. I would ask those responsible for political decisions affecting the relationships between North and South, between East and West, to be convinced that there can be ONLY ONE PEACE. Those upon whom the future of the world depends, regardless of their political philosophy, economic system or religious commitment, are all called to help construct a single peace on the basis of social justice and the dignity and rights of every human person.

This task requires a radical openness to all humanity and a conviction of the interrelatedness of all the nations of the world. This interrelatedness is expressed in an interdependence that can prove either profoundly advantageous or profoundly destructive. Hence, worldwide solidarity and cooperation constitute ethical imperatives that appeal to the consciences of individuals and to the responsibilities of all nations. And it is *in this context of ethical imperatives* that I address the whole world for 1 January 1986, proclaiming the universal value of peace.

Threats to peace

2.   In putting forward this vision of peace at the dawn of a new year we are deeply aware that in the present situation peace is also a value that rests on foundations that are very fragile. At first glance our goal to make peace an absolute imperative may seem to be utopian, since our world gives such ample evidence of *excessive self-interest* in the context of opposed political, ideological and economic groups. Caught in the grip of these systems, leaders and various groups are led to pursue their particular aims and their ambitions of power, progress and wealth, without taking sufficiently into account the necessity and duty of international solidarity and cooperation for the benefit of the common good of all peoples who make up the human family.

In this situation *blocs* are formed and maintained which divide and oppose peoples, groups and individuals, making peace precarious and setting up grave obstacles to development. Positions harden and the excessive desire to maintain one's advantage or to increase one's share often becomes the overriding rationale for action. This leads to exploitation of others and the spiral grows towards a polarization that feeds on the fruits of self-interest and the increasing mistrust of others. In such a situation, *it is the small and the weak, the poor and the voiceless who suffer most.* This can happen directly when a poor and comparatively defenceless people is held in subjection by the force of power. It can happen indirectly when economic power is used to disenfranchise people of their rightful share and to hold them in social and economic subjection, generating dissatisfaction and violence. The examples are sadly too numerous today.

The spectre of nuclear weapons, which has its origin precisely in the opposition of East and West, remains the most dramatic and compelling example of this. Nuclear weapons are so powerful in their destructive capacities, and nuclear strategies are so inclusive in their designs, that the popular imagination is often paralyzed by fear. This fear is not groundless. The only way to respond to this legitimate fear of the consequences of nuclear destruction is by *progress in negotiations* for the reduction of nuclear weapons and for mutually agreed upon measures that will lessen the likelihood of nuclear warfare. I would ask the nuclear powers once again to reflect on their very grave moral and political responsibility in this matter. It is an obligation that some have also juridically accepted in international agreements; for all it is an obligation by reason of a *basic co-responsibility for peace and development*.

But the threat of nuclear weapons is not the way that conflict is made permanent and increased. *The increasing sale and purchase of arms* – conventional but very sophisticated – is causing dire results. While the major powers have avoided direct conflict, their rivalries have often been acted out in other parts of the world. Local problems and regional difference are aggravated and perpetuated through armaments supplied by wealthier countries and by the ideologizing of local conflicts by powers that seek regional advantage by exploiting the condition of the poor and defenceless.

Armed conflict is not the only way that the poor bear an unjust share of the burden of today's world. The developing countries must face formidable challenges even when free of such a scourge. In its many dimensions, *underdevelopment remains an ever growing threat to world peace*.

In fact, between the countries which form the 'North bloc' and those of the 'South bloc' there is *a social and economic abyss* that separates rich from poor. The statistics of recent years show signs of improvement in a few countries but also evidence of a widening of the gap in too many others. Added to this is *the unpredictable and fluctuating financial situation* with its direct impact on countries with *large debts* struggling to achieve some positive development.

In this situation peace as a universal value is in great danger. Even if there is no actual armed conflict as such, where *injustice* exists, it is in fact a cause and potential factor of conflict. In any case a situation of peace in the full sense of its value cannot coexist with injustice. Peace cannot be reduced to the mere absence of conflict; it is the tranquillity and completeness of order. It is lost by the social and economic exploitation by special interest groups which operate internationally or function as elites within developing countries. It is lost by the social divisions that pit rich against poor between States or within States. It is lost when *the use of force* produces the bitter fruit of hatred and division. It is lost when economic exploitation and internal strains on the social fabric leave the people defenceless and disillusioned, a ready prey to the destructive forces of violence. As a value, peace is continually endangered by vested interests, by diverging and opposing interpretations, and even by clever manipulations for the service of ideologies and political systems that have domination as their ultimate aim.

Overcoming the current situation

3.   There are those who claim that the present situation is natural and inevitable. Relations between individuals and between States are said to be characterized by permanent conflict. This doctrinal and political outlook is translated into a model of society and a system of international relations that are dominated by competition and antagonism, in which the strongest prevails. Peace born from such an outlook can only be an 'arrangement', suggested by the principle of *Realpolitik*, and as an 'arrangement' it seeks not so much to resolve tensions through justice and equity *as to manage differences and conflicts* in order to maintain a kind of balance that will preserve whatever is in the interests of the dominating party. It is clear that 'peace' built and maintained on social injustices and ideological conflict will never become a true peace for the world. Such a 'peace' cannot deal with the substantial causes of the world's tensions or give to the world *the kind of vision*

and values which can resolve the divisions represented by the poles of North–South and East–West.

To those who think that blocs are inevitable we answer that it is possible, indeed necessary, to set up *new types of society and of international relations* which will ensure justice and peace on stable and universal foundations. Indeed, a healthy realism suggests that such types cannot be simply imposed from above or from outside, or effected only by methods and techniques. This is because the deepest roots of the opposition and tensions that mutilate peace and development are to be found in the heart of man. It is above all the hearts and the attitudes of people that must be changed, and this needs a renewal, *a conversion of individuals.*

If we study the evolution of society in recent years we can see, not only deep wounds, but also signs of a determination on the part of many of our contemporaries and of peoples to overcome the present obstacles in order to bring into being a new international system. This is *the path that humanity must take* if it is to enter into an age of universal peace and integral development.

The path of solidarity and dialogue

4.   Any new international system capable of overcoming the logic of blocs and opposing forces must be *based on the personal commitment of everyone to make the basic and primary needs of humanity the first imperative of international policy.* Today countless human beings in all parts of the world have acquired a vivid sense of their fundamental equality, their human dignity and their inalienable rights. At the same time there is a growing awareness that humanity has a profound unity of interests, vocation and destiny, and that all peoples, in the variety and richness of their different national characteristics, are called to form a single family. Added to this is the realization that resources are not unlimited and that needs are immense. Therefore, rather than waste resources or devote them to deadly weapons of destruction, it is necessary to use them above all to satisfy *the primary and basic needs of humanity.*

It is likewise important to note that an awareness is gaining ground of the fact that reconciliation, justice and peace between individuals and between nations given the stage that humanity has reached and the very grave threats that hang over its future – are not merely a noble appeal meant for a few idealists but a condition for survival of life itself. Consequently, the establishment of an order based on justice and peace is vitally needed today, as a clear moral imperative valid for all people and regimes; above ideologies and systems. Together with and above the particular common good of a nation, the need to consider *the common good of the entire family of nations* is quite clearly an ethical and juridical duty.

The right path to a world community in which justice and peace will reign without frontiers among all peoples and on all continents is *the path of solidarity, dialogue and universal brotherhood*. This is the only path possible. Political, economic, social and cultural relations and systems must be imbued with the values of solidarity and dialogue which, in turn, require an *institutional dimension* in the form of special organisms of the world community that will watch over the common good of all peoples.

It is clear that, in order effectively to achieve a world community of this kind, mental outlooks and political views contaminated by the lust for power, by ideologies, by the defence of one's own privilege and wealth must be abandoned, and replaced by *an openness to sharing and collaboration with all in a spirit of mutual trust*.

That call to recognize the unity of the human family has very real repercussions for our life and for our commitment to peace. It means first of all that we reject the kind of thinking that divides and exploits. It means that we commit ourselves to *a new solidarity*, the solidarity of the human family. It means looking at the North–South tensions and replacing them with a *new relationship, the social solidarity of all*. This social solidarity faces up honestly to the abyss that exists today but it does not acquiesce in any kind of economic determinism. It recognizes all the complexities of a problem that has been allowed to get out of hand for too long, but which can still be rectified by men and women who see themselves in fraternal solidarity with everyone else on this earth. It is true that changes in economic growth patterns have affected all parts of the world and not just the poorest. But the person who sees peace as a universal value will want to use this opportunity *to reduce the differences between North and South* and foster the relationships that will bring them closer together. I am thinking of the prices of raw materials, of the need for technological expertise, of the training of the work force, of the potential productivity of the millions of unemployed, of the debts poor nations are carrying, and of a better and more responsible use of funds within developing countries. I am thinking of so many elements which individually have created tensions and which combined together have polarized North–South relations. *All this can and must be changed.*

If social justice is the means to move towards a peace for all peoples, then it means that we see peace as an indivisible fruit of just and honest relations on every level – social, economic, cultural and ethical – of human life on this earth. This conversion to an attitude of social solidarity also serves to highlight the deficiencies in *the current East–West situation.* In my message to the Second Special Session of the United Nations General Assembly on Disarmament, I explored many of the elements that are needed to improve the situation between the two major power blocs of East and West. All of the measures recommended then and reaffirmed since that time rest on the solidarity of the human family travelling together *along the path of dialogue.* Dialogue can open many doors closed by the tensions that have marked East–West relations. Dialogue is a means by which people discover one another and discover the good hopes and peaceful aspirations that too often lie hidden in their hearts. True dialogue goes beyond ideologies, and people meet in the reality of their human lives. Dialogue breaks down preconceived notions and artificial barriers. Dialogue brings human beings into contact with one another as members of one human family, with all the richness of their various cultures and histories. A conversion of heart commits people to promoting universal brotherhood; dialogue helps to effect this goal.

Today this dialogue is more needed than ever. Left to themselves, weapons and weapons systems, military strategies and alliances become the instruments of intimidation, mutual recrimination and the consequent dread that affects so much of the human race today. Dialogue considers these instruments in their relationship to human life. I am thinking first of all of the various dialogues in Geneva that are seeking to negotiate reductions and limitations in armaments. But also there are the dialogues being conducted in the context of the multilateral process initiated with the Helsinki Final Act of the Conference on Security and Cooperation in Europe, a process which will be reviewed once again next year in Vienna and continued. Concerning the dialogue and cooperation between North and South one can think of the important role entrusted to certain bodies such as UNCTAD, and of the Conventions of Lomé, to which the European Community is committed. I am thinking too of the kinds of dialogue that take place when borders are open and people can travel freely. I am thinking of the dialogue that takes place when one culture is enriched by contact with another culture, when scholars are free to communicate, when workers are free to assemble, when young people join forces for the future, when the elderly are reunited with their loved ones. The path of dialogue is a path of discoveries, and the more we discover one another, the more we can replace the tensions of the past with bonds of peace.

New relationships built on solidarity and dialogue

5.   In the spirit of solidarity and with the instruments of dialogue we will learn:
• respect for every human person;
• respect for the true values and cultures of others;
• respect for the legitimate autonomy and self-determination of others;

- to look beyond ourselves in order to understand and support the good of others;
- to contribute our own resources in social solidarity for the development and growth that come from equity and justice;
- to build the structures that will ensure that social solidarity and dialogue are permanent features of the world we live in.

The tension born of the two blocs will be successfully replaced by the interconnected relations of solidarity and dialogue when we learn to insist on *the primacy of the human person*. The dignity of the person and the defence of his or her human rights are in the balance, because they always suffer in one way or another from those tensions and distortions of the blocs which we have been examining. This can happen in countries where many individual liberties are guaranteed but where individualism and consumerism warp and distort the values of life. It happens in societies where the person is submerged into the collectivity. It can happen in young countries which are eager to take control of their own affairs but which are often forced into certain policies by the powerful, or seduced by the lure of immediate gain at the expense of the people themselves. In all this we must insist on the primacy of the person.

The Christian vision and commitment

6.   My brothers and sisters in the Christian faith find *in Jesus Christ*, in the Gospel message and in the life of the Church lofty reasons and *even more inspiring motives for striving to bring about one single peace in today's world*. The Christian faith has as its focus Jesus Christ, who stretches out his arms on the Cross in order to unite the children of God who were scattered (cf. *Jn* 11:52), to break down the walls of division (cf. *Eph* 2:14), and to reconcile the peoples in fraternity and peace. The Cross raised above the world symbolically embraces and has the power to reconcile North and South, East and West.

Christians, enlightened by faith, know that *the ultimate reason* why the world is the scene of divisions, tensions, rivalries, blocs and unjust inequalities, instead of being a place of genuine fraternity, *is sin*, that is to say human moral disorder. But Christians also know that the grace of Christ, which can transform this human condition, is continually being offered to the world, since 'where sin increased, grace abounded all the more' (*Rom* 5:20). *The Church*, which carries on Christ's work and dispenses his redeeming grace, *has precisely as her purpose the reconciling of all individuals and peoples in unity, fraternity and peace*. 'The promotion of unity', says the Second Vatican Council, 'belongs to the innermost nature of the Church, since she is "by her relationship with Christ, both a sacramental sign and an instrument of intimate union with God, and of the unity of all mankind"' (*Gaudium et Spes*, 42). The Church, which is one and universal in the variety of the peoples that she brings together, 'can form a very close unifying effect on the various communities of individuals and nations, provided they have trust in the Church and guarantee her true freedom to carry out her mission' (*ibid.*).

This vision and these demands which arise from the very heart of faith, should above all cause all Christians to become more aware of situations that are out of harmony with the Gospel, in order to purify and rectify them. At the same time Christians should recognize and value the positive signs attesting that efforts are being made to remedy these situations, efforts which they must effectively support, sustain and strengthen.

Animated by a lively hope, capable of hoping against hope (cf. *Rom* 4:18), Christians must *go beyond the barriers of ideologies and systems*, in order to enter into dialogue with all people of good will, and create new relationships and new forms of solidarity. In this regard I would like to say a word of appreciation and praise to all those who are engaged in international volunteer work and other forms of activity aimed at creating links of sharing and fraternity at a level higher than the various blocs.

International Year of Peace and final appeal

7.   Dear friends, brothers and sisters all: at the beginning of a new year I renew my appeal to all of you to put aside hostilities, to break the fetters of the tensions that exist in the world. I appeal to you to turn those tensions of North and South, East and West into new relationships of social solidarity and dialogue. The United Nations Organization has proclaimed 1986 the International Year of Peace. This noble effort deserves our encouragement and support. What better way could there be to further the aims of the Year of Peace than to make the relationships of North–South and East–West the basis of a peace that is universal!

To you, politicians and statesmen, I appeal: to give the leadership that will incite people to renewed effort in this direction.

To you, businessmen, to you who are responsible for financial and commercial organizations, I appeal: to examine anew your responsibilities towards all your brothers and sisters.

To you, military strategists, officers, scientists and technologists, I appeal: to use your expertise in ways that promote dialogue and understanding.

To you, the suffering, the handicapped, those who are physically limited, I appeal: to offer your prayers and your lives in order to break down the barriers that divide the world.

To all of you who believe in God I appeal that you live your lives in the awareness of being one family under the fatherhood of God.

To all of you and to each one of you, young and old, weak and powerful, I appeal: embrace peace as the great unifying value of your lives. Wherever you live on this planet I earnestly exhort you to pursue in solidarity and sincere dialogue:

Peace as a value with no frontiers: North–South, East–West, everywhere one people united in only one Peace.

1 January 1987
DEVELOPMENT AND SOLIDARITY: TWO KEYS TO PEACE

On the twentieth anniversary of Paul VI's acclaimed encyclical, Populorum Progressio, with its famous phrase 'development is the new name for peace', Pope John Paul II devotes his 1987 message to development and links it to a key theme of his social teaching – solidarity. He comments positively on the growing realization of social solidarity but he notes obstacles to solidarity such as xenophobia, closing of barriers, ideologies and terrorism. He proposes effective solidarity as an antidote to all of this, noting that 'pride of place' should be given 'to the elements that unite, however small'. Referring to the theme of development and the need for integral development, he underlines how much people should always be the focus and centre of development. He warns, therefore, against aid packages that force countries to accept contraception programmes and abortion schemes as the price of economic growth. Linking solidarity and development as two keys to peace, he proposes increased ethical considerations regarding the problem of external debt as well as greater sharing of scientific and technological advances with countries less advanced in these areas. He comments on the contemporary phenomenon of the breakdown of the family. Finally, recalling the great Assisi gathering of representatives of World Religions who came together to pray for peace in 1986, he underlines the need for solidarity in prayer and meditation for peace.

✳ ✳ ✳

An appeal to all ...

1.   My predecessor Pope Paul VI issued an appeal to all people of good will to celebrate a World Day of Peace on the first day of each civil year, as both a hope and promise that peace 'would dominate the development of events to come' (*AAS* 59, 1967, p. 1098). Twenty years later, I repeat this appeal, addressing myself to every member of the human family. I invite you to join with me in reflecting on peace and in celebrating peace. To celebrate peace in the midst of difficulties – such as those of today – is to *proclaim our trust* in humanity.

Because of this trust, I address my appeal to everyone, confident that together we can learn to celebrate peace as the universal desire of all peoples everywhere. All of us who share that desire can thus become one in our thoughts and in our efforts to make peace a goal that can be attained by all for all.

The theme I have chosen for this year's Message takes its inspiration from that deep truth about humanity: *we are one human family*. By simply being born into this world, we are of one inheritance and one stock with every other human being. This oneness expresses itself in all the richness and diversity of the human family: in different races, cultures, languages and histories. And we are called to recognize the *basic solidarity* of the human family as the fundamental condition of our life together on this earth.

1987 also marks the twentieth anniversary of the publication of *Populorum Progressio*. This celebrated Encyclical of Paul VI was a solemn appeal for concerted action in favour of the integral development of peoples (cf. *Populorum Progressio*, 5). Paul VI's phrase – 'Development is the new name for peace' (ibid., 76, 87) – specifies one of the keys in our search for peace. Can true peace exist when men, women and children cannot live in full human dignity? Can there be a lasting peace in a world ruled by relations – social, economic and political – that favour one group or nation at the expense of another? Can genuine peace be established without an effective recognition of that wonderful truth that we are all equal in dignity, equal because we have been formed in the image of God who is our Father?

... *to reflect on solidarity* ...

2.   This Message for the Twentieth World Day of Peace is closely linked to the Message I addressed to the world last year on the theme *North–South, East–West: Only One Peace*. In that Message, I said: ' ... the unity of the human family has very real repercussions for our life and for our commitment to peace ... It means that we commit ourselves to *a new solidarity*, the solidarity of the human family ... a *new relationship*, the social solidarity of all' (No. 4).

To recognize the social solidarity of the human family brings with it the responsibility to build on what makes us one. This means promoting effectively and without exception the equal dignity of all as human beings endowed with certain fundamental and inalienable human rights. This touches all aspects of our individual life, as well as our life in the family, in the community in which we live, and in the world. Once we truly grasp that we are *brothers and sisters in a common humanity*, then we can shape our attitudes towards life in the light of the solidarity which makes us one. This is especially true in all that relates to the basic universal project: *peace*.

In the lifetime of all of us, there have been moments and events that have bound us together in a conscious recognition of the oneness of humanity. From the time that we were first able to see pictures of the world from space, a perceptible change has taken place in our understanding of our planet and of its immense beauty and fragility. Helped by the accomplishments of space exploration, we found that the expression 'the common heritage of all mankind' has taken on a new meaning from that date. The more we share in the artistic and cultural riches of one another, the more we discover our common humanity. Young people especially have deepened their sense of oneness through regional and worldwide sports events and similar activities, deepening their bonds of brotherhood and sisterhood.

... as put into practice ...

3.   At the same time, how often in recent years have we had occasion to reach out as brothers and sisters to help those struck by natural disaster or subjected to war and famine. We are witnessing a growing collective desire – across political, geographical or ideological boundaries – to help the less fortunate members of the human family. The suffering, still so tragic and protracted, of our brothers and sisters in Sub-Saharan Africa is giving rise to forms and concrete expressions of this solidarity of human beings everywhere. Two of the reasons why I was pleased in 1986 to confer the Pope John XXIII International Peace Prize on the Catholic Office for Emergency Relief and Refugees (COERR) of Thailand were first, to be able to call the attention of the world to the continuing plight of those who are forced from their homelands; and secondly to highlight the spirit of cooperation and collaboration that so many groups – Catholic and otherwise – have displayed in responding to the need of these sorely tried homeless people. Yes, the human spirit can and does respond with great generosity to the suffering of others. In these responses we can find a growing realization of the social solidarity that proclaims in word and deed that we are one, that we must recognize that oneness, and that it is an essential element for the common good of all individuals and nations.

These examples illustrate that we can and do cooperate in many ways, and that we can and do work together to advance the common good. However, we must do more. We need *to adopt a basic attitude towards* humanity and the relationships we have with every person and every group in the world. Here we can begin to see how the commitment to the solidarity of the whole human family is a key to peace. Projects that foster the good of humanity or good will among peoples are one step in the realization of solidarity. The bond of sympathy and charity that compels us to help those who suffer brings our oneness to the fore in another way. But the underlying challenge to all of us is to adopt *an attitude of social solidarity with the whole human family* and to face all social and political situations with this attitude.

Thus, for example, the United Nations Organization has designated 1987 as the International Year of Shelter for the Homeless. By so doing it is calling attention to a matter of great concern, and supporting an attitude of solidarity – human, political and economic – towards millions of families deprived of the environment essential for proper family life.

... and as obstructed

4.   Examples unfortunately abound of obstacles to solidarity, of political and ideological positions which do in fact affect the achievement of solidarity. These are positions or policies that ignore or deny the fundamental equality and dignity of the human person. Among these, I am thinking in particular of:

- *a xenophobia* that closes nations in on themselves or which leads governments to enact discriminatory laws against people in their own countries;
- *the closing of borders* in an arbitrary and unjustifiable way so that people are effectively deprived of the ability to move and to better their lot, to be reunited with their loved ones, or simply to visit their family or reach out in care and understanding to others;
- *ideologies* that preach hatred or distrust, systems that set up artificial barriers. Racial hatred, religious intolerance, class divisions are all too present in many societies, both openly and covertly. When political leaders erect such divisions into internal systems or into policies regarding relationships with other nations, then these prejudices strike at the core of human dignity. They become a powerful source of counteractions that further foster division, enmity, repression and warfare. Another evil, which in this past year

brought so much suffering to people and havoc to society, is terrorism.

To all of these, *effective solidarity* offers an antidote. For if the essential note of solidarity is to be found in the radical equality of all men and women, then any and every policy that contradicts the basic dignity and human rights of any person or group of persons is a policy that is to be rejected. On the contrary, policies and programmes that build open and honest relationships among peoples, that forge just alliances, that unite people in honourable cooperation, are to be fostered. Such initiatives do not ignore the real linguistic, racial, religious, social or cultural differences among peoples; nor do they deny the great difficulties in overcoming long-standing divisions and injustice. But they do give pride of place to the elements that unite, however small they may appear to be.

This spirit of solidarity is a spirit that is open to dialogue. It finds its roots in truth, and needs truth to develop. It is a spirit that seeks to build up rather than to destroy, to unite rather than to divide. Since solidarity is universal in its aspiration, it can take many forms. Regional agreements to promote the common good and encourage bilateral negotiations can serve to lessen tensions. The sharing of technology or information to avert disasters or to improve the quality of life of people in a particular area will contribute to solidarity and facilitate further measures on a wider level.

To reflect on development ...

5.   Perhaps in no other sector of human endeavour is there greater need of social solidarity than *in the area of development*. Much of what Paul VI said twenty years ago in his now celebrated Encyclical is especially applicable today. He saw with great clarity that the social question had become worldwide (cf. *Populorum Progressio*, 3). He was among the first to call attention to the fact that economic progress in itself is insufficient, that it demands social progress (cf. *ibid.*, 35). Above all, he insisted that development must be integral, that

is, the development of every person and of the whole person (cf. *ibid.*, 14–21). This was, for him, a complete humanism: the fully-rounded development of the person in all his or her dimensions and open to the Absolute, which 'gives human life its true meaning' (*ibid.*, 42). Such a humanism is the common goal that must be sought for everyone. 'There can be no progress towards the complete development of man', he said, 'without the simultaneous development of all humanity in the spirit of solidarity' (*ibid.*, 43).

Now, twenty years later, I wish to pay tribute to this teaching of Paul VI. In the changed circumstances of today, these profound insights, especially regarding the importance of a spirit of solidarity for development, are still valid and shed great light on new challenges.

... and its applications today

6.   When we reflect on commitment to solidarity in the field of development, the first and most basic truth is that *development is a question of people*. People are the *subjects* of true development, and the *aim* of true development is people. The integral development of people is the goal and measure of all development projects. That all people are at the centre of development is a consequence of the oneness of the human family; and this is irrespective of any technological or scientific discoveries that the future may hold. People must be the focus of all that is done to improve the conditions of life. People must be active agents, not passive recipients, in any true development process.

Another principle of development as it relates to solidarity is the need *to promote values that truly benefit individuals and society*. It is not enough to reach out and help those in need. We must help them to discover the values which enable them to build a new life and to take their rightful place in society with dignity and justice. All people have the right to pursue and attain what is good and true. All have the right to choose those things that enhance life, and life in society is by no means morally neutral. Social choices have consequences that either promote or debase the true good of the person in society.

In the field of development, and especially of development assistance, programmes have been offered which claim to be 'value free' but which in fact are countervalues to life. When one considers government programmes or aid packages that virtually force communities or countries to accept contraception programmes and abortion schemes as the price of economic growth, then one has to say clearly and forcefully that these offers violate the solidarity of the human family because they deny the values of human dignity and human freedom.

What is true of personal development through the choice of values that enhance life applies also to the development of society. Whatever impedes true freedom militates against the development of society and of social institutions. Exploitation, threats, forced subjection, denials of opportunities by one sector of society to another are unacceptable and contradict the very notion of human solidarity. Such activities, both within a society and among nations, may unfortunately seem successful for a while. However, the longer such conditions exist, the more likely they are to be the cause of still further repression and increasing violence. The seeds of destruction are already sown in institutionalized injustice. To deny the means of achieving development to any sector of a given society or to any nation can only lead to insecurity and social unrest. It breeds hatred and division and destroys the hope for peace.

The solidarity that fosters integral development is that which *protects and defends the legitimate freedom of every person and the rightful security of every nation*. Without this freedom and security, the very conditions for development are missing. Not only individuals but also nations must be able to share in the choices which affect them. The freedom that nations must have to ensure their growth and development as equal partners in the family of nations is dependent on reciprocal respect among them. Seeking economic, military or political superiority at the expense of the rights of other nations places in jeopardy any prospects for *true development or true peace*.

Solidarity and development: two keys to peace

7.   For these reasons, I have proposed that we reflect this year on *solidarity* and *development* as *keys to peace*. Each of these realities has its own specific meaning. Both are necessary for the goals we seek. *Solidarity is ethical* in nature because it involves an *affirmation of value* about humanity. For this reason, its implications for human life on this planet and for international relations are also ethical: our common bonds of humanity demand that we live in harmony and that we promote what is good for one another. These ethical implications are the reason why *solidarity is a basic key to peace*.

In this same light, *development* takes on its full meaning. It is no longer a question merely of improving certain situations or economic conditions. Development ultimately becomes a question of *peace*, because it helps to achieve what is good for others and for the human community as a whole.

In the context of true solidarity, there is no danger of exploitation or the misuse of development programmes for the benefit of the few. Rather, development thus becomes a process involving different members of the same human family and enriching them all. As solidarity gives us the ethical basis to act upon, development becomes the offer that brother makes to brother, so that both can live more fully in all the diversity and complementarity that are the hallmarks of human civilization. Out of this dynamic comes the harmonious 'tranquillity of order' which is true peace. Yes, solidarity and development are two keys to peace.

Some modern problems ...

8.   Many of the problems that face the world in this beginning of 1987 are indeed complex, and seem almost

insoluble. Yet, if we believe in the oneness of the human family, if we insist that peace is possible, our common reflection on solidarity and development as keys to peace can shed much light on these critical issues.

Certainly the continuing problem of the *external debt* of many of the developing countries could be looked at with new eyes if everyone concerned would consciously include these ethical considerations in the evaluations made and the solutions proposed. Many aspects of this issue – protectionism, prices of raw materials, priorities in investment, respect for obligations contracted as well as consideration of the internal condition of the debtor countries – would benefit from seeking *in solidarity* those solutions that promote stable development.

With reference to *science and technology*, new and powerful divisions are appearing between the technological haves and have-nots. Such inequalities do not promote peace and harmonious development, but rather compound already existing situations of inequality. If people are the subject of development and the goal to which it tends, a more open sharing of applicable technological advances with less technologically advanced countries becomes an ethical imperative of solidarity, as does a refusal to make of such countries the testing area for doubtful experiments or a dumping ground for questionable products. International agencies and various States are making notable efforts in these fields. Such efforts are an important contribution to peace.

Recent contributions on the relationship between *disarmament and development* – two of the most crucial problems facing the world today – point to the fact that current East–West tensions and North–South inequalities *present serious threats to world peace*. It is becoming increasingly clear that a peaceful world, one in which the security of peoples and of States is ensured, calls for active solidarity in efforts for both development and disarmament. All States are inevitably affected by the poverty of other States; all States inevitably suffer from the lack of results in disarmament negotiations. Nor can we forget the so-called local wars that take a heavy toll of human life. All States have responsibility for world peace and this peace cannot be ensured until a security based on arms is gradually replaced with a *security based on the solidarity of the human family.* Once again, I appeal for further efforts to reduce arms to the minimum necessary for legitimate defence, and for increased measures to aid the developing countries to become self-reliant. Only thus can the community of States live in true solidarity.

There is yet another threat to peace, one that throughout the world saps the very roots of every society: *the breakdown of the family.* The family is the basic cell of society. The family is the first place where development occurs or does not occur. If it is healthy and wholesome, then the possibilities for the integral development of the whole of society are great. Too often, however, this is not the case.

In too many societies, the family has become a secondary element. It is relativized by various forms of interference and it often fails to find in the State the protection and support that it needs. Not infrequently it is deprived of the just means to which it has a right so that it can grow and provide an atmosphere where its members can flourish. The phenomena of broken families, of family members forced to separate for survival, or unable even to find shelter to begin or to maintain themselves as families, are all signs of moral underdevelopment and of a society that has confused its values. A basic measure of the health of a people or nation is the importance it gives to conditions for the development of families. Conditions that are beneficial to families promote the harmony of the society and nation, and this in turn fosters peace at home and in the world.

Today we see the frightening spectre of young children who are abandoned or forced into the marketplace. We find children and young people in shanty towns and in large impersonal cities where they find meagre sustenance and little or no hope for the future. The breakdown of the family structure, the dispersal of its members, especially the very young, and the consequent ills visited upon them – drug abuse, alcoholism, transient and meaningless sexual relations, exploitation by others – all are countersigns to the development of the whole person that is fostered through the social solidarity of the human family. To look into the eyes of another person and to see the hopes and anxieties of a brother or sister is to discover the meaning of solidarity.

... that challenge us all

9.   *Peace is at stake*: civil peace within nations and world peace among States (cf. *Populorum Progressio*, 55). Paul VI saw this clearly twenty years ago. He saw the intrinsic connection between the demands of justice in the world and the possibility of peace for the world. It is no mere coincidence that the very year of the publication of *Populorum Progressio* also marked the institution of the annual World Day of Peace, an initiative which I was glad to continue.

Paul VI already expressed the heart of this year's reflection on solidarity and development as keys to peace when he stated: 'Peace cannot be limited to a mere absence of war, the result of an ever precarious balance of forces. No, peace is something that is built up day after day in pursuit of an order intended by God, which implies a more perfect form of justice among people' (*ibid.*, 76).

The commitment of believers and especially Christians

10.   All of us who believe in God are convinced that this harmonious order for which all peoples long cannot come about solely through human efforts, indispensable though they be. This peace – personal peace and peace for others – must at the same time be sought in prayer and meditation. In saying this, I have before my eyes and in my heart the deep experience of the recent World Day of Prayer for Peace in Assisi. Religious leaders and representatives of the Christian Churches and Ecclesial Communities and the World Religions gave living expression to solidarity in prayer and meditation for peace. It was a visible commitment on the part of every participant –

and of the many others who joined with us in spirit – to seek peace, to be peacemakers, to do everything possible, in the deep solidarity of the spirit to work for a society in which justice will flourish and peace abound (cf. *Ps* 72:7).

The Just Ruler whose description the Psalmist sets before us is one who deals out justice to the poor and suffering. 'He has pity on the weak and the needy, and saves the lives of the needy. From oppression and violence he redeems their life ...' (vv. 13–14). These words are before our eyes today as we pray that the longing for peace which marked the meeting in Assisi may be the moving force for all believers and in a special way for Christians.

For Christians can discern in these inspired words of the Psalms the figure of our Lord Jesus Christ, the One who brought his peace to the world, the One who healed the wounded and afflicted, announced good news to the poor and set at liberty those who were oppressed (cf. *Lk* 4:18). Jesus Christ is the One whom we call 'our peace', and who 'has broken down the dividing wall of hostility' (*Eph* 2:14), in order to make peace. Yes. Precisely this wish to make peace, seen at the Assisi meeting, also encourages us to give some thought to the manner of celebrating this World Day in the future.

We too are called to be like Christ, to be peacemakers through reconciliation, to be cooperators with him in the task of bringing peace to this earth by furthering the cause of justice for all peoples and nations. And we must never forget those words of his which summarize every perfect expression of human solidarity: 'Treat others the way you would have them treat you' (*Mt* 7:12). When this commandment is broken, Christians should realize that they are causing a division and committing a sin. This sin has serious effects on the community of believers and on the whole of society. It offends God himself, who is the creator of life and the one who keeps it in being.

The grace and wisdom that Jesus shows even from the time of his hidden life in Nazareth with Mary and Joseph (cf. *Lk* 2: 51f) is a model for our own relations with one another in the family, in our nations, in the world. The service of others through word and deed that marks the public life of Jesus is a reminder to us that the solidarity of the human family has been radically deepened. It has been given a transcendent aim that ennobles all our human efforts for justice and peace. Finally, the ultimate act of solidarity that the world has known – the death of Jesus Christ on the Cross for all – opens up to us Christians the way we are to follow. If our work for peace is to be fully effective, it must share in the transforming power of Christ, whose death gives life to all people born into this world, and whose triumph over death is the final guarantee that the justice which solidarity and development require will lead to lasting peace.

May the acceptance that Christians give to Jesus Christ as Saviour and Lord direct all their efforts. May their prayers sustain them in their commitment to the cause of peace through the development of peoples in the spirit of social solidarity.

Final appeal

11.   And so together we begin another year: 1987. May it be a year in which humanity finally puts aside the divisions of the past, a year in which people seek peace with all their heart. My hope is that this Message may be an occasion for each one to deepen his or her commitment to the oneness of the human family in solidarity. May it be a spur encouraging us all to seek the true good of all our brothers and sisters in an integral development that fosters all values of the human person in society.

At the beginning of this Message I explained that the theme of solidarity impelled me to address this to everyone, to every man and woman in this world. I now repeat this call to every one of you, but I wish to make a special appeal in the following way:

• to all of you, Government leaders and those responsible for international agencies: in order to ensure peace I appeal to you to redouble your efforts for the integral development of individuals and nations;

- to all of you who participated in the World Day of Prayer for Peace in Assisi or who were joined spiritually with us at that time: I appeal to you that we may bear witness together to peace in the world;
- to all of you who travel or who are involved in cultural exchanges: I appeal to you to be conscious instruments of greater mutual understanding, respect and esteem;
- to you, my younger brothers and sisters, the youth of the world: I appeal to you to use every means to forge new bonds of peace in fraternal solidarity with young people everywhere.

And dare I hope to be heard by those who practise violence and terrorism? Those of you who will at least listen to my voice, I beg you again, as I have in the past, to turn away from the violent pursuit of your goals – even if the goals themselves are just. I beg you to turn away from killing and harming the innocent. I beg you to stop undermining the very fabric of society. The way of violence cannot obtain true justice for you or for anyone else. If you want, you can still change. You can profess your own humanity and recognize human solidarity.

I appeal to all of you, wherever you are, whatever you are doing, to see the face of a brother or sister in every human being. What unites us is so much more than what separates and divides us: it is our common humanity.

Peace is always a gift of God, yet it depends on us too. And the keys to peace are within our grasp. It is up to us to use them to unlock all the doors!

1 January 1988

RELIGIOUS FREEDOM:
CONDITION FOR PEACE

Forty years after the Universal Declaration of Human Rights, the Pope in this message refers to religious freedom as a fundamental human right and condition for peace. The freedom of the individual in seeking the truth and in professing his or her religious convictions must be recognised as a personal, inalienable, human as well as civil and social right. Religious freedom is the raison d'être of other freedoms. It contributes to producing citizens who are genuinely free because it makes possible the quest for and acceptance of the truth about man and the world. And an honest relationship with truth is an essential condition for authentic freedom. Religious faith leads to a new understanding of our human condition: 'Faith brings people together and unites them, makes them see others as their brothers and sisters; it makes them more attentive, more responsible, more generous in their commitment to the common good'. While the state has duties regarding the exercise of the right of religious freedom, members of religions and religious leaders have grave responsibilities in ensuring that their teaching and living conforms to the requirements of peaceful coexistence and respect for the freedom of each individual. The Pope advocates the 'spirit of Assisi' referring to the 1986 gathering of prayer for peace. Finally he reminds Christians of the 'new' ways of seeing the world and others brought by Jesus Christ.

* * *

On the first day of the year, I am happy to fulfil a task, now twenty years old, of addressing the Leaders of the Nations and the Heads of the International Organizations, as well as all my brothers and sisters throughout the world who have at heart the cause of peace. For I am deeply convinced that to reflect together on the priceless treasure of peace is in a way to begin to build it.

The above mentioned theme which I would like to submit this year for everybody's consideration arises from three considerations.

In the first place, religious freedom, an essential requirement of the dignity of every person, is a cornerstone of the structure of human rights, and for this reason an irreplaceable factor in the good of individuals and of the whole of society, as well as of the personal fulfilment of each individual. It follows that the freedom of individuals and of communities to profess and practise their religion is an essential element for peaceful human coexistence. Peace, which is built up and consolidated at all levels of human association, puts down its roots in the freedom and openness of consciences to truth.

Moreover, every violation of religious freedom, whether open or hidden, does fundamental damage to the cause of peace, like violations of the other fundamental rights of the human person. Forty years after the *Universal Declaration of Human Rights*, to be commemorated next December, we have to admit that millions of people in various parts of the world are still suffering for their religious convictions: they are victims of repressive and oppressive legislation, victims sometimes of open persecution, but more often of subtle forms of discrimination aimed at believers and communities. This state of affairs, in itself intolerable, is also a bad omen for peace.

Furthermore, I wish to recall and hold up as a treasured memory the experience of the Day of Prayer held in Assisi on 27 October 1986. That great gathering of brothers and sisters, brought together in prayer for peace, was a sign for the world.

Without any confusion or syncretism, representatives of the major religious communities throughout the world sought to express together their conviction that *peace is a gift from on high*; they sought to evince an active commitment to pray for peace, to welcome it and make it fruitful through practical choices of respect, solidarity and fraternity.

The dignity and freedom of the human person

1.   Peace is not only the absence of conflict and war but 'the fruit of an order written into human society by its Divine Founder' (*Gaudium et Spes*, 78). It is a work of justice, and for that reason it demands respect for the rights of every person and the fulfilment of corresponding duties. There is an intrinsic connection between the demands of justice, truth and peace (cf. *Pacem in Terris*, I and III).

In accordance with this order, which is willed by the Creator, society is called upon to organize itself and to carry out its task at the service of man and the common good. The essential lines of this order can be examined by reason and recognized in historical experience. The modern development of the social sciences has enriched humanity's awareness of this order, despite all the ideological distortions and the conflicts which sometimes seem to obscure that awareness.

For this reason, the Catholic Church – while seeking to fulfil faithfully her mission of proclaiming the salvation that comes from Christ alone (cf. *Acts* 4:12) – turns to all people without distinction and invites them to recognize the laws of the natural order that govern human association and determine the conditions for peace.

The foundation and goal of the social order is the human person, as a subject of inalienable rights which are not conferred from outside but which arise from the person's very nature. Nothing and nobody can destroy them, and no external constraint can annihilate them, for they are rooted in what is most profoundly human. Likewise, the person is not merely the subject of social, cultural and historical conditioning, for it is proper to man, who has a spiritual soul, to tend towards a goal that transcends the changing conditions of his existence. No human power may obstruct the realization of man as a person.

From this first and fundamental principle of the social order, namely that society exists for the person, it follows that every society must be organized in such a way as to enable and indeed to help man to realize his vocation in full freedom.

Freedom is man's most noble prerogative. Beginning with the most private options, all individuals must be able to express themselves in an act of conscious choice, each following his or her own conscience. Without freedom, human acts are empty and valueless.

The freedom with which man has been endowed by the Creator is the capacity always given to him to seek what is true by using his intelligence and to embrace without reserve the good to which he naturally aspires, without being subjected to undue pressures, constraints or violence of any kind. It belongs to the dignity of the person to be able to respond to the moral imperative of one's own conscience in the search for truth. And the truth as the Second Vatican Council emphasized 'is to be sought after in a manner proper to the dignity of the human person and his social nature' (*Dignitatis Humanae*, 3) and 'cannot impose itself except by virtue of its own truth' (*ibid.*, 1).

The freedom of the individual in seeking the truth and in the corresponding profession of his or her religious convictions must be specifically guaranteed within the juridical structure of society; that is, it must be recognized and confirmed by civil law as a personal and inalienable right in order to be safeguarded from any kind of coercion by individuals, social groups or any human power (cf. *ibid.*, 2).

It is quite clear that freedom of conscience and of religion does not mean a relativization of the objective truth which every human being is morally obliged to seek. In an organized society, such freedom is only a translation, in institutional form, of that order within which God has ordained that his creatures should be able to know and accept his eternal offer of a covenant, and be able to correspond to it as free and responsible persons.

The civil and social right to religious freedom, inasmuch as it touches the most intimate sphere of the spirit, is a point of reference of the other fundamental rights and in some way becomes a measure of them. For it is a matter of respecting the individual's most jealously guarded autonomy, thus making it possible to act according to the dictates of conscience both in private choices and in social life. The State cannot claim authority, direct or indirect, over a person's religious convictions. It cannot arrogate to itself the right to impose or to impede the profession or public practice of religion by a person or a community. In this matter, it is the duty of civil authorities to ensure that the rights of individuals and communities are equally respected, and at the same time it is their duty to safeguard proper public order.

Even in cases where the State grants a special juridical position to a particular religion, there is a duty to ensure that the right to freedom of conscience is legally recognized and effectively respected for all citizens, and also for foreigners living in the country even temporarily for reasons of employment and the like.

In no case may the civil organization set itself up as the substitute for the conscience of the citizens, nor may it remove or take the place of the freedom of action of religious associations. A right social order requires that all – as individuals and in groups – should be able to profess their religious convictions with full respect for others.

On 1 September 1980, when I addressed the Heads of State who signed the *Helsinki Final Act*, I intended to emphasize, among other things, that authentic religious freedom requires that the rights deriving from the social and public dimension of the profession of faith and of belonging to an organized religious community must also be guaranteed.

In this regard, speaking to the General Assembly of the United Nations, I expressed my conviction that 'respect for the dignity of the human person would seem to demand that, when the exact tenor of the exercise of religious freedom is being discussed or determined with a view to national laws or

international conventions, the institutions that are by their
nature at the service of religion should also be brought in'
(*AAS* [1979], p. 1158).

A common patrimony

2.   It must be acknowledged that the principles of which
we have spoken are the common patrimony of most civil
societies today, as also of the organization of international
society, which has drawn up appropriate norms. These form
part of the culture of our time, as is demonstrated by the ever
more accurate and detailed discussion which, especially in
recent years, has taken place in meetings and congresses of
scholars and experts on every practical aspect of religious
freedom. Nonetheless, it frequently happens that the right to
religious freedom is incorrectly understood and insufficiently
respected.

In the first place there are spontaneous outbreaks of
intolerance, more or less haphazard, sometimes the result of
ignorance or mistaken ideas, which attack individuals or
communities and cause disputes, bad feelings and hostility, to
the detriment of peace and a united commitment to the
common good.

In various countries, laws and administrative practices limit
or in fact annul the rights formally recognized by the
Constitution for individual believers and religious groups.

Furthermore, there still exist today laws and regulations
which do not recognize the fundamental right to religious
freedom, or which envisage completely unjustified limitations,
not to mention cases of provisions which are actually
discriminatory in nature and which sometimes amount to open
persecution.

Various organizations, public and private, national and
international, have been established, especially in recent years,
for the defence of those who in many parts of the world are –
by reason of their religious convictions – victims of situations
which are illegal and detrimental to the whole human family.
Before public opinion these bodies rightly express the

complaints and protests of those brothers and sisters who often have no voice of their own.

The Catholic Church, for her part, constantly shows her solidarity with all those suffering from discrimination and persecution because of their faith. She works with steady resolve and patient persistence for the remedying of such situations. For this purpose the Holy See seeks to make its own specific contribution in international assemblies which discuss the safeguarding of human rights and of peace. In the same sense is to be understood the action, necessarily more discreet but no less solicitous, of the Apostolic See and its Representatives in contacts with the political authorities of the whole world.

Religious freedom and peace

3.   Everybody is aware that the religious dimension, rooted in the human conscience, has a specific impact on the subject of peace, and that every attempt to impede or to coerce its free expression inevitably has grave negative effects upon the possibility of a peaceful society.

An obvious consideration presents itself. As I wrote in the already mentioned Letter to the Heads of State who signed the *Helsinki Final Act*, religious freedom, in so far as it touches the most intimate sphere of the spirit, sustains and is as it were the *raison d'etre* of other freedoms. And the profession of a religion, although it consists primarily in interior acts of the spirit, involves the entire experience of human life, and thus all its manifestations.

Religious freedom also contributes decisively to producing citizens who are genuinely free: for by making possible the quest for and acceptance of the truth about man and the world it helps all individuals to gain a full understanding of their own dignity. It also helps them to take up their duties with greater responsibility. An honest relationship with the truth is an essential condition for authentic freedom (cf. *Redemptor Hominis*, 12).

In this sense it can be said that religious freedom is a very important means of strengthening a people's moral integrity.

Civil society can count on believers who, because of their deep convictions, will not only not succumb readily to dominating ideologies or trends but will endeavour to act in accordance with their aspirations to all that is true and right, an essential condition for securing peace (cf. *Dignitatis Humanae*, 8).

But there is more. By leading people to a new understanding of their human condition, religious faith brings people, through a sincere gift of themselves, to a complete fellowship with other human beings (cf. *Dominum et Vivificantem*, 59). Faith brings people together and unites them, makes them see others as their brothers and sisters; it makes them more attentive, more responsible, more generous in their commitment to the common good. It is not just a matter of feeling better disposed to collaborating with others by reason of the fact that one's own rights are ensured and protected; it is rather a matter of drawing from the deepest resources of a right conscience higher incentives for the task of building a more just and more human society.

Within each State – or rather within each people – this need for a shared sense of common responsibility is more keenly felt today. But, as my predecessor Pope Paul VI had occasion to ask, how can a State call for total trust and collaboration when, in a kind of 'negative confessionalism', it proclaims itself atheistic and when, within a certain framework, it declares its respect for the beliefs of individuals but in fact takes up an attitude opposed to the faith of a part of its citizens (cf. *Speech to the Diplomatic Corps*, 14 January 1978)? On the contrary, an effort should be made to ensure that the opposition between the religious view of the world and the agnostic or even atheistic view, which is one of the 'signs of the times' of our age, should be kept within human limits of fairness and respect, without doing harm to the fundamental rights of conscience of any man or woman living on this planet (cf. John Paul II, *Speech to the United Nations*, 2 October 1979, No. 20).

Above and beyond persisting situations of war and injustice, we are witnessing today a movement towards an increasing union of peoples and nations, on the various levels of politics, economics, culture, etc. This tendency, which appears to be unstoppable but which meets with continuous and serious obstacles, receives a profound and not insignificant impulse from religious conviction. For the latter, by excluding recourse to violent methods for resolving conflicts and by educating to fraternal solidarity and love, fosters understanding and reconciliation, and can provide fresh moral resources for the solution of questions in the face of which humanity today seems weak and powerless.

The responsibility of religious people

4.   The State's duties regarding the exercise of the right of religious freedom are matched by the precise and grave responsibilities of men and women for both their individual religious profession and the organization and life of the communities to which they belong.

In the first place, the leaders of religious bodies are obliged to present their teaching without allowing themselves to be conditioned by personal, political or social interests, and in ways that conform to the requirements of peaceful coexistence and respect for the freedom of each individual.

Similarly, the followers of the various religions should, individually and collectively, express their convictions and organize their worship and all other specific activities with respect for the rights of those who do not belong to that religion or do not profess any creed.

And it is precisely with regard to peace, mankind's supreme aspiration, that every religious community and every individual believer can test the genuineness of their commitment to solidarity with their brothers and sisters. Today as perhaps never before, the world looks expectantly to the various religions, precisely in matters concerning peace.

At the same time there is reason to rejoice that both the leaders of the religious bodies and the ordinary faithful are showing an ever keener interest and a livelier desire to work for peace. These intentions deserve to be encouraged and appropriately coordinated in order to increase their effectiveness. For this purpose, it is necessary to go to the roots.

That is what happened last year at Assisi. In response to my fraternal invitation, the leaders of the world's main religions gathered in order to affirm together – while remaining faithful to each one's religious conviction – their common commitment to building peace.

In the spirit of Assisi there is here a question of a binding and demanding gift, a gift to be cultivated and brought to maturity: in mutual acceptance and respect, renouncing ideological intimidation and violence, promoting institutions and methods of joint action and cooperation between peoples and nations, but especially in education for peace, considered at a level well above the necessary and hoped for reform of structures – peace that presupposes the conversion of hearts.

The commitment of the followers of Christ

5.   We recognize with joy that among the *Christian Churches and Ecclesial Communions* this process is already happily begun. I would like to express the hope that it will continue to receive a fresh impulse and that it will spread and bring about a broader involvement of all the adherents of the world's religions, in the great challenge of peace.

As the Pastor of the universal Church I would be failing in my duty if I did not speak out in favour of respect for the inalienable right of the Gospel to be proclaimed 'to the whole creation' (*Mk* 16:15), and if I did not repeat that God has ordered civil society to the service of the human person, to whom belongs the freedom to seek and embrace the truth. The commitment to truth, freedom, justice and peace is a mark of the followers of Christ the Lord. For we bear in our hearts the revealed certainty that God the Father, through his crucified Son, who 'is our peace' (*Eph* 2:14), has made of us a new People, which has as a condition the freedom of the children of God and as a statute the precept of fraternal love.

As the People of the New Covenant, we know that our freedom finds its highest expression in total acceptance of the

144

divine call to salvation, and with the Apostle John we profess: 'we know and believe the love God has for us ' (1 *Jn* 4:16), the love manifested in his Word made flesh. From this free and liberating act of faith there flows a new vision of the world, a new approach to our brethren, a new way of existing as a leaven in society. It is the 'new commandment' (*Jn* 13:34) which the Lord has given us; it is 'his peace' (cf. *Jn* 14:27) – not the peace of the world that is always imperfect – which he has left us.

We have to live completely and responsibly the freedom which comes to us from being children of God and which opens our eyes to transcendent prospects. We have to commit ourselves with all our strength to living the new commandment, allowing ourselves to be enlightened by the peace which has been given to us and radiating it to those around us. 'By this', the Lord admonishes us, 'all men will know that you are my disciples' (*Jn* 13:35).

I am well aware that this formidable commitment is beyond our poor powers. How many divisions and misunderstandings we Christians bear a certain responsibility for, and how much more remains for us to build, in our own spirits, in our families and communities, beneath the banner of reconciliation and fraternal charity! And, as we have to admit, the conditions of the world make the task no easier. The temptation to violence is always there. Selfishness, materialism and pride make man ever less free and society ever less open to the demands of brotherhood. Be this as it may, we must not become discouraged: Jesus, our Master and Lord, is with us always, to the close of the age (cf. *Mt* 28:20).

My thoughts turn with particular affection to those brothers and sisters who are deprived of the freedom to profess their Christian faith, to all who are suffering persecution for the name of Christ, to those who for his sake must suffer rejection and humiliation. I want these brothers and sisters of ours to feel our spiritual closeness, our solidarity, and the comfort of our prayer. We know that their sacrifice, to the extent that it is joined to Christ's, bears fruits of true peace.

Brothers and sisters in the faith: the commitment to peace is one of the testimonies which today makes us credible in the eyes of the world, and especially in the eyes of the younger generation. The great challenge facing modern man, the challenge to his true freedom, is found in the Gospel Beatitude: 'Blessed are the peacemakers' (*Mt 5:9*).

The world needs peace, the world ardently desires peace. Let us pray that all men and women, enjoying religious freedom, may be able to live in peace.

1 January 1989
TO BUILD PEACE,
RESPECT MINORITIES

In the context of increased international détente, Pope John Paul turns his attention to the question of minority groups that exist in almost all societies today. These groups 'take their origin from separate cultural traditions, racial and ethnic stock, religious beliefs, or historical experiences'. He outlines fundamental principles that need to be kept in mind when it comes to social organization within nations. He advocates respect for human diversity while also stressing the need to know the cultural heritage of minority groups better and so foster healthy social relations. He lists both minority rights (to exist, to preserve and develop their culture, right to religious freedom) and duties (to cooperate for the common good, promote freedom and dignity of each of its members, judge correctness of their claims in light of historical developments). The translation of law that enshrines fundamental human rights into behaviour needs initiatives, programmes and exchanges aimed at mutual understanding. He praises voluntary groups, religious organizations and people of good will that find work and decent housing for minority groups. He advocates dialogue as the way to solve problems. Again he reminds Christians of their mission of unifying love.

* * *

Introduction

1.   'From the nineteenth century a certain political trend has spread and taken hold in all parts of the world according to which people of the same extraction wish to be independent and to set themselves up as a nation apart. But since, for various reasons, this cannot always be achieved, it follows that ethnic minorities are often included within the national borders of a different ethnic group, and this leads to quite complex problems' (Encyclical *Pacem in Terris*, III).

With these words, twenty-five years ago, my venerable predecessor Pope John XXIII pointed to one of the most delicate questions affecting contemporary society, a question which, with the passing of time, has become even more pressing since it is related to the organization of social and civil life within each country, as well as to the life of the international community.

It is for this reason that, in choosing a specific theme for the World Day of Peace, I think it appropriate to present for general reflection the problem of minorities. For we are all aware that, as the Second Vatican Council affirms, 'peace is not merely the absence of war, nor can it be reduced solely to the maintenance of a balance of power between enemies' (*Gaudium et Spes*, 78). Rather, peace is a dynamic process which must take account of the many conditions and factors that can either favour it or disturb it.

It is clear that at this time of increased international *détente* resulting from agreements and mediations which allow us to look forward to solutions in favour of peoples who have been the victims of bloody conflicts, the question of minorities is assuming a notable importance. Consequently, it constitutes a matter for careful reflection on the part of political and religious leaders and all men and women of good will.

2.   As communities which take their origin from separate cultural traditions, racial and ethnic stock, religious beliefs, or historical experiences, minority groups exist in almost all societies today. Some go very far back in time, others are of

148

recent origin. The situations in which they live are so diverse that it is almost impossible to draw up a complete picture of them. On the one hand there are groups, even very small ones, which are able to preserve and affirm their own identity and are well integrated within the societies to which they belong. In some cases, such minority groups even succeed in imposing their control on the majority in public life. On the other hand one sees minorities which exert no influence and do not fully enjoy their rights, but rather find themselves in situations of suffering and distress. This can lead them either to passive resignation or to unrest and even rebellion. Yet, neither passivity nor violence represents the proper path for creating conditions of true peace.

Some minority groups share another experience: that of separation or exclusion. While it is true that at times a group may deliberately choose to remain apart in order to protect its own way of life, it is more often true that minorities are confronted by barriers that keep them apart from the rest of society. While in such a context the minority group tends to become closed within itself, the majority group may foster a feeling of rejection towards this group as a whole or towards its individual members. When this happens, the latter are no longer in a position actively and creatively to contribute to building a peace based on the acceptance of legitimate differences.

Fundamental principles

3.   In a nation made up of various groups of people there are two general principles which can never be abrogated and which constitute the basis of all social organization.

The first of these principles is the inalienable dignity of every human person, irrespective of racial, ethnic, cultural or national origin, or religious belief. Individuals do not exist for themselves alone, but achieve their full identity in relation to others. The same can be said about groups of people. They indeed have a right to a collective identity that must be safeguarded, in accordance with the dignity of each member.

Such a right remains intact even in cases in which the group, or one of its members, acts against the common good. In such situations, the alleged abuse must be addressed by the competent authorities, without the whole group being condemned, since that would be against justice. At the same time, the members of minority groups have the duty to treat others with the same respect and sense of dignity.

The second principle concerns the fundamental unity of the human race, which takes its origin from the one God, the Creator, who, in the language of Sacred Scripture, 'made from one every nation of men to live on all the face of the earth' (*Acts* 17:26). The unity of the human family requires that the whole of humanity, beyond its ethnic, national, cultural and religious differences, should form a community that is free of discrimination between peoples and that strives for reciprocal solidarity. Unity also requires that differences between the members of the human family should be used to strengthen unity, rather than serve as a cause of division.

The obligation to accept and defend diversity belongs not only to the State and to the groups themselves. Every individual, as a member of the one human family, ought to understand and respect the value of human diversity and direct it to the common good. A mind that is open and desirous of knowing better the cultural heritage of the minority groups with which it comes into contact will help to eliminate attitudes of prejudice which hinder healthy social relations. This is a process which has to be continuously fostered, since such attitudes tend to reappear time and again under new forms.

Peace within the one human family requires a constructive development of what distinguishes us as individuals and peoples, and of what constitutes our identity. Furthermore, on the part of all social groups, whether constituted as States or not, peace requires a readiness to contribute to the building of a peaceful world. The micro-community and the macro-community are bound by reciprocal rights and duties, the observance of which serves to consolidate peace.

Rights and duties of minorities

4.   One of the objectives of a State ruled by law is that all its citizens may enjoy the same dignity and the same equality before the law. Nonetheless, the existence of minorities as identifiable groups within a State raises the question of their specific rights and duties.

Many of these rights and duties have to do precisely with the relationship of minority groups to the State. In some cases, these rights have been codified and minorities enjoy specific legal protection. But not infrequently, even where the State guarantees such protection, minorities can suffer discrimination and exclusion. In these cases, the State itself has an obligation to promote and foster the rights of the minority groups, since peace and internal security can only be guaranteed through respect for the rights of all those for whom the State has responsibility.

5.   The first right of minorities is the right to exist. This right can be ignored in many ways, including such extreme cases as its denial through overt or indirect forms of genocide. The right to life as such is inalienable, and the State which perpetrates or tolerates acts aimed at endangering the lives of its citizens belonging to minority groups violates the fundamental law governing the social order.

6.   The right to exist can be undermined also in more subtle ways. Certain peoples, especially those identified as native or indigenous, have always maintained a special relationship to their land, a relationship connected with the group's very identity as a people having their own tribal, cultural and religious traditions. When such indigenous peoples are deprived of their land they lose a vital element of their way of life and actually run the risk of disappearing as a people.

7.   Another right which must be safeguarded is the right of minorities to preserve and develop their own culture. It is not unheard of that minority groups are threatened with

151

cultural extinction. In some places, in fact, laws have been enacted which do not recognize their right to use their own language. At times people are forced to change their family and place names. Some minorities see their artistic and literary expressions ignored, with their festivals and celebrations given no place in public life. All this can lead to the loss of a notable cultural heritage. Closely connected with this right is the right to have contact with groups having a common cultural and historical heritage but living in the territory of another State.

8.　　Here I will make only a brief mention of the right to religious freedom, since this was the theme of my Message for last year's World Day of Peace. This right applies to all religious communities, as well as to individuals, and includes the free manifestation of religious beliefs, both individually and collectively. Consequently, religious minorities must be able to worship as a community, according to their own rites. They must also be in a position to provide religious education through appropriate teaching programmes and to utilize the necessary means to this end.

Moreover, it is very important that the State should effectively ensure and promote the observance of religious freedom, especially when, alongside the great majority who follow one religion, there exist one or more minority groups of another faith.

Finally, religious minorities must be guaranteed a legitimate freedom of exchange and contacts with other communities, both within and outside their own national borders.

9.　　Today, fundamental human rights are enshrined in many international and national declarations. However essential these juridical instruments may be, they are still not enough to overcome deep-seated attitudes of prejudice and distrust, or to eliminate ways of thinking which lead to actions directed against minority groups. The translation of law into behaviour constitutes a long and slow process, especially with a view to eradicating such attitudes. This does not make the process any less urgent. Not only the State, but also each individual has the obligation to do everything possible to achieve this goal. The State, though, can play an important role by favouring the promotion of cultural initiatives and exchanges which aid mutual understanding, as well as educational programmes which help to train young people to respect others and reject all prejudices, many of which stem from ignorance. Parents too have a great responsibility, since children learn much from observation and tend to adopt their parents' attitudes towards other peoples and groups.

There is no doubt that the development of a culture based on respect for others is essential to the building of a peaceful society. But unfortunately the evidence today is that the effective exercise of this respect meets with considerable difficulties.

In practice, the State must be alert to prevent new forms of discrimination, as for example in access to housing or employment. In this respect the policies of public authorities are often laudably complemented by the generous initiatives of voluntary groups, religious organizations and people of good will, working to lower tensions and promote greater social justice by helping so many brothers and sisters to find work and decent housing.

10.   Delicate problems arise when a minority group puts forward claims which have particular political implications. A group may sometimes be seeking independence or at least greater political autonomy.

I wish to restate that, in such delicate circumstances, dialogue and negotiation are the obligatory path to peace. The willingness of parties involved to meet and talk to one another is the indispensable condition for reaching an equitable solution to the complex problems that can seriously obstruct peace. And a refusal to enter into dialogue can open the door to violence.

In some situations of conflict, terrorist groups unduly arrogate to themselves the exclusive right to speak in the name of a minority, depriving it of the possibility of freely and openly choosing its own representatives and of seeking a solution without intimidation. In addition, the members of such minority communities too often suffer from the acts of violence wrongfully committed in their name.

May those who follow the inhuman path of terrorism hear my voice: to strike blindly, kill innocent people or carry out bloody reprisals does not help a just evaluation of the claims advanced by the minorities for whom they claim to act (cf. *Sollicitudo Rei Socialis*, 24)!

11. Every right carries with it corresponding duties. Members of minority groups also have their own duties towards society and the State in which they live: in the first place, the duty to cooperate, like all citizens, for the common good. Minorities, in fact, must offer their own specific contribution to the building of a peaceful world that will reflect the rich diversity of all its inhabitants.

Secondly, a minority group has the duty to promote the freedom and dignity of each one of its members and to respect the decisions of each one, even if someone were to decide to adopt the majority culture.

In situations of real injustice it may be the duty of groups which have emigrated to other countries to demand respect for the legitimate rights of the members of their group who remain oppressed in their place of origin and who cannot themselves make their voice heard. In such cases great prudence and enlightened discernment must be exercised, especially when it is difficult to have objective information about the changing conditions of life of the people involved.

All members of minority groups, wherever they may be, must conscientiously judge the correctness of their claims in the light of historical developments and present reality. Not to do so would involve the risk of remaining prisoners of the past without prospects for the future.

Building peace

12. In the above reflections one can perceive the outline of a just and peaceful society, to the achievement of which all

have a responsibility to contribute with every possible effort. Building this society requires a wholehearted commitment to eliminate not only evident discrimination but also all barriers that divide groups. Reconciliation according to justice and with respect for the legitimate aspirations of all sectors of the community must be the rule. Above all and in all, the patient effort to build a peaceful society finds strength and fulfilment in the love that embraces all peoples. Such a love can be expressed in countless concrete ways of serving the rich diversity of the human race, which is one in origin and destiny.

The increased awareness which is found today at every level regarding the situation of minority groups constitutes for our own times a hopeful sign for the coming generations and for the aspirations of minority groups themselves. Indeed, in a sense, respect for minorities is to be considered the touchstone of social harmony and the index of the civic maturity attained by a country and its institutions. In a truly democratic society, to guarantee the participation of minorities in political life is a sign of a highly developed civilization, and it brings honour upon those nations in which all citizens are guaranteed a share in national life in a climate of true freedom.

13.   Finally, I wish to address a special appeal to my brothers and sisters in Christ. Whatever our origin and wherever we live, all of us know through faith that in Christ 'we all have access in one Spirit to the Father' for we have become 'members of the household of God' (*Eph* 2:18, 19). As members of the one family of God we can tolerate no division or discrimination in our midst. When the Father sent his Son into the world he entrusted him with a mission of universal salvation. Jesus came that 'all may have life and have it abundantly' (*Jn* 10:10). No person, no group is excluded from this mission of unifying love which has now been entrusted to us. We too must pray as Jesus did on the very eve of his death, with the simple and sublime words: 'Father may they be one in us, as you are in me and I am in you' (*Jn* 17:21).

This prayer must be our life's work, our witness, since as Christians we acknowledge that we have a common Father who makes no distinction of persons and 'loves the sojourner, giving him food and clothing' (*Dt* 10:18).

14.   When the Church speaks of discrimination in general or, as in this Message, of the particular discrimination that affects minority groups, she addresses her own members first of all, whatever their position or responsibility in society. Just as there can be no place for discrimination within the Church, so no Christian can knowingly foster or support structures and attitudes that unjustly divide individuals or groups. This same teaching must be applied to those who have recourse to violence or support it.

15.   In closing, I would like to express my spiritual closeness to those members of minority groups who are suffering. I know their moments of pain and their reasons for legitimate pride. My prayer is that their trials may soon cease and that all may be secure in the enjoyment of their rights. I in turn ask for prayers, that the peace we seek may be an ever more genuine peace, built on the 'cornerstone' which is Christ himself (cf. *Eph* 2:20–22).

May God bless everyone with the gift of his peace and his love!

1 January 1990

PEACE WITH GOD THE CREATOR, PEACE WITH ALL OF CREATION

This message focuses on ecology. Basing his comments on the biblical account of creation, the Pope describes the earth as 'suffering' because of the lack of respect shown it. Indiscriminate application of advances in science and technology such as biological and genetic manipulation as well as unacceptable experimentation regarding the origins of human life result in damage: 'We cannot interfere in one area of the ecosystem without paying due attention both to the consequences of such interference in other areas and to the well-being of future generations.' No peaceful society can afford to neglect respect for life nor the fact that creation has an integrity. He proposes a more internationally co-ordinated approach to the management of the earth's goods. Each individual State bears responsibility in this area. A new solidarity is needed to avoid the damage that comes about through industrial pollutants, radical deforestation and unlimited exploitation of non-renewable resources. A new solidarity is needed and this could present new opportunities for strengthening co-operative and peaceful relations among States. The Pope also highlights how structural forms of poverty need to be addressed if the proper ecological balance is to be found. War too is an ecological menace. But the Pope addresses each one of us personally when he says that we all need to 'take a serious look at our lifestyle'. Finally, the Pope highlights the 'aesthetic value of creation' and its deep restorative power. He points us to the example of Francis of Assisi, the Patron of those who promote ecology.

✳ ✳ ✳

Introduction

1.   In our day, there is a growing awareness that world peace is threatened not only by the arms race, regional conflicts and continued injustices among peoples and nations, but also by a lack of *due respect for nature*, by the plundering of natural resources and by a progressive decline in the quality of life. The sense of precariousness and insecurity that such a situation engenders is a seedbed for collective selfishness, disregard for others and dishonesty.

Faced with the widespread destruction of the environment, people everywhere are coming to understand that we cannot continue to use the goods of the earth as we have in the past. The public in general as well as political leaders are concerned about this problem, and experts from a wide range of disciplines are studying its causes. Moreover, a new *ecological awareness* is beginning to emerge which, rather than being downplayed, ought to be encouraged to develop into concrete programmes and initiatives.

2.   Many ethical values, fundamental to the development of a *peaceful society*, are particularly relevant to the ecological question. The fact that many challenges facing the world today are interdependent confirms the need for carefully coordinated solutions based on a morally coherent world view.

For Christians, such a world view is grounded in religious convictions drawn from Revelation. That is why I should like to begin this Message with a reflection on the biblical account of creation. I would hope that even those who do not share these same beliefs will find in these pages a common ground for reflection and action.

I.   'AND GOD SAW THAT IT WAS GOOD'

3.   In the Book of Genesis, where we find God's first self-revelation to humanity (*Gen* 1–3), there is a recurring refrain: '*And God saw that it was good*'. After creating the heavens,

the sea, the earth and all it contains, God created man and woman. At this point the refrain changes markedly: 'And God saw everything that he had made, and behold, *it was very good* (*Gen* 1:31). God entrusted the whole of creation to the man and woman, and only then – as we read – could he rest 'from all his work' (*Gen* 2:3).

Adam and Eve's call to share in the unfolding of God's plan of creation brought into play those abilities and gifts which distinguish the human being from all other creatures. At the same time, their call established a fixed relationship between mankind and the rest of creation. Made in the image and likeness of God, Adam and Eve were to have exercised their dominion over the earth (*Gen* 1:28) with wisdom and love. Instead, they destroyed the existing harmony *by deliberately going against the Creator's plan*, that is, by choosing to sin. This resulted not only in man's alienation from himself, in death and fratricide, but also in the earth's 'rebellion' against him (cf. *Gen* 3: 17–19; 4:12). All of creation became subject to futility, waiting in a mysterious way to be set free and to obtain a glorious liberty together with all the children of God (cf. *Rom* 8:20–21).

4.   Christians believe that the Death and Resurrection of Christ accomplished the work of reconciling humanity to the Father, who 'was pleased ... through (Christ) to reconcile to himself *all things*, whether on earth or in heaven, making peace by the blood of his cross' (*Col* 1:19–20). Creation was thus made new (cf. *Rev* 21:5). Once subjected to the bondage of sin and decay (cf. *Rom* 8:21), it has now received new life while 'we wait for new heavens and a new earth in which righteousness dwells' (2 *Pt* 3:13). Thus, the Father 'has made known to us in all wisdom and insight the mystery ... which he set forth in Christ as a plan for the fulness of time, to unite *all things* in him, all things in heaven and things on earth' (*Eph* 1:9–10).

5.   These biblical considerations help us to understand better *the relationship between human activity and the whole of*

creation. When man turns his back on the Creator's plan, he provokes a disorder which has inevitable repercussions on the rest of the created order. If man is not at peace with God, then earth itself cannot be at peace: 'Therefore the land mourns and all who dwell in it languish, and also the beasts of the field and the birds of the air and even the fish of the sea are taken away' (*Hos* 4:3).

The profound sense that the earth is 'suffering' is also shared by those who do not profess our faith in God. Indeed, the increasing devastation of the world of nature is apparent to all. It results from the behaviour of people who show a callous disregard for the hidden, yet perceivable requirements of the order and harmony which govern nature itself.

People are asking anxiously if it is still possible to remedy the damage which has been done. Clearly, an adequate solution cannot be found merely in a better management or a more rational use of the earth's resources, as important as these may be. Rather, we must go to the source of the problem and face in its entirety that profound moral crisis *of which the destruction of the environment is only one troubling aspect*.

II.   THE ECOLOGICAL CRISIS: A MORAL PROBLEM

6.   Certain elements of today's ecological crisis reveal its moral character. First among these is the *indiscriminate* application of advances in science and technology. Many recent discoveries have brought undeniable benefits to humanity. Indeed, they demonstrate the nobility of the human vocation to participate *responsibly* in God's creative action in the world. Unfortunately, it is now clear that the application of these discoveries in the fields of industry and agriculture have produced harmful long-term effects. This has led to the painful realization that *we cannot interfere in one area of the ecosystem without paying due attention both to the consequences of such interference in other areas and to the well-being of future generations*.

The gradual depletion of the ozone layer and the related 'greenhouse effect' has now reached crisis proportions as a

160

consequence of industrial growth, massive urban concentrations and vastly increased energy needs. Industrial waste, the burning of fossil fuels, unrestricted deforestation, the use of certain types of herbicides, coolants and propellants: all of these are known to harm the atmosphere and environment. The resulting meteorological and atmospheric changes range from damage to health to the possible future submersion of low-lying lands.

While in some cases the damage already done may well be irreversible, in many other cases it can still be halted. It is necessary, however, that the entire human community – individuals, States and international bodies – take seriously the responsibility that is theirs.

7.   The most profound and serious indication of the moral implications underlying the ecological problem is the lack of *respect for life* evident in many of the patterns of environmental pollution. Often, the interests of production prevail over concern for the dignity of workers, while economic interests take priority over the good of individuals and even entire peoples. In these cases, pollution or environmental destruction is the result of an unnatural and reductionist vision which at times leads to a genuine contempt for man.

On another level, delicate ecological balances are upset by the uncontrolled destruction of animal and plant life or by a reckless exploitation of natural resources. It should be pointed out that all of this, even if carried out in the name of progress and well-being, is ultimately to mankind's disadvantage.

Finally, we can only look with deep concern at the enormous possibilities of biological research. We are not yet in a position to assess the biological disturbance that could result from indiscriminate genetic manipulation and from the unscrupulous development of new forms of plant and animal life, to say nothing of unacceptable experimentation regarding the origins of human life itself. It is evident to all that in any area as delicate as this, indifference to fundamental ethical norms, or their rejection, would lead mankind to the very threshold of self-destruction.

Respect for life, and above all for the dignity of the human person, is the ultimate guiding norm for any sound economic, industrial or scientific progress.

The complexity of the ecological question is evident to all. There are, however, certain underlying principles, which, while respecting the legitimate autonomy and the specific competence of those involved, can direct research towards adequate and lasting solutions. These principles are essential to the building of a peaceful society; *no peaceful society can afford to neglect either respect for life or the fact that there is an integrity to creation.*

III.   IN SEARCH OF A SOLUTION

8.   Theology, philosophy and science all speak of a harmonious universe, of a 'cosmos' endowed with its own integrity, its own internal, dynamic balance. *This order must be respected.* The human race is called to explore this order, to examine it with due care and to make use of it while safeguarding its integrity.

On the other hand, the earth is ultimately *a common heritage, the fruits of which are for the benefit of all.* In the words of the Second Vatican Council, 'God destined the earth and all it contains for the use of every individual and all peoples' (*Gaudium et Spes*, 69). This has direct consequences for the problem at hand. It is manifestly unjust that a privileged few should continue to accumulate excess goods, squandering available resources, while masses of people are living in conditions of misery at the very lowest level of subsistence. Today, the dramatic threat of ecological breakdown is teaching us the extent to which greed and selfishness – both individual and collective – are contrary to the order of creation, an order which is characterized by mutual interdependence.

9. The concepts of an ordered universe and a common heritage both point to the necessity of a *more internationally coordinated approach to the management of the earth's goods.* In many cases the effects of ecological problems transcend the borders of individual States; hence their solution cannot be found solely on the national level. Recently there have been some promising steps towards such international action, yet the existing mechanisms and bodies are clearly not adequate for the development of a comprehensive plan of action. Political obstacles, forms of exaggerated nationalism and economic interests – to mention only a few factors – impede international cooperation and long-term effective action.

The need for joint action on the international level *does not lessen the responsibility of each individual State.* Not only should each State join with others in implementing internationally accepted standards, but it should also make or facilitate necessary socio-economic adjustments within its own borders, giving special attention to the most vulnerable sectors of society. The State should also actively endeavour within its own territory to prevent destruction of the atmosphere and biosphere, by carefully monitoring, among other things, the impact of new technological or scientific advances. The State also has the responsibility of ensuring that its citizens are not exposed to dangerous pollutants or toxic wastes. *The right to a safe environment* is ever more insistently presented today as a right that must be included in an updated Charter of Human Rights.

IV. THE URGENT NEED FOR A NEW SOLIDARITY

10. The ecological crisis reveals the *urgent moral need for a new solidarity,* especially in relations between the developing nations and those that are highly industrialized. States must increasingly share responsibility, in complimentary ways, for the promotion of a natural and social environment that is both peaceful and healthy. The newly industrialized States cannot, for example, be asked to apply restrictive environmental

standards to their emerging industries unless the industrialized States first apply them within their own boundaries. At the same time, countries in the process of industrialization are not morally free to repeat the errors made in the past by others, and recklessly continue to damage the environment through industrial pollutants, radical deforestation or unlimited exploitation of non-renewable resources. In this context, there is urgent need to find a solution to the treatment and disposal of toxic wastes.

No plan or organization, however, will be able to effect the necessary changes unless world leaders are truly convinced of the absolute need for this new solidarity, which is demanded of them by the ecological crisis and which is essential for peace. *This need presents new opportunities for strengthening cooperative and peaceful relations among States.*

11. It must also be said that the proper ecological balance will not be found without *directly addressing the structural forms of poverty* that exist throughout the world. Rural poverty and unjust land distribution in many countries, for example, have led to subsistence farming and to the exhaustion of the soil. Once their land yields no more, many farmers move on to clear new land, thus accelerating uncontrolled deforestation, or they settle in urban centres which lack the infrastructure to receive them. Likewise, some heavily indebted countries are destroying their natural heritage, at the price of irreparable ecological imbalances, in order to develop new products for export. In the face of such situations it would be wrong to assign responsibility to the poor alone for the negative environmental consequences of their actions. Rather, the poor, to whom the earth is entrusted no less than to others, must be enabled to find a way out of their poverty. This will require a courageous reform of structures, as well as new ways of relating among peoples and States.

12. But there is another dangerous menace which threatens us, namely *war*. Unfortunately, modern science already has the

capacity to change the environment for hostile purposes. Alterations of this kind over the long term could have unforeseeable and still more serious consequences. Despite the international agreements which prohibit chemical, bacteriological and biological warfare, the fact is that laboratory research continues to develop new offensive weapons capable of altering the balance of nature.

Today, any form of war on a global scale would lead to incalculable ecological damage. But even local or regional wars, however limited, not only destroy human life and social structures, but also damage the land, ruining crops and vegetation as well as poisoning the soil and water. The survivors of war are forced to begin a new life in very difficult environmental conditions, which in turn create situations of extreme social unrest, with further negative consequences for the environment.

13.   Modern society will find no solution to the ecological problem unless it *takes a serious look at its lifestyle*. In many parts of the world society is given to instant gratification and consumerism while remaining indifferent to the damage which these cause. As I have already stated, the seriousness of the ecological issue lays bare the depth of man's moral crisis. If an appreciation of the value of the human person and of human life is lacking, we will also lose interest in others and in the earth itself. Simplicity, moderation and discipline, as well as a spirit of sacrifice, must become a part of everyday life, lest all suffer the negative consequences of the careless habits of a few.

An education in ecological responsibility is urgent: responsibility for oneself, for others, and for the earth. This education cannot be rooted in mere sentiment or empty wishes. Its purpose cannot be ideological or political. It must not be based on a rejection of the modern world or a vague desire to return to some 'paradise lost'. Instead, a true education in responsibility entails a genuine conversion in ways of thought and behaviour. Churches and religious bodies, non-governmental and governmental organizations, indeed all members of society, have a precise role to play in such education. The first educator, however, is the family, where the child learns to respect his neighbour and to love nature.

14. *Finally, the aesthetic value of creation cannot be overlooked.* Our very contact with nature has a deep restorative power; contemplation of its magnificence imparts peace and serenity. The Bible speaks again and again of the goodness and beauty of creation, which is called to glorify God (cf. *Gen* l:4ff; *Ps* 8:2; 104:1ff; *Wis* 13:3–5; *Sir* 39:16, 33; 43:1, 9). More difficult perhaps, but no less profound, is the contemplation of the works of human ingenuity. Even cities can have a beauty all their own, one that ought to motivate people to care for their surroundings. Good urban planning is an important part of environmental protection, and respect for the natural contours of the land is an indispensable prerequisite for ecologically sound development. The relationship between a good aesthetic education and the maintenance of a healthy environment cannot be overlooked.

V. THE ECOLOGICAL CRISIS: A COMMON RESPONSIBILITY

15. Today the ecological crisis has assumed such proportions as to be *the responsibility of everyone*. As I have pointed out, its various aspects demonstrate the need for concerted efforts aimed at establishing the duties and obligations that belong to individuals, peoples, States and the international community. This not only goes hand in hand with efforts to build true peace, but also confirms and reinforces those efforts in a concrete way. When the ecological crisis is set within the broader context of *the search for peace* within society, we can understand better the importance of giving attention to what the earth and its atmosphere are telling us: namely, that there is an order in the universe which must be respected, and that the human person, endowed with the capability of choosing freely, has a grave responsibility to preserve this order for the well-being of future generations. I wish to repeat that *the*

ecological crisis is a moral issue.

Even men and women without any particular religious conviction, but with an acute sense of their responsibilities for the common good, recognize their obligation to contribute to the restoration of a healthy environment. All the more should men and women who believe in God the Creator, and who are thus convinced that there is a well-defined unity and order in the world, feel called to address the problem. Christians, in particular, realize that their responsibility within creation and their duty towards nature and the Creator are an essential part of their faith. As a result, they are conscious of a vast field of ecumenical and interreligious cooperation opening up before them.

16.   At the conclusion of this Message, I should like to address directly my brothers and sisters in the Catholic Church, in order to remind them of their serious obligation to care for all of creation. The commitment of believers to a healthy environment for everyone stems directly from their belief in God the Creator, from their recognition of the effects of original and personal sin, and from the certainty of having been redeemed by Christ. Respect for life and for the dignity of the human person extends also to the rest of creation, which is called to join man in praising God (cf. *Ps* 148:96).

In 1979, I proclaimed Saint Francis of Assisi as the heavenly Patron of those who promote ecology (cf. Apostolic Letter *Inter Sanctos*: *AAS* 71 [1979], 1509f.). He offers Christians an example of genuine and deep respect for the integrity of creation. As a friend of the poor who was loved by God's creatures, Saint Francis invited all of creation – animals, plants, natural forces, even Brother Sun and Sister Moon – to give honour and praise to the Lord. The poor man of Assisi gives us striking witness that when we are at peace with God we are better able to devote ourselves to building up that peace with all creation which is inseparable from peace among all peoples.

It is my hope that the inspiration of Saint Francis will help us to keep ever alive a sense of 'fraternity' with all those good and beautiful things which Almighty God has created. And may he remind us of our serious obligation to respect and watch over them with care, in light of that greater and higher fraternity that exists within the human family.

1 January 1991

IF YOU WANT PEACE, RESPECT THE CONSCIENCE OF EVERY PERSON

In the light of the events that followed the fall of the Berlin Wall, Pope John Paul returns to the theme of freedom recalling his 1988 message that: 'peace...puts down its roots in the freedom and openness of consciences to truth'. He zeroes in on respect for freedom of conscience because in its relation to objective truth conscience bears witness to the transcendence of the human person. We can never impose our own 'truth' or personal opinion on others: Truth imposes itself solely by the force of its own truth. Important agents in the task of forming consciences include the family, schools, mass media as well as the Catholic Church, Christian communities and other religious institutions that contribute to religious education. While warning against the recurring temptation of yielding to fundamentalism, the Pope underlines how much religious freedom can be a force for peace and so stresses the need to strengthen juridical instruments capable of promoting freedom of conscience in the areas of political and social life. In the new multi-cultural and multi-religious societies, the Pope affirms that it is through educating people to respect the conscience of others that we can tackle the difficult questions concerning peaceful co-existence. He notes the increased cooperation and dialogue among world religions. He comments: 'Man needs to develop his spirit and his conscience'. The mark of those who are 'in the truth' is the ability to love humbly in the freedom that leads to peace for all.

* * *

Today the many peoples who make up the one human family are increasingly concerned that freedom of conscience, which is essential for the freedom of every human being, be recognized in practice and safeguarded by law. I have already devoted two Messages for the World Day of Peace to various aspects of this freedom, which remains fundamental for peace in the world.

In 1988 I proposed some reflections on religious freedom. It is essential that the right to express one's own religious convictions publicly and in all domains of civil life be ensured if human beings are to live together in peace. I noted on that occasion that 'peace...puts down its roots in the freedom and openness of consciences to truth'[1]. The following year I continued this reflection by proposing some thoughts on the need to respect the rights of civil and religious minorities, 'one of the most delicate questions affecting contemporary society... since it is related to the organization of social and civil life within each country, as well as to the life of the international community'[2]. This year I wish to consider specifically the importance of *respect for the conscience of every person*, as a necessary basis for peace in the world.

Freedom of conscience and peace

1.   The need to take concrete steps towards ensuring full respect for freedom of conscience, both legally and in ordinary human relations, has become even more urgent in the light of the events of last year. The rapid changes which have taken place show very clearly that a person may not be treated as a kind of object governed solely by forces outside of his or her control. Rather, the individual person, despite human frailty, has the ability to seek and freely know the good, to recognize and reject evil, to choose truth and to oppose error. In creating the person, God wrote on the human heart a law which everyone can discover (cf. Rom 2:15). Conscience for its part is the ability to judge and act according to that law: 'To obey it is the very dignity of man'[3].

No human authority has the right to interfere with a

person's conscience. Conscience bears witness to the *transcendence of the person,* also in regard to society at large, and, as such, is inviolable. Conscience, however, is not an absolute placed above truth and error. Rather, by its very nature, it implies *a relation to objective truth,* a truth which is universal, the same for all, which all can and must seek. It is in this relation to objective truth that freedom of conscience finds its justification, inasmuch as it is a necessary condition for seeking the truth worthy of man, and for adhering to that truth once it is sufficiently known. This in turn necessarily requires that each individual's conscience be respected by everyone else; people must not attempt to impose their own 'truth' on others. The right to profess the truth must always be upheld, but not in a way which involves contempt for those who may think differently. *Truth imposes itself solely by the force of its own truth.* To deny an individual complete freedom of conscience – and in particular the freedom to seek the truth – or to attempt to impose a particular way of seeing the truth, constitutes a violation of that individual's most personal rights. This also aggravates animosities and tensions, which can easily lead to strained and hostile relations within society or even to open conflict. In the end, it is *on the level of conscience* that the difficult task of ensuring a firm and lasting peace is most effectively confronted.

Absolute truth is found only in God

2.   The guarantee that objective truth exists is found in God, who is Absolute Truth; objectively speaking, the search for truth and the search for God are one and the same. This alone is enough to show the *intimate relationship between freedom of conscience and religious freedom.* It also explains why the systematic denial of God and the establishment of a regime which incorporates this denial in its very constitution are diametrically opposed to both freedom of conscience and freedom of religion. However, those who acknowledge the relationship between ultimate truth and God himself will also acknowledge the right, as well as the duty, of non-believers to

seek the truth which can lead them to discover the Mystery of God and humbly accept it.

The formation of conscience

3. *Every individual has the grave duty to form his or her own conscience* in the light of that objective truth which everyone can come to know, and which no one may be prevented from knowing. To claim that one has a right to act according to conscience, but without at the same time acknowledging the duty to conform one's conscience to the truth and to the law which God himself has written on our hearts, in the end means nothing more than imposing one's limited personal opinion. This hardly contributes in any useful way to the cause of world peace. On the contrary, the truth must be passionately pursued and lived to the best of one's ability. This sincere search for the truth will lead not only to respect for the search that others are making, but also to a desire to seek the truth together.

The family plays a primary role in the important task of forming consciences. Parents have a grave duty to help their children to seek the truth from their earliest years and to live in conformity with the truth, to seek the good and to promote it.

The school is also fundamental to the formation of conscience. It is there that children and young people come into contact with a world which is larger and often unlike the family environment. Education is in fact never morally indifferent, even when it claims to be neutral with regard to ethical and religious values. The way in which children and young people are brought up and educated will necessarily reflect certain values which in turn influence their understanding of others and of society as a whole. Hence, in a way consonant with the nature and dignity of the human person and with the law of God, young people should be helped during their years of schooling to discern and to seek the truth, to accept its demands and the limits of authentic freedom, and to respect the right of others to do the same.

The formation of conscience is compromised if a thorough *religious education* is lacking. How can a young person fully understand the demands of human dignity if no reference is made to the source of that dignity, namely, God the Creator? In this regard, the role of the family, the Catholic Church, Christian communities and other religious institutions remains essential. The State, in compliance with international norms and Declarations,[4] must guarantee their rights in this field and make it possible for them to exercise those rights. For their part, families and communities of believers ought to appreciate and ever deepen their commitment to the human person and to the objective values of the person.

Among the many other institutions and bodies which play a specific role in forming consciences, *the means of social communication* must also be mentioned. In today's world of rapid communication, the mass media can play an extremely important and indeed essential role in furthering the search for the truth, provided that they avoid presenting merely the limited interests of certain individuals, groups or ideologies. For more and more people the media are often their only source of information. How important, then, that the media be used responsibly in the service of the truth!

Intolerance: A serious threat to peace

4.   A serious threat to peace is posed by intolerance, which manifests itself in the denial of freedom of conscience to others. The excesses to which intolerance can lead has been one of history's most painful lessons.

Intolerance can creep into every aspect of social life. It becomes evident when individuals or minorities who seek to follow their conscience in regard to legitimate expressions of their own way of life are oppressed or relegated to the margins of society. In public life, intolerance leaves no room for a plurality of political or social options, and thus imposes a monolithic vision of civil and cultural life.

As for religious intolerance, it cannot be denied that, despite the firm teaching of the Catholic Church according to which no one ought to be compelled to believe,[5] throughout the centuries not a few misunderstandings and even conflicts have occurred between Christians and members of other religions[6]. This fact was formally acknowledged by the Second Vatican Council, which stated that 'in the life of the People of God as it has made its pilgrim way through the vicissitudes of human history, there have at times appeared ways of acting which were less in accord with the ways of the Gospel'[7].

Even today much remains to be done to overcome religious intolerance, which in different parts of the world is closely connected with the oppression of minorities. Unfortunately, we are still witnessing attempts to impose a particular religious idea on others, either directly, by a proselytism which relies on means which are truly coercive, or indirectly, by the denial of certain civil or political rights. Extremely sensitive situations arise when a specifically religious norm becomes, or tends to become, the law of the State, without due consideration for the distinction between the domains proper to religion and to political society. In practice, the identification of religious law with civil law can stifle religious freedom, even going so far as to restrict or deny other inalienable human rights. In this regard, I wish to repeat what I stated in the Message for the 1988 World Day of Peace: 'Even in cases where the State grants a special juridical position to a particular religion, there is a duty to ensure that the right to freedom of conscience is legally recognized and effectively respected for all citizens, and also for foreigners living in the country even temporarily for reasons of employment and the like'[8]. This holds true also for the civil and political rights of minorities, and for those situations in which an extreme and uncompromising separation of religion and political life, in the name of respect for conscience, effectively hinders believers from exercising their right to give public expression to their faith.

Intolerance can also result from the recurring temptation to fundamentalism, which easily leads to serious abuses such as the radical suppression of all public manifestations of diversity, or even the outright denial of freedom of expression. Fundamentalism can also lead to the exclusion of others from civil society; where religion is concerned, it can lead to forced 'conversions'. However much one may remain convinced of the truth of one's own religion, no person or group has the right to attempt to repress the freedom of conscience of those who have other religious convictions, or to induce them to betray their consciences by the offer or denial of certain social privileges and rights, should they change their religion. There are cases in which individuals are prevented – even through the imposition of severe penalties – from freely choosing a religion different from the one to which they presently belong. Manifestations of intolerance such as these clearly do not advance the cause of world peace.

To eliminate the effects of intolerance, it is not sufficient for ethnic or religious minorities to be 'protected', and thus reduced to the category of legal minors or wards of the State. This could result in a form of discrimination which hinders or even prevents the development of a harmonious and peaceful society. Rather, *the inalienable right to follow one's conscience and to profess and practise one's own faith,* individually or within a community, is to be acknowledged and guaranteed, always provided that the demands of public order are not violated.

Paradoxically, those who were once victims of various forms of intolerance can in their turn be in danger of creating new situations of intolerance. In certain parts of the world, the end of long years of repression – years when the conscience of individuals was not respected and everything that was most precious to the person was stifled – must not prove an occasion for new forms of intolerance, no matter how difficult reconciliation with the former oppressor may be.

Freedom of conscience, rightly understood, is by its very nature *always ordered to the truth.* As a result, it does not lead to intolerance, but to tolerance and reconciliation. This tolerance is not a passive virtue, but is rooted in active love and is meant to be transformed into a positive commitment to ensuring freedom and peace for all.

Religious freedom: A force for peace

5.   The importance of religious freedom leads me to stress once more that the right to religious freedom is not merely one human right among many others; 'rather, [it] is the most fundamental, since the dignity of every person has its first source in his essential relationship with God the Creator and Father, in whose image and likeness he was created, since he is endowed with intelligence and freedom'[9]. 'Religious freedom, an essential requirement of the dignity of every person, is a cornerstone of the structure of human rights'[10]. It is thus the most profound expression of freedom of conscience.

It cannot be denied that the right to religious freedom has a bearing on a person's very identity. One of the most significant aspects of today's world is the role that religion has played in the awakening of peoples and in the search for freedom. In many cases it was religious faith that preserved intact and even strengthened the identity of entire peoples. In nations where religion was hindered or even persecuted in an attempt to treat it as a relic of the past, it has once more proved to be a powerful force for liberation.

Religious faith is so important for individuals and peoples that in many cases a person is ready to make any sacrifice in order to preserve it. In the end, every attempt to ban or crush what a person holds most dear risks fuelling open or latent rebellion.

The need for a just legal order

6.   Despite the various national and international Declarations which proclaim the right to freedom of conscience and religion, we still find too many attempts at religious repression. In the absence of corresponding legal guarantees expressed in appropriate forms, these Declarations are all too frequently doomed to remain a dead letter. Valuable indeed are the renewed efforts being made to confirm the existing legal order[11] by creating new and effective agreements aimed at strengthening religious freedom. This sort of full legal protection must exclude the practice of any religious coercion as being a serious obstacle to peace. For 'this freedom means

that all men are to be immune from coercion on the part of individuals or of social groups and of any human power, in such wise that in matters religious no one is to be forced to act in a manner contrary to his beliefs. Nor is anyone to be restrained from acting in accordance with his own beliefs, whether privately or publicly, whether alone or in association with others, within due limits'[12].

It is urgently necessary at this moment of history to strengthen juridical instruments capable of promoting freedom of conscience in the areas of political and social life. The gradual and constant development of an internationally recognized legal order could well provide one of the surest bases for the peace and orderly progress of the human family. It is likewise essential that comparable efforts be undertaken nationally and regionally to ensure that all individuals, wherever they live, enjoy the protection of internationally recognized legal norms.

The State is obliged not only to recognize the basic freedom of conscience, but also to foster it, always with a view to the natural moral law and the requirements of the common good, and with respect for the dignity of every human being. It should be noted that freedom of conscience does not confer a right to indiscriminate recourse to conscientious objection. When an asserted freedom turns into licence or becomes an excuse for limiting the rights of others, the State is obliged to protect, also by legal means, the inalienable rights of its citizens against such abuses.

I wish to address a special and urgent appeal to all who are in positions of public responsibility – Heads of State or of government, legislators, magistrates and others – to ensure by every means necessary the *authentic freedom of conscience* of all those who live within the limits of their jurisdictions, and pay special attention to the rights of minorities. Besides being an issue of justice, this serves to promote the development of a peaceful and harmonious society. Finally, it goes without saying that States are bound by a strict moral and legal obligation to observe international agreements which they have signed.

A pluralistic society and world

7.   The existence of recognized international norms does not preclude the existence of regimes or systems of government which correspond to certain socio-cultural situations. Such regimes, however, must ensure complete freedom of conscience for every citizen, and may in no way be used as an excuse for denying or restricting universally recognized rights.

This is especially true when one considers that in today's world it is rare for the entire population of a country to have the same religious beliefs and to belong to the same ethnic group or culture. Mass migration and population shifts are resulting in the growth of multi-cultural and multi-religious societies in various parts of the world. In this context, respect for the conscience of everyone takes on added urgency and presents new challenges to every sector and structure within society, as well as to legislators and government leaders.

How can a country show respect for different traditions, customs, ways of life, and religious obligations, and yet maintain the integrity of its own culture? How can the culture which is predominant in a given society accept and integrate new elements without losing its own identity and without creating conflicts? The answer to these difficult questions can be found in a *thorough education with regard to the respect due to the conscience of others;* for example, through greater knowledge of other cultures and religions, and through a balanced understanding of such diversity as already exists. What better means is there of building unity within diversity than a commitment on the part of all to a common search for peace and a common affirmation of freedom which enlightens and esteems the conscience of everyone? For the sake of an orderly society, it is also to be hoped that the various cultures existing in a given area will show mutual respect and experience mutual enrichment. A genuine commitment to inculturation also serves to increase understanding between religions.

In recent years much has been accomplished in the realm of inter-religious understanding to promote an active cooperation in the common tasks facing humanity, on the basis of the many values shared by the great religions. I wish to encourage this cooperation wherever it is possible, as well as the official dialogues currently underway between representatives of the major religious groups. In this regard, the Holy See has an Office – the Pontifical Council for Interreligious Dialogue – the specific purpose of which is to promote dialogue and cooperation with other religions, maintaining absolute fidelity to its own Catholic identity while fully respecting the identity of others.

When undertaken in a spirit of trust, and with respect and sincerity, interreligious cooperation and dialogue make a real contribution to peace. 'Man needs to develop *his spirit and his conscience*. This is often the very thing which is missing in people's lives these days. The lack of concern for values and the overall identity crisis which our world is now experiencing demand that we move beyond our present situation and make renewed efforts to ask important questions and to seek understanding. An inner light will then start to shine in our conscience and will enable us to understand development in a meaningful way, directing it towards the good of each person and of all mankind, in accordance with God's plan'[13]. This common search – carried out in the light of the law of conscience and of the precepts of one's own religion, and confronting the causes of present-day social injustices and wars – will lay a solid foundation for cooperation in the search for needed solutions.

The Catholic Church has willingly sought to encourage every form of honest cooperation for the sake of promoting peace. She will continue to make her own contribution towards this cooperation by forming the consciences of her members in openness towards others and respect for them, in that tolerance which accompanies the search for truth, and in a spirit of solidarity[14].

Conscience and the Christian

8.   Faced with the obligation of following their own consciences in the search for the truth, the disciples of Jesus

Christ know that they may not trust only in their personal capacity for moral discernment. Revelation enlightens their consciences and enables them to know that freedom which is God's great gift to mankind[15]. Not only has he inscribed the natural law within the heart of each individual, in that 'most secret core and sanctuary of a man (where) he is alone with God',[16] but he has also revealed his own law in the Scriptures. Here we find the call, or rather the command, to love God and to observe his law.

God has enabled us to know his will. He has revealed his commandments to us, and has set before us 'life and good, death and evil'; he calls us to 'choose life...loving the Lord your God, obeying his voice, and cleaving to him; for that means life to you and length of days...'[17]. In *the fullness of his love*, God respects a person's free choice regarding the highest values he or she seeks, and he thus reveals *his full respect* for the precious gift of freedom of conscience. God's laws bear witness to this, since they seek to assist and not hinder our use of freedom. In themselves, God's laws remain the perfect expression of his will and his absolute opposition to moral evil, and it is through them that he wishes to guide us in the search for our final end.

Yet it was not enough for God to demonstrate his great love in the created world and in man. God 'so loved the world that he gave his only Son, that whoever believes in him should not perish but have eternal life...He who does what is true comes to the light, that it may be clearly seen that his deeds have been wrought in God'[18]. The Son did not hesitate to proclaim that he is the Truth,[19] and to assure us that this Truth would make us free[20].

In searching for the truth the Christian has recourse to divine revelation, which in Christ is present in all its fullness. Christ has entrusted the Church with the mission of proclaiming this truth, and the whole Church has the duty of remaining faithful to that truth. My most serious responsibility as the Successor of Peter is precisely this: to ensure this constant fidelity by confirming my brothers and sisters in their faith[21].

More than anyone else, the Christian ought to feel the obligation *to conform his conscience to the truth*. Before the splendour of the free gift of God's revelation in Christ, how humbly and attentively must he listen to the voice of conscience! How modest must he be in regard to his own limited insight! How quick must he be to learn, and how slow to condemn! One of the constant temptations in every age, even among Christians, is to make oneself the norm of truth. In an age of pervasive individualism, this temptation takes a variety of forms. But the mark of those who are 'in the truth' is the ability to love humbly. This is what God's word teaches us: truth is expressed in love[22].

The very truth that we profess calls us to promote unity rather than division; reconciliation rather than hatred and intolerance. The free gift of our coming to know the truth places upon us the serious responsibility of proclaiming only that truth which leads to freedom and peace for all: the Truth which became flesh in Jesus Christ.

At the conclusion of this Message, I invite all people, within their own situation and in the light of their specific responsibilities, to reflect well on the need to respect the conscience of each individual. In every sphere of social, cultural and political life, *respect for freedom of conscience*, ordered to the truth, has many important and immediate applications. As we seek the truth together, with respect for the conscience of others, we will be able to go forward along the paths of freedom which lead to peace, in accordance with the will of God.

Notes

1   *Message for the 1988 World Day of Peace,* Introduction.
2   *Message for the 1989 World Day of Peace,* 1.
3   Pastoral Constitution *Gaudium et spes,* 16.
4   For the most recent recognition of this right, see the 1981 Declaration of the United Nations on Eliminating all Forms of Intolerance and Discrimination Based on Religion or Beliefs, art. 1.
5   Cf. for example, the Declaration *Dignitatis humanae,* 12.
6   Cf. for example, the Declaration *Nostra aetate,* 3.
7   Declaration *Dignitatis humanae,* 12.
8   No. 1.
9   *Address to the participants in the Fifth International Colloquium of Juridical Studies,* 10 March 1984, 5.
10   *Message for the 1988 World Day of Peace,* Introduction.
11   Cf., among other documents, the Universal Declaration of Human Rights, art. 18; Helsinki Final Act, 1, a) VII; Convention on the Rights of the Child, art. 14.
12   (Declaration *Dignitatis humanae,* 2.
13   Address to Muslim Youth, Casablanca, 19 August 1985, 9: *AAS* 78 (1986) 101–102.
14   Cf. *Address to the Diplomatic Corps,* 11 January 1986, 12.
15   Cf. Sir 17:6.
16   Pastoral Constitution *Gaudium et spes,* 16.
17   Cf. Dt 30:15-20.
18   Jn 3:16, 21.
19   Cf. Jn 14:6.
20   Cf. Jn 8:32.
21   Cf. Lk 22:32.
22   Cf. Eph 4:15.

1 January 1992
BELIEVERS UNITED IN BUILDING PEACE

The World Day of Peace message for 1992 was the twenty-fifth such message since Pope Paul VI began them in 1967. It offered Pope John Paul II an opportunity to extend a renewed, fraternal invitation to consider present human events and consider an ethical and religious vision, one that 'believers should be the first to live by'. He notes the universal natural longing for peace. References to peace are to be found in the Jewish and Islamic sacred books. In encouraging us to make a serious examination of conscience, the Pope recalls tragic events 'of recent months' (these would seem to be events in the Balkans and Rwanda). He advocates a rekindling and fostering of the genuine 'Spirit of Assisi'. Spiritual foundations are important and so the Pope writes of elements that can be profitably developed and put into practice with the followers of other faiths and confessions. He even refers to instances that 'activity would have proved more effective had it been carried out jointly and in a coordinated manner'. The Pope knows there is still a long way to go to reach the goal of active cooperation in the cause of peace. He comments that individual believers, perhaps more than their leaders 'must face the hard work and at the same time have the satisfaction of building peace together'. He reminds believers and even more Christians that they must feel the commitment to living values of justice, crowned by the supreme law of love: 'you shall love your neighbour as yourself' (Mt 22:39).

* * *

1.   As is now customary, on 1 January next the annual World Day of Peace will be celebrated.

Twenty-five years will have passed since this celebration was begun, and it is entirely natural that on this anniversary I should recall with undimmed admiration and gratitude the beloved figure of my venerable predecessor Paul VI, whose keen pastoral and pedagogical insight led him to invite all 'true friends of peace' to join together in order to reflect on this 'primary good' of humanity.

But it is likewise natural, a quarter of a century later, to look back at this period as a whole, in order to determine if the cause of peace in the world has actually made progress or not, and if the tragic events of recent months – some of which are regrettably still going on – have marked a substantial setback, revealing how real is the danger that human reason can allow itself to be dominated by destructive self-interest or inveterate hatred. At the same time, the progressive rise of new democracies has given back hope to entire peoples, inspired confidence in more fruitful international dialogue and made possible a long-awaited era of peace.

Against this background of light and shadows, this yearly Message is not meant to offer either a progress report or a judgment, but only a new, fraternal invitation to consider present human events, in order to raise them to an *ethical and religious vision,* a vision which believers should be the first to live by. Precisely because of their faith, believers are called – as individuals and as a body – to be messengers and artisans of peace. Like others and even more than others, they are called to seek with humility and perseverance appropriate responses to the yearnings for security and freedom, solidarity and sharing, which are common to everyone in this world, which as it were has become smaller. A commitment to peace of course concerns every person of good will, and this is the reason why the various Messages have been addressed to all the members of the human family. Yet, *this is a duty* which is especially *incumbent upon all who profess faith in God* and even more so *upon Christians,* who have as their guide and master the 'Prince of Peace' (Is 9:5).

The moral and religious nature of peace

2.   The longing for peace is deeply rooted in human nature and is found in the different religions. It expresses itself in the desire for order and tranquillity, in an attitude of readiness to help others, in cooperation and sharing based on mutual respect. These values, which originate in the natural law and are propounded by the world's religions, require, if they are to develop, the support of everyone – politicians, leaders of international organizations, businessmen and workers, associations and private citizens. What we are speaking of is a precise duty incumbent on everyone, and more so if one is a believer: bearing witness to peace and working and praying for peace are a normal part of good religious behaviour.

This also explains why in the sacred books of the different religions references to peace occupy a prominent place in the context of man's life and his relationship with God. For example, we Christians believe that Jesus Christ, the Son of the One who has 'plans for welfare and not for evil' (*Jer* 29:11) is 'our peace' (*Eph* 2:14); for our Jewish brothers and sisters, the word 'shalom' expresses both a wish and blessing in a situation in which man is in harmony with himself, with nature and with God; and for the followers of Islam the term 'salam' is so important that it constitutes one of the glorious divine names. It can be said that a religious life, if it is lived authentically, cannot fail to bring forth fruits of peace and brotherhood, for it is in the nature of religion to foster an ever closer bond with the Godhead and to promote an increasingly fraternal relationship among people.

Rekindling the 'spirit of Assisi'

3.   Convinced of this agreement about this value, five years ago I wrote to the leaders of the Christian Churches and the major world religions in order to invite them to a *special meeting of prayer for peace,* which was held in Assisi. The memory of that significant event has led me to return to and

suggest once more *the theme of the solidarity of believers* in the same cause.

At Assisi the spiritual leaders of the major religions from the different continents gathered together: the meeting was a concrete witness to the universal dimension of peace, and confirmed that peace is not only the result of skilful political and diplomatic negotiations or a compromise between economic interests, but depends in a fundamental way upon the One who knows human hearts and guides and directs the steps of all mankind. As people concerned for the future of humanity, we fasted together, meaning thereby to express our compassion and solidarity with the millions and millions who are victims of hunger throughout the world. As believers concerned with the events of human history, we went on pilgrimage together, meditating silently on our common origin and our common destiny, our limitations and our responsibilities, and on the prayers and expectations of all our many brothers and sisters who look to us for help in their needs.

What we did on that occasion by praying and demonstrating our firm commitment to peace on earth, we must continue to do now. We must foster the genuine 'spirit of Assisi' not only out of a duty to be consistent and faithful, but also in order to offer a reason for hope to future generations. In the town of Saint Francis, the Poor Man of Assisi, we began *a common journey which must now continue,* obviously without excluding the search for other ways and new means for a solid peace, built on spiritual foundations.

The power of prayer

4. But before having recourse to human resources, I wish to reaffirm the need for intense, humble, confident and persevering prayer, if the world is finally to become a dwelling-place of peace. Prayer is *par excellence* the power needed to implore that peace and obtain it. It gives courage and support to all who love this good and desire to promote it in accordance with their own possibilities and in the various situations in which they live.

186

Prayer not only opens us up to a meeting with the Most High but also disposes us to a meeting with our neighbour, helping us to establish with everyone, without discrimination, relationships of respect, understanding, esteem and love.

Religious sentiment and a prayerful spirit not only help us to grow inwardly; they also enlighten us about the true meaning of our presence in the world. It can also be said that the religious dimension encourages us to make an even more committed contribution to the building of a well-ordered society in which peace reigns.

Prayer is the bond which most effectively unites us: it is through prayer that believers meet one another at a level where inequalities, misunderstandings, bitterness and hostility are overcome, namely before God, the Lord and Father of all. Prayer, as the authentic expression of a right relationship with God and with others, is already a positive contribution to peace.

Ecumenical dialogue and inter-religious relations

5.   Prayer cannot remain isolated and needs to be accompanied by other concrete actions. Each religion has its own outlook regarding the actions to be accomplished and the paths to be followed in order to attain peace. The Catholic Church, while clearly affirming her own identity, her own doctrine and her saving mission for all humanity, 'rejects nothing of those things which are true and holy' in other religions; 'she regards with respect those ways of acting and living and those precepts and teachings which, though often at variance with what she holds and expounds, frequently reflect a ray of that truth which enlightens everyone' (Nostra aetate, n. 2).

Without ignoring differences or playing them down, the Church is convinced that, in promoting peace, there are certain elements or aspects which can be profitably developed and put into practice with the followers of other faiths and confessions. Inter-religious contacts and, in a unique way, ecumenical dialogue lead to this. Thanks to these forms of encounter and exchange the various religions have been able to attain a clearer awareness of their considerable responsibilities with regard to the true good of humanity as a whole. Today they all seem to be more firmly determined not to allow themselves to be used by particularistic interests or for political aims, and they are tending to assume a more conscious and decisive attitude in the shaping of social and cultural realities in the community of peoples. This enables them to be an active force in the process of development and thus to offer a sure hope to humanity. In a number of instances, it has become evident that their activity would have proved more effective had it been carried out jointly and in a coordinated manner. Such a way of working among believers can have a decisive effect in fostering peace among peoples and overcoming the still existing divisions between 'zones' and 'worlds'.

The path to be travelled

6.   There is still a long way to go to reach this goal of active cooperation in the cause of peace: there is the path of mutual knowledge, assisted today by the development of the means of social communication and facilitated by the beginning of a frank and wider dialogue; there is the path of generous forgiveness, fraternal reconciliation, and collaboration in areas which though limited or secondary are nonetheless directed to the same cause; finally, there is the path of daily coexistence, sharing efforts and sacrifices in order to reach the same goal. Perhaps it is on this path that individual believers, people who profess a religion, even more than their leaders, must face the hard work and at the same time have the satisfaction of building peace together.

Inter-religious contacts, together with ecumenical dialogue, now seem to be obligatory paths, in order to ensure that the many painful wounds inflicted over the course of centuries will not be repeated, and indeed that any such wounds still remaining will soon be healed. Believers must work for peace, above all by the personal example of their own right interior attitude, which shows outwardly in consistent action and behaviour. Serenity, balance, self-control, and acts of understanding, forgiveness and generosity have a peace-making influence on people's surroundings and on the religious and civil community.

It is for this reason that on the next World Day of Peace I invite all believers to make a serious *examination of conscience,* in order to be better disposed to listen to the voice of the 'God of peace' (cf. 1 *Cor* 14:33) and to devote themselves to this great undertaking with renewed trust. I am convinced that they – and, I hope, all people of good will – will respond to this renewed appeal of mine, which I make with an insistence which matches the seriousness of the moment.

Building peace in justice together

7.   The prayer of believers and their joint action for peace must face the problems and legitimate aspirations of individuals and peoples.

Peace is a fundamental good which involves respecting and promoting essential human values: the right to life at every stage of its development; the right to be respected, regardless of race, sex or religious convictions; the right to the material goods necessary for life; the right to work and to a fair distribution of its fruits for a well-ordered and harmonious coexistence. As individuals, as believers and even more as Christians, we must feel the commitment to living these *values of justice,* which are crowned by the *supreme law of love:* 'You shall love your neighbour as yourself' (*Mt* 22:39).

Once more I wish to emphasize that rigorous respect for religious freedom, and for the corresponding right to it, is the source and foundation of peaceful coexistence. I look forward to the time when it will be commitment which is not merely affirmed but really put into practice both by political and religious leaders, and by believers themselves: it is on the basis of the recognition of this right that the transcendent dimension of the human person assumes importance.

It would be a mistake if religions or groups of their followers, in the interpretation and practice of their respective beliefs, were to fall into forms of fundamentalism and fanaticism, justifying struggles and conflicts with others by adducing religious motives. If there exists a struggle worthy of man, it is the struggle against his own disordered passions, against every kind of selfishness, against attempts to oppress others, against every type of hatred and violence: in short, against everything that is the exact opposite of peace and reconciliation.

Necessary support from world leaders

8.   Finally, I call upon the Leaders of the Nations and of the international community always to show *the greatest respect for the religious conscience of every man and woman* and for the special contribution of religion to the progress of civilization and to the development of peoples. They should not succumb to the temptation of exploiting religion as a means of power, particularly when it is a matter of opposing an adversary by military means.

Civil and political authorities ought to accord the various religions respect and juridical guarantees – at the national and international levels – ensuring that their contribution to peace is not rejected, or relegated to the private sphere, or ignored altogether.

Again I call upon public authorities to strive with vigilant responsibility to prevent war and conflict, to work for the triumph of justice and right, and at the same time to support development which benefits everyone, and primarily those oppressed by poverty, hunger and suffering. The progress already made in the reduction of arms is worthy of praise. The economic and financial resources hitherto devoted to the production and sale of so many instruments of death can be used from now on for man and not against him! I am certain that millions of men and women throughout the world, who have no way of making their voices heard, share my positive judgment.

A special word for Christians

9.   At this point I cannot fail to address a particular invitation to all Christians. Our common faith in Christ the Lord obliges us to bear a united witness to 'the Gospel of peace' (*Eph* 6:15). It falls to us, first of all, to be open to other believers so as to undertake together with them, courageously and perseveringly, the immense work of building that peace which the world desires but which in the end it does not know how to achieve. 'Peace I leave with you; my peace I give to you', Christ has said to us (*Jn* 14:27). This divine promise fills us with the hope, indeed the certainty of divine hope, that peace is possible, because nothing is impossible with God (cf. *Lk* 1:37). For true peace is always God's gift, and for us Christians it is a precious gift of the Risen Lord (*Jn* 20:19–26).

Dear brothers and sisters of the Catholic Church, we must respond to the great challenges of the contemporary world by joining forces with all those who share with us certain basic values, beginning with religious and moral ones. And among these challenges still to be faced is that of peace. To build peace together with other believers is already to live in the spirit of the Gospel Beatitude: 'Blessed are the peacemakers, for they shall be called sons of God' (*Mt* 5:9).

1 January 1993

IF YOU WANT PEACE,
REACH OUT TO THE POOR

Referring initially to the post cold-war situation of local conflicts breaking out in various parts of the world such as Bosnia-Hercegovina, the Pope goes on to highlight another threat to peace – the fact that so many are living today in conditions of extreme poverty in Europe, Africa, Asia and America. He invites everyone to reflect together on the many links between poverty and peace. He also outlines the indispensable premises for building true peace described in the Latin American Bishops' Conference held in Santo Domingo: defence of the dignity of the person, commitment to a fair distribution of resources, the harmonious and united promotion of a society in which everyone feels welcomed and loved. War is clearly a major cause of poverty and the Pope cries out his conviction: 'nothing is resolved by war; on the contrary, everything is placed in jeopardy by war'. Poverty is itself often a source of conflict. The Pope recommends new economic mechanisms reflecting a new solidarity to ensure a more just and equitable distribution of goods. He draws our attention to problems such as foreign debt, drug trafficking, mass migrations. He invites people in industrialized countries to adopt moderation and simplicity as criteria of daily living. Addressing Christians, the Pope offers a meditation on evangelical poverty. Indeed at the Last Judgement because of their practical love of their neighbour 'many will discover that they have in fact met Christ, although without having known him before in an explicit way'.

❋ ❋ ❋

'If you want peace...'

1.   What person of good will does not long for peace? Today, peace is universally recognized as one of the highest values to be sought and defended. And yet, as the spectre of a deadly war between opposing ideological blocs fades away, grave local conflicts continue to engulf various parts of the world. In particular, everyone is aware of the *situation in Bosnia-Hercegovina*, where hostilities are daily claiming new victims, especially among the defenceless civil population, and causing enormous destruction to property and territory. Nothing seems able to halt the senseless violence of arms: neither the joint efforts to promote an effective truce, nor the humanitarian activity of the International Organizations, nor the chorus of appeals for peace which rise from the lands stained by the blood of battle. Sadly, the aberrant logic of war is prevailing over the repeated and authoritative calls for peace.

Our world also shows increasing evidence of *another grave threat to peace:* many individuals and indeed whole peoples are living today *in conditions of extreme poverty.* The gap between rich and poor has become more marked, even in the most economically developed nations. *This is a problem which the conscience of humanity cannot ignore,* since the conditions in which a great number of people are living are an insult to their innate dignity and as a result are a threat to the authentic and harmonious progress of the world community.

The gravity of this situation is being felt in many countries of the world: in Europe as well as in Africa, Asia and America. In various regions the social and economic challenges which believers and all people of good will have to face are many. Poverty and destitution, social differences and injustices, some of them even legalized, fratricidal conflicts and oppressive regimes – all of these appeal to the conscience of whole peoples in every part of the world.

The recent Conference of Latin American Bishops, held in Santo Domingo in October, carefully examined the situation in Latin America, and while urgently calling on Christians to undertake *the task of the new evangelization* earnestly invited the faithful and all those committed to justice and righteousness *to serve the cause of man,* without failing to take into account any of his deepest needs. The Bishops spoke of the great mission which must draw together the efforts of everyone: defence of the dignity of the person, commitment to a fair distribution of resources, the harmonious and united promotion of a society in which everyone feels welcomed and loved. It is apparent to all that these are *the indispensable premises for building true peace.*

To say 'peace' is really to speak of much more than the simple absence of war. It is to postulate a condition of authentic respect for the dignity and rights of every human being, a condition enabling him to achieve complete fulfilment. The exploitation of the weak and the existence of distressing pockets of poverty and social inequality constitute so many delays and obstacles to the establishment of stable conditions for an authentic peace.

Poverty and *peace:* at the beginning of the New Year, I would like to invite everyone to reflect together on the many different links between these two realities.

In particular, I would like to call attention to the threat to peace posed by poverty, especially when it becomes destitution. There are millions of men, women and children suffering every day from hunger, insecurity and emargination. These situations constitute a grave affront to human dignity and contribute to social instability.

The inhuman choice of war

2.   At the present time, there exists yet another situation which is a source of poverty and destitution: the situation caused by war between nations and by conflicts within a given country. In the face of the tragedies which have caused and are still causing bloodshed, especially for ethnic reasons, in various regions of the world, I feel the duty to recall what I said in my Message for the 1981 World Day of Peace, the theme of which was: 'To serve peace, respect freedom'. At that time, I

emphasized that the indispensable premise for building true peace is respect for the freedom and rights of other individuals and groups. Peace is obtained by promoting free peoples in a world of freedom. The appeal I made then is still valid today: 'Respect for the freedom of peoples and nations is an integral part of peace. Wars continue to break out and destruction has fallen upon peoples and whole cultures because the sovereignty of a people or a nation was not respected. Every continent has seen and suffered from wars and struggles caused by one nation's attempts to limit another's autonomy' (n. 8).

I went on to say: 'Without a willingness to respect the freedom of every people, nation and culture, and without a world-wide consensus on this subject, it will be difficult to create the conditions for peace... This presupposes a conscious public commitment on the part of each nation and its government to renounce claims and designs injurious to other nations. In other words, it presupposes a refusal to accept any doctrine of national or cultural supremacy' (ibid., n. 9).

The consequences deriving from such a commitment are easy to see, also with regard to economic relations between States. To reject all temptations to secure economic dominance over other nations means to renounce a policy inspired by the prevailing criterion of profit, and to replace it with a policy guided by the criterion of solidarity towards all and especially towards the poorest.

Poverty as a source of conflict

3.   The number of people living in conditions of extreme poverty is enormous. I am thinking, for example, of the tragic situations *in certain countries of Africa, Asia and Latin America*. There exist vast groups, often whole sectors of the population, which find themselves on the margins of civil life within their own countries. Among them is a growing number of children who in order to survive can rely on nobody except themselves. Such a situation is not only an affront to human dignity but also represents *a clear threat to peace*. A State, whatever its political organization or economic system,

remains fragile and unstable if it does not give constant attention to its weakest members and if it fails to do everything possible to ensure that at least their primary needs are satisfied.

The poorest countries' *right to development* imposes upon the developed countries a clear duty to come to their aid. The Second Vatican Council said in this regard: 'Everyone has the right to have a part of the earth's goods that is sufficient for each and his or her dependents... We are obliged to support the poor, and not just from our surplus' (Pastoral Constitution *Gaudium et spes,* n. 69). The Church's admonition is clear, and it is a faithful echo of the voice of Christ: earthly goods are meant for the whole human family and cannot be reserved for the exclusive benefit of a few (cf. Encyclical Letter *Centesimus annus,* nn. 31 and 37).

In the interest of the individual – and thus of peace – it is therefore urgently necessary to introduce into the mechanisms of the economy the necessary correctives which will enable those mechanisms to ensure a more just and equitable distribution of goods. By itself the rules of the market are not sufficient to accomplish this; society must accept its own responsibilities (cf. ibid., n. 48). It must do so by increasing its efforts, which are often already considerable, to eliminate the causes of poverty and their tragic consequences. No country by itself can succeed in such an undertaking. For this very reason it is necessary to work together, with that solidarity demanded by a world which has become ever more interdependent. To allow situations of extreme poverty to persist is to create social conditions ever more exposed to the threat of violence and conflict.

All individuals and social groups have a right to live in conditions which enable them to provide for personal and family needs and to share in the life and progress of the local community. When this right is not recognized, it easily happens that the people concerned feel that they are victims of a structure which does not welcome them, and they react strongly. This is especially the case with young people, who, being deprived of adequate education and employment opportunities, are most exposed to the risk of being marginalized and exploited. Everybody is aware of the world-wide problem of unemployment, especially among the young, with the consequent impoverishment of an ever greater number of individuals and whole families. Moreover, unemployment is often the tragic result of the destruction of the economic infrastructure of a country affected by war or internal conflicts.

Here I would like to mention briefly a number of particularly disturbing problems which beset the poor and hence threaten peace.

First of all, there is the problem of *foreign debt*, which for some countries, and within them for the less well-off social strata, continues to be an intolerable burden, despite efforts made to lighten it by the international community, governments and financial institutions. Is it not the poorest groups in these countries which often have to bear the major burden of repayment? Such an unjust situation can open the door to growing resentment, to a sense of frustration and even desperation. In many cases the governments themselves share the widespread discomfort of their people, and this influences relations with other States. Perhaps the time has come to *re-examine the problem of foreign debt and to give it the priority which it deserves*. The conditions for total or partial repayment need to be reviewed, with an effort to find definitive solutions capable of fully absorbing the burdensome social consequences of adjustment programmes. Furthermore it will be necessary to act on the causes of indebtedness, by making the granting of aid conditional upon concrete commitments on the part of governments to reduce excessive or unnecessary expenditures – here one thinks particularly of expenditures on arms – and to guarantee that subsidies do in fact reach the needy.

Another grave problem is *drugs*. Sadly and tragically, everyone knows of their connection with violence and crime. Similarly, everyone knows that in some parts of the world, because of pressure from drug traffickers, it is precisely the very poor who cultivate the plants for drug-production. The lavish profits promised – which in fact represent only a tiny part of the profits deriving from this cultivation – are a temptation difficult to resist by those who gain a markedly insufficient income from the production of traditional crops. The first thing to be done in order to help growers to overcome this situation is therefore to offer them adequate means to escape from their poverty.

A further problem stems from the situations of grave economic difficulty in some countries. These situations encourage *mass migrations* to more fortunate countries, in which there then arise tensions which disturb the social order. In order to respond to such reactions of xenophobic violence, it is not enough simply to have recourse to provisional emergency measures. Rather, what is needed is to tackle the causes, by promoting through new forms of international solidarity the progress and development of the countries from which the migrant movements originate.

Destitution therefore is a hidden but real threat to peace. By impairing human dignity, it constitutes a serious attack on the value of life and strikes at the heart of the peaceful development of society.

Poverty as a result of conflict

4. In recent years we have witnessed on almost every continent local wars and internal conflicts of savage intensity. Ethnic, tribal and racial violence has destroyed human lives, divided communities that previously lived together in peace and left in its wake anguish and feelings of hatred. Recourse to violence, in fact, aggravates existing tensions and creates new ones. *Nothing is resolved by war; on the contrary, everything is placed in jeopardy by war.* The results of this scourge are the suffering and death of innumerable individuals, the disintegration of human relations and the irreparable loss of an immense artistic and environmental patrimony. War worsens the sufferings of the poor; indeed, it creates new poor by destroying means of subsistence, homes and property, and by

eating away at the very fabric of the social environment. Young people see their hopes for the future shattered and too often, as victims, they become irresponsible agents of conflict. Women, children, the elderly, the sick and the wounded are forced to flee and become refugees who have no possessions beyond what they can carry with them. Helpless and defenceless, they seek refuge in other countries or regions often as poor and turbulent as their own.

While acknowledging that the international and humanitarian organizations are doing much to alleviate the tragic fate of the victims of violence, I feel it is my duty *to urge all people of good will to intensify their efforts*. In some instances, in fact, the future of refugees depends entirely on the generosity of people who take them in – people who are as poor, if not poorer, than they are. It is only through the concern and cooperation of the international community that satisfactory solutions will be found.

After so many unnecessary massacres, it is in the final analysis of fundamental importance to recognize, once and for all, that *war never helps the human community*, that violence destroys and never builds up, that the wounds it causes remain long unhealed, and that as a result of conflicts the already grim condition of the poor deteriorates still further, and new forms of poverty appear. The disturbing spectacle of tragedies caused by war is before the eyes of world public opinion. May the distressing pictures quite recently transmitted by the media at least serve as an effective warning to all – individuals, societies and States – and remind everyone that money ought not to be used for war, nor for destroying and killing, but for defending the dignity of man, for improving his life and for building a truly open, free and harmonious society.

A spirit of poverty as a source of peace

5.   In today's industrialized countries people are dominated by the frenzied race for possessing material goods. The consumer society makes the gap separating rich from poor even more obvious, and the uncontrolled search for a

comfortable life risks blinding people to the needs of others. In order to promote the social, cultural, spiritual and also economic welfare of all members of society, it is therefore absolutely essential to stem the unrestrained consumption of earthly goods and to control the creation of artificial needs. *Moderation and simplicity ought to become the criteria of our daily lives.* The quantity of goods consumed by a tiny fraction of the world population produces a demand greater than available resources. A reduction of this demand constitutes a first step in alleviating poverty, provided that it is accompanied by effective measures to guarantee a fair distribution of the world's wealth.

In this regard, the Gospel invites believers not to accumulate the goods of this passing world: 'Do not lay up for yourselves treasures on earth, where moth and rust consume and where thieves break in and steal, but lay up for yourselves treasures in heaven' (*Mt* 6:19–20). This is a duty intrinsic to the Christian vocation, no less than the duty of working to overcome poverty; and it is also a very effective means for succeeding in this task.

Evangelical poverty is very different from socio-economic poverty. While the latter has harsh and often tragic characteristics, since it is experienced as a form of coercion, evangelical poverty is chosen freely by the person who intends in this way to respond to Christ's admonition: 'Whoever of you does not renounce all that he has cannot be my disciple' (*Lk* 14:33).

Such evangelical poverty is the source of peace, since through it the individual can establish a proper relationship with God, *with others and with creation.* The life of the person who puts himself in this situation thus witnesses to humanity's absolute dependence on God who loves all creatures, and material goods come to be recognized for what they are: *a gift of God for the good of all.*

Evangelical poverty is something that transforms those who accept it. They cannot remain indifferent when faced with the suffering of the poor; indeed, they feel impelled to share actively with God his preferential love for them (cf. Encyclical Letter *Sollicitudo rei socialis*, n. 42). Those who are poor in the Gospel sense are ready to sacrifice their resources and their own selves so that others may live. Their one desire is to live in peace with everyone, offering to others the gift of Jesus' peace (cf. *Jn* 14:27).

The divine Master has taught us by his life and words the demanding features of this poverty which leads us to true freedom. He 'who, though he was in the form of God, did not count equality with God a thing to be grasped but emptied himself, taking the form of a servant' (*Phil* 2:6–7). He was born in poverty; as a child he was forced to go into exile with his family in order to escape the cruelty of Herod; he lived as one who had 'nowhere to lay his head' (*Mt* 8:20). He was denigrated as a 'glutton and a drunkard, a friend of tax collectors and sinners' (*Mt* 11:19) and suffered the death reserved for criminals. He called the poor blessed and assured them that the kingdom of God belonged to them (cf. *Lk* 6:20). He reminded the rich that the snare of wealth stifles God's word (cf. *Mt* 13:22), and that it is difficult for them to enter the kingdom of God (cf. Mk 10:25).

Christ's example, no less than his words, is normative for Christians. We know that, at the Last Judgment, we shall all be judged, without distinction, on our practical love of our brothers and sisters. Indeed, it will be in the practical love they have shown that, on that day, many will discover that they have in fact met Christ, although without having known him before in an explicit way (cf. *Mt* 25:35–37).

'If you want peace, reach out to the poor!' May rich and poor recognize that they are brothers and sisters; may they share what they have with one another as children of the one God who loves everyone, who wills the good of everyone, and who offers to everyone the gift of peace!

1 January 1994

THE FAMILY CREATES THE PEACE OF THE HUMAN FAMILY

For the International Year of the Family, the Pope proposes a reflection on the close relationship between the family and peace. He considers what Genesis tells us about the family. He also refers to the Universal Declaration of Human Rights that calls the family the 'natural and fundamental nucleus' of society. He sees the family as 'an active agent of peace' in building up a civilization of love 'through the values which it expresses and transmits within itself and through the participation of each of its members in the life of society'. The Pope reviews the difficulties families have to face today. He calls for 'specific structures to be set up to actively support families affected by unexpected and devastating misfortunes'. He laments the plight of children deprived of the warmth of a family (e.g. street children and those led into drugs, prostitution and criminal organizations). The State has duties to the family including upholding the right of the family to the full support of the State in carrying out its mission. Referring to proposals for alternative forms of union as legally equivalent to the union of spouses, he writes of the State's duty to encourage and protect the authentic institution of the family, respecting its natural structure and its innate and inalienable rights. Finally, he repeats his exhortation to Christian families in Familiaris Consortio: 'Families, become what you are'. And to those who for various reasons feel they have no family, he reminds them the Church is home and family.

* * *

202

1.   The world longs for peace and has a desperate need of peace. Yet wars, conflicts, increasing violence and situations of social unrest and endemic poverty continue to reap innocent victims and to cause divisions between individuals and peoples. At times peace appears a truly unattainable goal! In a climate made cold by indifference and occasionally poisoned by hatred, how can one hope for the dawn of an era of peace, which only feelings of solidarity and of love can usher in?

We must not lose heart. We know that, in spite of everything, peace is possible, because it is part of the original divine plan.

God wished humanity to live in harmony and peace, and laid the foundations for this in the very nature of the human being, created 'in his image'. The divine image develops not only in the individual but also in that unique communion of persons formed by a man and a woman so united in love that they become 'one flesh' (*Gen* 2:24). It is written: 'in the image of God he created them; male and female he created them' (*Gen* 1:27). This specific community of persons has been entrusted by the Lord with the mission of giving life and of nurturing it by the formation of a family. It thus makes a decisive contribution to the work of stewardship over creation and provides for the very future of humanity.

The initial harmony was disrupted by sin, but God's original plan continues. The family therefore remains the true foundation of society,[1] constituting, in the words of the Universal Declaration of Human Rights, its 'natural and fundamental nucleus'.[2]

The contribution which the family can offer preserving and promoting peace is so important that I would like, on the occasion of the International Year of the Family, to devote this World Day of Peace Message to a reflection on the close relationship between the family and peace. I am confident that this year will be a useful occasion for all who wish to contribute to the quest for true peace – Churches, Religious Organizations, Associations, Governments, International Agencies – to study together ways of helping the family to carry out fully its irreplaceable task as a builder of peace.

The family: a community of life and love

2.   The family, as the fundamental and essential educating community, is the privileged means for transmitting the religious and cultural values which help the person to acquire his or her own identity. Founded on love and open to the gift of life, the family contains in itself the very future of society; its most special task is to contribute effectively to a future of peace.

This it will achieve, in the first place, through the mutual love of married couples, called to full and complete communion of life by marriage in its natural meaning and even more, if they are Christians, by its having been raised to a sacrament, and then through the efforts of parents to carry out properly their task as educators, committed to training their children to respect the dignity of every person and the values of peace. These values, more than being 'taught', must be witnessed to in a family setting which lives out that self-giving love which is capable of accepting those who are different, making their needs and demands its own, and allowing them to share in its own benefits. The domestic virtues, based upon a profound respect for human life and dignity, and practiced in understanding, patience, mutual encouragement and forgiveness, enable the community of the family to live out the first and fundamental experience of peace. Outside this context of affectionate relationships and of fruitful mutual solidarity, the human being 'remains a being that is incomprehensible for himself, his life is senseless, if love is not revealed to him ... if he does not experience it and make it his own'.[3] This love is not a fleeting emotion, but an intense and enduring moral force which seeks the good of others, even at the cost of self-sacrifice. Furthermore, true love always goes together with justice, so necessary for peace. It reaches out to those experiencing hardship: those who have no family, children who lack guidance and affection, the lonely and the outcast. The family which lives this love, even though imperfectly, and opens itself generously to the rest of society, is the primary agent of a future of peace. A civilization of peace is not possible if love is lacking.

The family: victim of the lack of peace

3.　　In contrast with its original vocation of peace, the family is sadly, and not infrequently, seen to be the scene of tension and oppression, or the defenseless victim of the many forms of violence marking society today.

Tensions are sometimes seen in relations within the family. These are often due to the difficulty of efforts to harmonize family life when work keeps spouses far from each other, or the lack or uncertainty of employment causes them to worry about survival and to be haunted by uncertainty about the future. There are also tensions deriving from patterns of behavior inspired by hedonism and consumerism, family members who seek personal gratification rather than a happy and fruitful life together. Frequent arguments between parents, the refusal to have children, and the abandonment and ill-treatment of minors are the sad symptoms that family peace is already seriously endangered; certainly it cannot be restored by the sad solution of a separation of the spouses, much less by recourse to divorce, a true 'plague' of present day society.[4]

Likewise, in many parts of the world, whole nations are caught in the spiral of bloody conflicts, of which families are often the first victims: either they are deprived of the main if not the only breadwinner, or they are forced to abandon home, land and property and flee into the unknown; in any event they are subjected to painful misfortunes which threaten all security. How can we fail to recall, in this regard, the bloody conflict between ethnic groups which is still going on in Bosnia-Hercegovina? And this is only one case, amid so many situations of war throughout the world!

In the face of such distressing situations, society often appears incapable of offering effective help, or even culpably indifferent. The spiritual and psychological needs of those who have experienced the effects of armed conflict are as pressing and serious as their need for food or shelter. Specific structures need to be set up for actively supporting families affected by unexpected and devastating misfortunes, so that in spite of them they will not yield to the temptation to discouragement and revenge, but will react in a spirit of forgiveness and reconciliation. How often, unfortunately, there is no sign of this!

4.   Nor can one forget that war and violence not only constitute divisive forces which weaken and destroy family structures; they also exercise a pernicious influence on people's minds, suggesting and practically imposing models of behavior diametrically opposed to peace. In this regard, one must deplore a very sad fact: these days unfortunately a growing number of boys and girls and even small children are playing a direct part in armed conflicts. They are forced to join armed militias and have to fight for causes they do not always understand. In other cases, they become involved in a real culture of violence in which life counts for very little and killing does not seem wrong. It is in the interests of the whole of society to ensure that these young people give up violence and take the path of peace, but this presupposes patient education given by people who sincerely believe in peace.

At this point I cannot fail to mention another serious obstacle to the development of peace in our society: many, too many children are deprived of the warmth of a family. Sometimes the family is absent: in fact, the parents, taken up by other interests, leave their children to their own devices. In other cases the family simply does not exist: thus there are thousands of children who have no home but the street and who can count on no resources except themselves. Some of these street children die tragically. Others are led into the use and even the sale of drugs and into prostitution, and not infrequently they end up in criminal organizations. Such scandalous and widespread situations cannot be ignored! The very future of society is at stake. A community which rejects children, or marginalizes them, or reduces them to hopeless situations, can never know peace.

In order to count on a peaceful future, every child needs to experience the warmth of caring and constant affection, not betrayal and exploitation. And although the State can do much by providing means and structures of support, the contribution of the family to ensuring that climate of security and trust cannot be replaced, so important is it in helping young children to look to the future with serenity, and in preparing them to take a responsible part in building a society of true progress when they grow up. Children are the future already present among us; they need to experience what peace means, so that they will be able to create a future of peace.

The family: an agent for peace

5.   An enduring peaceful order needs institutions which express and consolidate the values of peace. The institution which most immediately responds to the nature of the human being is the family. It alone ensures the continuity and the future of society. The family is therefore called to become an active agent for peace, through the values which it expresses and transmits within itself, and through the participation of each of its members in the life of society.

As the fundamental nucleus of society, the family has a right to the full support of the State in order to carry out fully its particular mission. State laws, therefore, must be directed to promoting its well-being, helping it to fulfill its proper duties. In the face of increasing pressure nowadays to consider, as legally equivalent to the union of spouses, forms of union which by their very nature or their intentional lack of permanence are in no way capable of expressing the meaning and ensuring the good of the family, it is the duty of the State to encourage and protect the authentic institution of the family, respecting its natural structure and its innate and inalienable rights.[5] Among these, the fundamental one is the right of parents to decide, freely and responsibly, on the basis of their moral and religious convictions and with a properly formed conscience, when to have a child, and then to educate that child in accordance with those convictions.

The State also has an important role in creating the conditions in which families can provide for their primary needs in a way befitting human dignity. Poverty, indeed destitution – a perennial threat to social stability, to the development of people and to peace – in our day affects too many families. It sometimes happens that, because of a lack of means, young couples put off having a family or are even prevented from having one, while needy families cannot participate fully in the life of society, or are forced into total emargination.

The duty of the State does not, however, excuse individual citizens: the real reply to the gravest questions in every society is in fact ensured by the harmonious solidarity of everyone. In effect, no one can be at ease until an adequate solution has been found to the problem of poverty, which strikes families and individuals. Poverty is always a threat to social stability, to economic development and ultimately therefore to peace. Peace will always be at risk so long as individuals and families are forced to fight for their very survival.

The family at the service of peace

6.   I would now like to speak directly to families, in particular to Christian families.

'Families, become what you are!', I wrote in my Apostolic Exhortation *Familiaris Consortio*.[6] Become an 'intimate sharing of married life and love',[7] called to give love and to transmit life!

Families, you have a mission of prime importance: that of contributing to the construction of peace, indispensable for respect for human life and its development.[8] Knowing that peace is never secured once and for all,[9] you must never grow weary of seeking it! Jesus, through his death on the Cross, has left to humanity his peace, assuring us of his enduring presence.[10] Ask for this peace, pray for this peace, work for this peace!

To you parents falls the responsibility for forming and educating your children to be people of peace: for this purpose, you in the first place must be workers for peace.

You children, facing the future with the eagerness of youth, full of hopes and dreams, value the gift of the family, prepare for the responsibility of building it or promoting it according to the particular callings that God will give you in due course. Develop a desire for good and thoughts of peace.

You grandparents, who with the other family members represent unique and precious links between the generations, make a generous contribution of your experience and your witness in order to link the past to the future in a peaceful present.

Families, live out your mission in harmony and to the full!

Finally, how can we forget the many people who for various reasons feel that they have no family? To them I would like to say that there is a family for them too: the Church is home and family for all.[11] She opens wide her doors and welcomes in all who are alone or abandoned; in them she sees the specially beloved children of God, whatever their age, and whatever their aspirations, difficulties or hopes.

May the family so live in peace that from it peace may spread throughout the whole human family!

This is the prayer which, through the intercession of Mary, Mother of Christ and of the Church, I offer to him 'from whom every family in heaven and on earth is named' (Eph 3:15), at the beginning of the International Year of the Family.

Notes

1   Cf. Second Vatican Ecumenical Council, Pastoral Constitution *Gaudium et Spes*, 52.
2   Article 16, 3.
3   Encyclical *Redemptor Hominis*, 10.
4   Cf. Pastoral Constitution *Gaudium et Spes*, 47.
5   Cf. in this regard the 'Charter of the Rights of the Family presented by the Holy See to all Persons, Institutions and Authorities Interested in the Mission of the Family in Today's World' (22 October 1983).
6   No. 17.
7   *Gaudium et Spes*, 48.
8   Cf. *Catechism of the Catholic Church*, No. 2304.
9   Cf. *Gaudium et Spes*, 78.
10   Cf. *Jn* 14:27; 20:19–21; *Mt* 28:20.
11   Cf. *Familiaris Consortio*, 85.

1 January 1995
WOMEN: TEACHERS OF PEACE

With the new millennium fast approaching and the realization that 'the time has come to move from words to deeds' the Pope directs his 1995 message to women and invites them to 'become teachers of peace with their whole being and in all their actions'. He does so on the basis that if we review God's plan as outlined in the bible we see that God entrusts the human being in a special way to women. This plan speaks of a reciprocity and complementarity between man and woman. There is a need to rediscover this plan so that women in particular 'who have suffered more in its failure to be fulfilled' can give full expression to their womanhood and their dignity. While noting positive developments he also points out that there are many obstacles that still prevent women from being respected in their own special dignity. He urges everyone 'to reflect on the critical importance of the role of women in the family and in society' and also as teachers of peace. Mothers have a singular important role in rearing children but no mother should be left alone in parenting. The Pope praises the work of congregations of women who promoted the education of girls and women. In the face of all kinds of violence today, he appeals to all women to take their place on the side of life. Finally, he points to Mary as an example.

* * *

1.   At the beginning of 1995, with my gaze fixed on the new millennium now fast approaching, I once again address to you, men and women of goodwill, a pressing appeal for peace in the world.

The violence which so many individuals and peoples continue to experience, the wars which still cause bloodshed in many areas of the world, and the injustice which burdens the life of whole continents can no longer be tolerated.

The time has come to move from words to deeds: may individual citizens and families, believers and Churches, States and International Organizations all recognize that they are called to renew their commitment to work for peace!

Everyone is aware of the difficulty of this task. If it is to be effective and long-lasting, work for peace cannot be concerned merely with the external conditions of coexistence; rather, it must affect people's hearts and appeal to a new awareness of human dignity. It must be forcefully repeated: authentic peace is only possible if the dignity of the human person is promoted at every level of society, and every individual is given the chance to live in accordance with this dignity. 'Any human society, if it is to be well-ordered and productive, must lay down as a foundation this principle, namely, that *every human being is a person,* that is, his nature is endowed with intelligence and free will. Indeed, precisely because he is a person he has rights and obligations which flow directly and immediately from his very nature. And these rights and obligations are universal, inviolable and inalienable'.[1]

The truth about man is the keystone in the resolution of all the problems involved in promoting peace. To teach people this truth is one of the most fruitful and lasting ways to affirm the value of peace.

Women and the teaching of peace

2.   To educate in the ways of peace means to open minds and hearts to embrace the values which Pope John XXIII indicated in the Encyclical *Pacem in terris* as essential to a peaceful society: truth, justice, love and freedom.[2] This is an

educational programme which involves every aspect of life and is lifelong. It trains individuals to be responsible for themselves and for others, capable of promoting, with boldness and wisdom, the welfare of the whole person and of all people, as Pope Paul VI emphasized in the Encyclical *Populorum progressio*.[3] The effectiveness of this education for peace will depend on the extent to which it involves the co-operation of those who, in different ways, are responsible for education and for the life of society. Time dedicated to education is time truly well spent, because it determines a person's future, and therefore the future of the family and of the whole of society.

In this context, I wish to direct my Message for this year's World Day of Peace especially to *women*, and to invite them to become *teachers of peace with their whole being and in all their actions*. May they be witnesses, messengers and teachers of peace in relations between individuals and between generations, in the family, in the cultural, social and political life of nations, and particularly in situations of conflict and war. May they continue to follow the path which leads to peace, a path which many courageous and far-sighted women have walked before them!

In communion of love

3.   This invitation to become teachers of peace, directed particularly to women, is based on a realization that to them God *'entrusts the human being in a special way'*.[4] This is not however to be understood in an exclusive sense, but rather according to the logic of the complementary roles present in the common vocation to love, which calls men and women to seek peace with one accord and to work together in building it. Indeed, from the very first pages of the Bible God's plan is marvellously expressed: he willed that there should be a relationship of profound communion between man and woman, in a perfect reciprocity of knowledge and of the giving of self.[5] In woman, man finds a partner with whom he can dialogue in complete equality. This desire for dialogue, which was not satisfied by any other living creature, explains the

man's spontaneous cry of wonder when the woman, according to the evocative symbolism of the Bible, was created from one of his ribs: 'This at last is bone of my bones and flesh of my flesh' (*Gn* 2:23). This was the first cry of love to resound on the earth!

Even though man and woman are made for each other, this does not mean that God created them incomplete. God 'created them to be a communion of persons, in which each can be a 'helpmate' to the other, for they are equal as persons ('bone of my bones...') and complementary as masculine and feminine'.[6] Reciprocity and complementarity are the two fundamental characteristics of the human couple.

4.   Sadly, a long history of sin has disturbed and continues to disturb God's original plan for the couple, for the male and the female, thus standing in the way of its complete fulfilment. We need to return to this plan, to proclaim it forcefully, so that women in particular – who have suffered more from its failure to be fulfilled – can finally give full expression to their womanhood and their dignity.

In our day women have made great strides in this direction, attaining a remarkable degree of self-expression in cultural, social, economic and political life, as well as, of course, in family life. The journey has been a difficult and complicated one and, at times, not without its share of mistakes. But it has been substantially a positive one, even if it is still unfinished, due to the many obstacles which, in various parts of the world, still prevent women from being acknowledged, respected, and appreciated in their own special dignity.[7] The work of building peace can hardly overlook the need to acknowledge and promote the dignity of women as persons, called to play a unique role in educating for peace. I urge everyone to reflect on the critical importance of the role of women in the family and in society, and to heed the yearning for peace which they express in words and deeds and, at times of greatest tragedy, by the silent eloquence of their grief.

Women of peace

5.   In order to be a teacher of peace, a woman must first of all nurture peace within herself. Inner peace comes from knowing that one is loved by God and from the desire to respond to his love. History is filled with marvellous examples of women who, sustained by this knowledge, have been able successfully to deal with difficult situations of exploitation, discrimination, violence and war.

Nevertheless, many women, especially as a result of social and cultural conditioning, do not become fully aware of their dignity. Others are victims of a materialistic and hedonistic outlook which views them as mere objects of pleasure, and does not hesitate to organize the exploitation of women, even of young girls, into a despicable trade. Special concern needs to be shown for these women, particularly by other women who, thanks to their own upbringing and sensitivity, are able to help them discover their own inner worth and resources. *Women need to help women,* and to find support in the valuable and effective contributions which associations, movements and groups, many of them of a religious character, have proved capable of making in this regard.

6.   In rearing children, mothers have a singularly important role. Through the special relationship uniting a mother and her child, particularly in its earliest years of life, she gives the child that sense of security and trust without which the child would find it difficult to develop properly its own personal identity and, subsequently, to establish positive and fruitful relationships with others. This primary relationship between mother and child also has a very particular educational significance in the religious sphere, for it can direct the mind and heart of the child to God long before any formal religious education begins.

In this decisive and sensitive task, no mother should be left alone. *Children need the presence and care of both parents,* who carry out their duty as educators above all through the influence of the way they live. The quality of the relationship

215

between the spouses has profound psychological effects on children and greatly conditions both the way they relate to their surroundings and the other relationships which they will develop throughout life.

This primary education is extremely important. If relationships with parents and other family members are marked by affectionate and positive interaction, children come to learn from their own experience the values which promote peace: love of truth and justice, a sense of responsible freedom, esteem and respect for others. At the same time, as they grow up in a warm and accepting environment, they are able to perceive, reflected in their own family relationships, the love of God himself; this will enable them to mature in a spiritual atmosphere which can foster openness to others and to the gift of self to their neighbour. Education in the ways of peace naturally continues throughout every period of development; it needs particularly to be encouraged during the difficult time of adolescence, when the passage from childhood to adulthood is not without some risks for young people, who are called to make choices which will be decisive for life.

7.   Faced with the challenge of education, the family becomes 'the first and fundamental school of social living',[8] the first and fundamental *school of peace*. And so it is not difficult to imagine the tragic consequences which occur when the family experiences profound crises which undermine or even destroy its inner equilibrium. Often, in these circumstances, women are left alone. It is then, however, that they most need to be assisted, not only by the practical solidarity of other families, of communities of a religious nature and of volunteer groups, but also by the State and by International Organizations through appropriate structures of human, social and economic support which will enable them to meet the needs of their children without being forced to deprive them unduly of their own indispensable presence.

8.   Another serious problem is found in places where the intolerable custom still exists of discriminating, from the

earliest years, between boys and girls. If, from the very beginning, girls are looked down upon or regarded as inferior, their sense of dignity will be gravely impaired and their healthy development inevitably compromised. Discrimination in childhood will have lifelong effects and will prevent women from fully taking part in the life of society.

In this regard, how can we fail to acknowledge and encourage the invaluable efforts of so many women, including so many congregations of women religious, who on different continents and in every cultural context make the education of girls and women the principal goal of their activity? Similarly, how can we fail to acknowledge with gratitude all those women who have worked and continue to work in providing health services, often in very precarious circumstances, and who are frequently responsible for the very survival of great numbers of female children?

Women, teachers of peace in society

9.   When women are able fully to share their gifts with the whole community, the very way in which society understands and organizes itself is improved, and comes to reflect in a better way the substantial unity of the human family. Here we see the most important condition for the consolidation of authentic peace. The growing presence of women in social, economic and political life at the local, national and international levels is thus a very positive development. Women have a full right to become actively involved in all areas of public life, and this right must be affirmed and guaranteed, also, where necessary, through appropriate legislation.

This acknowledgment of the public role of women should not however detract from their unique role within the family. Here their contribution to the welfare and progress of society, even if its importance is not sufficiently appreciated, is truly incalculable. In this regard I will continue to ask that more decisive steps be taken in order to recognize and promote this very important reality.

10.   With astonishment and concern we are witnessing today a dramatic increase in all kinds of violence. Not just individuals but whole groups seem to have lost any sense of respect for human life. Women and even children are unfortunately among the most frequent victims of this blind violence. We are speaking of outrageous and barbaric behaviour which is deeply abhorrent to the human conscience.

We are all called upon to do everything possible to banish from society not only the tragedy of war but also every violation of human rights, beginning with the indisputable right to life, which every person enjoys from the very moment of conception. The violation of the individual human being's right to life contains the seeds of the extreme violence of war. For this reason, I appeal to all women ever to take their place on the side of life. At the same time I urge everyone to help women who are suffering, and particularly children, in a special way those scarred by the painful trauma of having lived through war. Only loving and compassionate concern will enable them once again to look to the future with confidence and hope.

11.   When my beloved predecessor Pope John XXIII indicated the participation of women in public life as one of the signs of our times, he also stated that, being aware of their dignity, they would no longer tolerate being exploited.[9]

Women have the right to insist that their dignity be respected. At the same time, they have the duty to work for the promotion of the dignity of all persons, men as well as women.

In view of this, I express the hope that the many international initiatives planned for 1995 – of which some will be devoted specifically to women, such as the Conference sponsored by the United Nations in Beijing on work for equality, development and peace – will provide a significant opportunity for making interpersonal and social relationships ever more human, under the banner of peace.

Mary, model of peace

12.   Mary, Queen of Peace, is close to the women of our day because of her motherhood, her example of openness to others' needs and her witness of suffering. Mary lived with a deep sense of responsibility the plan which God willed to carry out in her for the salvation of all humanity. When she was made aware of the miracle which God had worked in her by making her the Mother of his Incarnate Son, her first thought was to visit her elderly kinswoman Elizabeth in order to help her. That meeting gave Mary the chance to express, in the marvellous canticle of the Magnificat (Lk 1:46–55), her gratitude to God who, with her and through her, had begun a new creation, a new history.

I implore the Most Holy Virgin Mary to sustain those men and women who, in the service of life, have committed themselves to building peace. With her help, may they bear witness before all people, especially those who live in darkness and suffering and who hunger and thirst for justice, to the loving presence of the God of peace!

Notes

1   John XXIII, Encyclical Letter *Pacem in terris* (11 April 1963), n. 1: *AAS* 55 (1963), 259.
2   Cf. loc. cit., 259–264.
3   Cf. Paul VI, Encyclical Letter *Populorum progressio* (26 March 1967), n. 14: *AAS* (1967), 264.
4   John Paul II, Apostolic Letter *Mulieris dignitatem* (15 August 1988), n. 30: *AAS* 80 (1988), 1725.
5   Cf. *Catechism of the Catholic Church*, n. 371.
6   Ibid., n. 372.
7   Cf. John Paul II, Apostolic Letter *Mulieris dignitatem* (15 August 1988), n. 29: *AAS* 80 (1988), 1723.
8   Cf. John Paul II, Apostolic Exhortation *Familiaris consortio* (22 November 1981), n. 37: *AAS* 74 (1982), 127.
9   John XXIII, Encyclical Letter *Pacem in terris* (11 April 1963), n. 1: *AAS* 55 (1963), 267–268.

1 January 1996
LET US GIVE CHILDREN A FUTURE OF PEACE

In this message Pope John Paul II strongly emphasises the tragic conditions in which many children are living today. He lists, for instance, forms of war and violence against them: ethnic cleansings, forcing them to take an active part in war resulting in awful memories of violence and death. Children are used for begging and 'sex tourism', enlisted in criminal activities, and abandoned to the street as their only home. He also observes that violence is found even in wealthy and affluent families where children experience dismal loneliness and lack of suitable moral formation. In praising humanitarian and religious organizations, he encourages Catholic charitable and educational institutions to adopt a co-ordinated strategy that gives priority to issues concerning children and young women, especially those in need. In the second part of his message he notes the many positive signs of hope, especially the many families all over the world where children grow up in an atmosphere of peace. He believes that 'if children are properly helped and loved, they themselves can become peacemakers, builders of a world of fraternity and solidarity'. The mutual love between parents is itself an education for peace for children. He summarises: 'Everything possible should be done to help children to become messengers of peace.' Finally, the Pope underlines how Jesus turned around our way of thinking by showing us the need to learn the ways of God from children and become like little children with complete trust in God the Father.

✳ ✳ ✳

1.   At the end of 1994, the International Year of the Family, I wrote a Letter to the children of the whole world, asking them to pray that humanity would increasingly become *God's family*, living in harmony and peace. I have frequently expressed my heartfelt concern for children who are victims of armed conflicts and other kinds of violence, and I have not failed to call these serious situations to the attention of world public opinion.

At the beginning of this new year, my thoughts turn once again to children and to their *legitimate hope for love and peace*. I feel bound to mention in a particular way *children who are suffering* and those who often grow to adulthood without ever having experienced peace. Children's faces should always be happy and trusting, but at times they are full of sadness and fear: how much have these children already seen and suffered in the course of their short lives!

Let us give children a future of peace! This is the confident appeal which I make to men and women of good will, and I invite everyone to help children to grow up in an environment of authentic peace. This is their right, and it is our duty.

Children who are victims of war

2.   I begin by thinking of the great crowds of children whom I have met during the years of my Pontificate, especially during my Apostolic Visits to every continent: joyful children who are full of happiness. My thoughts turn to them at the beginning of this new year.

It is my hope that all children of the world will be able to begin 1996 in happiness and to enjoy a peaceful childhood, with the help of responsible adults.

I pray that everywhere a harmonious relationship between adults and children will promote a climate of peace and authentic well-being. Sadly, many of the world's children are innocent victims of war. In recent years millions of them have been wounded or killed: a veritable slaughter.

The special protection accorded to children by international law[1] has been widely disregarded, and the dramatic increase of regional and inter-ethnic conflicts has made it difficult to implement the protective measures called for by humanitarian regulations. Children have even become targets of snipers, their schools deliberately destroyed, and the hospitals where they are cared for bombed. In the face of such horrendous misdeeds, how can we fail to speak out with one voice in condemnation? The deliberate killing of a child is one of the most disturbing signs *of the breakdown of all respect for human life*.[2] In addition to the children who have been killed, my thoughts also turn to those who have been maimed during or after these conflicts. I likewise think of young people who are systematically hunted down, raped or killed during so-called 'ethnic cleansings'.

3.   Children are not only victims of the violence of wars; many *are forced to take an active part in them*. In some countries of the world it has come to the point where even very young boys and girls are compelled to serve in the army of the warring parties. Enticed by the promise of food and schooling, they are confined to remote camps, where they suffer hunger and abuse and are encouraged to kill even people from their own villages. Often they are sent ahead to clear minefields. Clearly, the life of children has little value for those who use them in this way!

The future of young people who have taken up arms is often compromised.

After years of military service, some are simply discharged and sent home, where they often fail to fit into civilian life. Others, ashamed of having survived when their companions have not, frequently end up as criminals or drug addicts. Who knows what nightmares must continue to afflict them! Will their minds ever be free of the memories of violence and death?

The humanitarian and religious organizations which attempt to relieve these inhuman sufferings deserve heartfelt respect. Thanks are also owed to those generous individuals and families who welcome orphans with love, and do everything they can to heal their traumas and to help them to fit once more into the communities from which they came.

4.   The memory of the millions of children who have been killed, and the sad faces of so many others who are suffering compel us to *take every possible measure* to safeguard or re-establish peace, and to bring conflicts and wars to an end.

Before the Fourth World Conference on Women which took place in Beijing last September, I asked Catholic charitable and educational institutions to adopt a co-ordinated strategy which gives priority to issues concerning children and young women, especially those most in need.[3] Now I wish to renew that appeal, and to extend it in a special way to Catholic institutions and organizations which deal with children. I ask them to help girls who have suffered as a result of war and violence, to teach boys to acknowledge and respect the dignity of women, and to help all children to rediscover the tenderness of the love of God who took flesh, and who by dying left the world the gift of his peace (cf. *Jn* 14:27).

I will continue to point out that all, from the most prominent international organizations to local associations, from Heads of State to ordinary citizens, in everyday actions and at the most significant moments of life, are called upon *to make a contribution to peace and to give no support to war.*

Children who are victims of various forms of violence

5.   Millions of children suffer from other kinds of violence present both in poverty-stricken and in developed societies. These kinds of violence are often less obvious, but they are no less terrible.

The International Summit for Social Development which took place this year in Copenhagen stressed the connection between poverty and violence,[4] and on that occasion States committed themselves to a greater battle against poverty through initiatives at the national level, beginning in 1996.[5] Similar suggestions were made by the earlier World Conference of the United Nations on Children, held in New York in 1990. Poverty is indeed the cause of inhuman living and working conditions. In some countries children are forced to work at a tender age and are often badly treated, harshly punished, and paid absurdly low wages.

Because they have no way of asserting their rights, they are the easiest to blackmail and exploit.

In other circumstances children are bought and sold,[6] so that they can be used for begging or, even worse, forced into prostitution, as in the case of so-called 'sex tourism'. This utterly despicable trade degrades not only those who take part in it but also those who in any way promote it. Some do not hesitate to enlist children in criminal activities, especially the selling of narcotics, thus exposing them to the risk of personal involvement in drug use.

Many children end up with the street as their only home. Having run away, or having been abandoned by their families, or never having known a family environment, these young people live by their wits and in a state of total neglect, and they are considered by many as refuse to be eliminated.

6.   Sadly, violence towards children is found even in wealthy and affluent families. Such cases are infrequent, but it is important not to overlook them. Sometimes children are taken advantage of and suffer abuse within the home itself, at the hands of people whom they should be able to trust, to the detriment of their development.

Many children are also compelled to endure the trauma caused by fighting between their parents, or by the actual breakup of the family. Concern for the children's welfare does not prevent solutions which are often dictated by the selfishness and hypocrisy of adults. Behind an appearance of normality and peacefulness, masked even further by an abundance of material possessions, children are at times forced to grow up in dismal loneliness, without firm and loving guidance and a suitable moral formation. Left to themselves, such children usually find their main contact with reality in television programmes which often present unreal and immoral situations which they are still too young to assess properly.

It is no wonder if this kind of widespread and pernicious violence also has its effect on their young hearts, changing their natural enthusiasm into disillusionment or cynicism, and their instinctive goodness into indifference or selfishness. When young people chase after false ideals, they can experience bitterness and humiliation, hostility and hatred, absorbing the discontent and emptiness all around them. Everyone is well aware of how childhood experiences can have profound and sometimes irreparable consequences on an individual's whole life.

It can hardly be hoped that children will one day be able to build a better world, unless there is a specific commitment to their *education for peace*. Children need to 'learn peace': it is their right, and one which cannot be disregarded.

Children and hope for peace

7.   I have sought to emphasize strongly the often tragic conditions in which many children are living today. I consider this my duty: they will be the adults of the Third Millennium. But *I have no intention of yielding to pessimism* or ignoring the signs of hope. How can I fail to mention, for example, the many families in every part of the world in which children grow up in an atmosphere of peace? And how can we not note the efforts being made by so many individuals and organizations to enable children in difficulty to grow up in peace and happiness? Public and private associations, individual families and particular communities have taken initiatives the only purpose of which is to help children who have suffered some traumatic event to return to a normal life. In particular, educational programmes have been developed for encouraging children and young people to use fully their personal talents, in order to become true peacemakers.

There is also a growing awareness in the international community which, in recent years, despite difficulties and hesitation, has made efforts to deal decisively and systematically with problems connected with childhood.

The results achieved thus far encourage us to continue these praiseworthy endeavours. If children are properly helped and loved, they themselves can become *peacemakers,* builders of a world of fraternity and solidarity. With their enthusiasm and youthful idealism, young people can become 'witnesses' and 'teachers' of hope and peace to adults. Lest these possibilities be lost, children should be offered, in a way adapted to their individual needs, every opportunity for a balanced personal growth.

A peaceful childhood will enable boys and girls to face the future with confidence. Let no one stifle their joyful enthusiasm and hope.

Children in the school of peace

8.   Little children very soon learn about life. They watch and imitate the behaviour of adults. They rapidly learn love and respect for others, but they also quickly absorb the poison of violence and hatred. Family experiences strongly condition the attitudes which children will assume as adults. Consequently, if the family is the place where children first encounter the world, *the family must be for children the first school of peace.*

Parents have an extraordinary opportunity to help their sons and daughters to become aware of this great treasure: *the witness of their mutual love.* It is by loving each other that they enable the child, from the very first moment of its existence, to grow up in peaceful surroundings, imbued with the positive values which make up the family's true heritage: mutual respect and acceptance, listening, sharing, generosity, forgiveness. Thanks to the sense of working together which these values foster, they provide a true education for peace and make the child, from its earliest years, an active builder of peace.

Children share with their parents and brothers and sisters the experience of life and hope. They see how life's inevitable trials are met with humility and courage, and they grow up in an atmosphere of esteem for others and respect for opinions different from their own.

It is above all in the home that, before ever a word is spoken, children should experience God's love in the love which surrounds them. In the family they learn that God wants peace and mutual understanding among all human beings, who are called to be one great family.

9.   Besides the basic education provided by the family, children have a right to *a specific training for peace at school* and in other educational settings.

These institutions have a duty to lead children gradually to understand the nature and demands of peace within their world and culture. Children need to learn *the history of peace* and not simply the history of victory and defeat in war.

Let us show them examples of peace and not just examples of violence! Fortunately many positive examples of this can be found in every culture and period of history. Suitable new educational opportunities must be created, especially in those situations where cultural and moral poverty has been most oppressive. Everything possible should be done to help *children to become messengers of peace.*

Children are not a burden on society; they are not a means of profit or people without rights. Children are precious members of the human family, for they embody its hopes, its expectations and its potential.

Jesus, the way of peace

10.   Peace is a gift of God; but men and women must first accept this gift in order to build a peaceful world. People can do this *only if they have a childlike simplicity of heart.* This is one of the most profound and paradoxical aspects of the Christian message: to become child-like is more than just a moral requirement but a dimension of the mystery of the Incarnation itself.

The Son of God did not come in power and glory, as he will at the end of the world, but as a child, needy and poor.

Fully sharing our human condition in all things but sin (cf. *Heb* 4:15), *he also took on the frailty and hope for the future which are part of being a child.*

After that decisive moment for the history of humanity, to despise childhood means to despise the One who showed the greatness of his love by humbling himself and forsaking all glory in order to redeem mankind.

Jesus identified with the little ones. When the Apostles were arguing about who was the greatest, he 'took a child and put him by his side, and said to them, "Whoever receives this child in my name, receives me; and whoever receives me receives him who sent me"' (*Lk* 9:47–48). The Lord also forcefully warned us against giving scandal to children: 'Whoever causes one of these little ones who believe in me to sin, it would be better for him to have a great millstone fastened round his neck and to be drowned in the depth of the sea' (*Mt* 18:6).

Jesus asked the disciples to become 'children' again. When they tried to turn away the little ones who were pressing in upon him, he said indignantly: 'Let the children come to me, do not hinder them; for to such belongs the Kingdom of God. Truly, I say to you, whoever does not receive the Kingdom of God like a child shall not enter it' (*Mk* 10:14–15). Jesus thus turned around our way of thinking. *Adults need to learn from children the ways of God*: seeing children's capacity for complete trust, adults can learn to cry out with true confidence, 'Abba, Father!'.

11.   To become like a little child – with complete trust in the Father and with the meekness taught by the Gospel – is not only an ethical imperative; *it is a reason for hope*. Even where the difficulties are so great as to lead to discouragement and the power of evil so overwhelming as to dishearten, those who can rediscover the simplicity of a child can begin to hope anew. This is possible above all for those who know they can trust in a God who desires harmony among all people in the peaceful communion of his Kingdom. It is also possible for those who, though not sharing the gift of faith, believe in the values of forgiveness and solidarity and see in them – not without the hidden action of the Spirit – the possibility of renewing the face of the earth.

It is therefore to men and women of good will that I address this confident appeal. Let us all unite to fight every kind of violence and to conquer war!

Let us create the conditions which will ensure that children can receive as the legacy of our generation a more united and fraternal world!

Let us give children a future of peace!

Notes

1   Cf. United Nations Convention of 20 November 1989 on the rights of children, especially Article 38; the Fourth Geneva Convention of 12 August 1949 for the protection of civilians in wartime, Article 24; Protocols I and II of 12 December 1977, etc.

2   Cf. John Paul II, Encyclical Letter *Evangelium vitae* (25 March 1995), n. 3: *AAS* 87 (1995), 404.

3   Cf. Message to the Delegation of the Holy See at the Fourth World Conference on Women (29 August 1995): *L'Osservatore Romano*, 30 August 1995, p. 1.

4   Cf. Copenhagen Declaration, n. 16.

5   Cf. Programme of Action, Chapter II.

6   Cf. Programme of Action, n. 39 (e).

1 January 1997

OFFER FORGIVENESS AND RECEIVE PEACE

Since 'no process of peace can ever begin unless the attitude of sincere forgiveness takes root in human hearts', Pope John Paul appeals in his 1997 message to all, and especially to Christians, to seek peace along the paths of forgiveness. He proposes forgiveness as a social and political category. Inspired by the logic of love that runs through God's merciful plan of love, the Pope believes forgiveness is key in a wounded world with many imprisoned in a deep inner loneliness. They yearn for healing. Conscience calls us to promote a culture of peace born of forgiveness because asking and granting forgiveness is sometimes the only way out of situations marked by age-old and violent hatred. Forgiveness is a free act of love based on respect for truth and justice. It neither eliminates nor lessens the need for reparation. The Pope comments both positively and with a note of prudence on situations where procedures have been set up to ascertain the truth regarding crimes between ethnic groups or nations. A first step in building a culture born of forgiveness is to learn to read the history of others, making an effort to understand their point of view. Religions too play a role in this. On the fiftieth anniversary of the UN, the Pope reaffirms its role but also calls for a review so that it will be able 'to face effectively the new challenges of our time'. In this message reference is made to the 'healing of memories' needed also by Christians as they enter the first of three years preparation for the new millennium.

✳ ✳ ✳

1.   Only three years separate us from the dawn of a new millennium. This time of expectation is a time for reflection, inviting us to make an assessment, as it were, of mankind's journey in the sight of God, the Lord of history. If we look back on the last millennium, and on this century in particular, it must be acknowledged that mankind's path has been greatly illuminated by progress in the socio-cultural, economic, scientific and technological spheres. Unfortunately, this new light coexists with persistent dark shadows, especially in the areas of morality and solidarity. Then there is the real scandal of violence, which in old and new ways still strikes many human lives, and tears apart families and communities.

The time has come for a resolute decision to set out together on a true *pilgrimage of peace*, starting from the concrete situation in which we find ourselves. At times the difficulties can be daunting: ethnic origin, language, culture and religious beliefs are often obstacles to such a pilgrimage. To go forward together, when we have behind us traumatic experiences or even age-old divisions, is not an easy thing to do. This, then, is the question: which path must we follow, what direction should we take?

Certainly there are many factors which can help restore peace, while safeguarding the demands of justice and human dignity. But no process of peace can ever begin unless an attitude of sincere forgiveness takes root in human hearts. When such forgiveness is lacking, wounds continue to fester, fuelling in the younger generation endless resentment, producing a desire for revenge and causing fresh destruction. Offering and accepting forgiveness is the essential condition for making the journey towards authentic and lasting peace.

With deep conviction therefore I wish to appeal to everyone to *seek peace along the paths of forgiveness*. I am fully aware that forgiveness can seem contrary to human logic, which often yields to the dynamics of conflict and revenge. But forgiveness is inspired by the logic of love, that love which God has for every man and woman, for every people and nation, and for the whole human family. If the Church dares to proclaim what, from a human standpoint, might appear to be sheer folly, it is precisely because of her unshakable confidence in the infinite love of God. As Scripture bears witness, God is rich in mercy and full of forgiveness for those who come back to him (cf. *Ez* 18:23; *Ps* 32:5; *Ps* 103:8–14; *Eph* 2:4–5; *2 Cor* 1:3). God's forgiveness becomes in our hearts an inexhaustible source of forgiveness in our relationships with one another, helping us to live together in true brotherhood.

A wounded world yearns for healing

2.   As I have said, the modern world, despite its many successes, continues to be marked by contradictions. Progress in industry and agriculture has brought a higher standard of living to millions of people and offers great hope for many others. Technology has shrunk distances, while information has become instantaneous and has made possible new advances in human knowledge. Respect for the environment is growing and becoming a way of life. A great army of volunteers, whose generosity often remains hidden, is working tirelessly in every part of the world for the good of humanity, sparing no effort especially in meeting the needs of the poor and the suffering.

How can we fail to acknowledge with joy these positive aspects of our times? Unfortunately, however, the present world scene also presents *more than a few negative signs*. These include materialism and a growing contempt for human life, which have now assumed disturbing proportions. Many people live their lives with no other allegiance than to the laws of profit, prestige and power.

As a result, many feel imprisoned in a deep inner loneliness. Others continue to be deliberately discriminated against on grounds of race, nationality or sex. Poverty is driving masses of people to the margins of society, or even worse, to extinction. For too many people war has become a harsh everyday reality. A society interested only in material and ephemeral goods is tending to marginalize those who are not useful to its purposes. Faced with situations like these, involving real human tragedies, some prefer simply to close their eyes, taking refuge in indifference. Theirs is the attitude of Cain: 'Am I my brother's keeper?' (*Gen* 4:9). But the Church has the duty to remind everyone of God's severe admonishment: 'What have you done? The voice of your brother's blood is crying to me from the ground!' (*Gen* 4:10).

When so many of our brothers and sisters are suffering, we cannot remain indifferent! *Their distress appeals to our conscience*, the inner sanctuary where we come face to face with ourselves and with God. How can we fail to see that, to different degrees, we are all involved in this revision of life to which God is calling us? We all need forgiveness from God and from our neighbour. Therefore we must all be ready to forgive and to ask for forgiveness.

The burden of history

3.   The difficulty of forgiving does not only arise from the circumstances of the present. History carries with it a heavy burden of violence and conflict which cannot easily be shed. Abuses of power, oppression and wars have brought suffering to countless human beings and, even if the causes of these sad events are lost in the distant past, their destructive effects live on, fuelling fear, suspicion, hatred and division among families, ethnic groups and whole peoples. These are facts which sorely try the good will of those who are seeking to overcome their past conditioning. The truth is that *one cannot remain a prisoner of the past*, for individuals and peoples need a sort of 'healing of memories', so that past evils will not come back again. This does not mean forgetting past events; it means re-examining them with a new attitude and learning precisely from the experience of suffering that only love can build up, whereas hatred produces devastation and ruin. The deadly cycle of revenge must be replaced by the new-found liberty of forgiveness.

For this to happen, we must learn to read the history of other peoples without facile and partisan bias, making an effort to understand their point of view. This is a real challenge also on the level of education and culture. This is a challenge for civilization! If we agree to set out on this journey, we shall come to see that mistakes are not all on one side. We shall see how history has sometimes been presented in a distorted and even manipulated way, with tragic results.

A correct reading of history will make it easier to accept and appreciate the social, cultural and religious differences between individuals, groups and peoples. This is the first step towards reconciliation, since respect for differences is an inherently necessary condition for genuine relationships between individuals and between groups. The suppression of differences can result in apparent peace, but it creates a volatile situation which is in fact the prelude to fresh outbreaks of violence.

Practical mechanisms for reconciliation

4.   Wars, even when they 'solve' the problems which cause them, do so only by leaving a wake of victims and destruction which weighs heavily upon ensuing peace negotiations. Awareness of this should encourage peoples, nations and States once and for all to rise above the 'culture of war', not only in its most detestable form, namely, the power to wage war used as an instrument of supremacy, but also in the less odious but no less destructive form of recourse to arms as an expeditious way to solve a problem. Precisely in a time such as ours, which is familiar with the most sophisticated technologies of destruction, it is urgently necessary to develop a consistent 'culture of peace', which will forestall and counter the seemingly inevitable outbreaks of armed violence, including taking steps to stop the growth of the arms industry and of arms trafficking.

But even before this, the sincere desire for peace has to be translated into a firm decision to remove every obstacle to achieving peace. Here, *the various religions* can make an important contribution, as they have often done in the past, by speaking out against war and bravely facing the consequent risks. But are not all of us called to do still more, by drawing upon the genuine patrimony of our religious traditions?

234

At the same time, the duty of *governments* and the *international community* remains essential in these matters. It is for them to contribute to the building of peace through the establishment of solid structures capable of withstanding the uncertainties of politics, thus guaranteeing to everyone freedom and security in every circumstance. The *United Nations Organization,* for example, in fidelity to its founding inspiration, has recently taken on ever more extensive responsibility for maintaining or restoring peace. In this regard, fifty years after its establishment, it seems fitting to hope that the means at its disposal will be appropriately reviewed in order to enable that Organization to face effectively the new challenges of our time.

Other *organizations at the continental and regional level* also have great importance as instruments for promoting peace: it is reassuring to see them committed to developing practical mechanisms for reconciliation, working actively to help peoples divided by war to rediscover the reasons for peaceful and harmonious coexistence. These are forms of mediation which offer hope to peoples in apparently helpless situations. Nor should we underestimate the activity of *local organizations:* present as they are in places where the seeds of conflict are sown, they can reach individuals directly, mediating between opposing factions and promoting mutual trust.

Lasting peace however is not just a matter of structures and mechanisms. It rests above all on the adoption of a style of human coexistence marked by mutual acceptance and a capacity to forgive from the heart. We all need to be forgiven by others, so we must all be ready to forgive. *Asking and granting forgiveness* is something profoundly worthy of man; sometimes it is the only way out of situations marked by age-old and violent hatred.

Certainly, forgiveness does not come spontaneously or naturally to people. Forgiving from the heart can sometimes be actually heroic. The pain of losing a child, a brother or sister, one's parents or whole family as a result of war, terrorism or criminal acts can lead to the total closing of oneself to others. People who have been left with nothing because they have been deprived of their land and home, refugees and those who have endured the humiliation of violence, cannot fail to feel the temptation to hatred and revenge. Only the warmth of human relationships marked by respect, understanding and acceptance can help them to overcome such feelings. The liberating encounter with forgiveness, though fraught with difficulties, can be experienced even by a wounded heart, thanks to the healing power of love, which has its first source in God who is Love.

Truth and justice: prerequisites for forgiveness

5.   Forgiveness, in its truest and highest form, is a free act of love. But precisely because it is an act of love, it has its own intrinsic demands: the first of which is *respect for the truth*. God alone is absolute truth. But he made the human heart open to the desire for truth, which he then fully revealed in his Incarnate Son. *Hence we are all called to live the truth*. Where lies and falsehood are sown, there suspicion and division flourish. Corruption too, and political or ideological manipulation, are essentially contrary to the truth: they attack the very foundations of social harmony and undermine the possibility of peaceful social relationships.

Forgiveness, far from precluding the search for truth, actually requires it. The evil which has been done must be acknowledged and as far as possible corrected. It is precisely this requirement which has led to the establishment in various parts of the world of appropriate procedures for ascertaining the truth regarding crimes between ethnic groups or nations, as a first step towards reconciliation. There is no need to insist on the great prudence which all parties must observe in this necessary process, in order not to accentuate contrasts, which would then make reconciliation even more difficult. Not uncommon are cases of countries whose leaders, looking to the fundamental good of consolidating peace, have agreed to grant an amnesty to those who have publicly admitted crimes committed during a period of turmoil. Such an initiative can be regarded favourably as an effort to promote good relations between groups previously opposed to one another.

Another essential requisite for forgiveness and reconciliation is *justice*, which finds its ultimate foundation in the law of God and in his plan of love and mercy for humanity.[1] Understood in this way, justice is not limited to establishing what is right between the parties in conflict but looks above all to re-establishing authentic relationships with God, with oneself and with others. Thus there is no contradiction between forgiveness and justice. *Forgiveness neither eliminates nor lessens the need for the reparation* which justice requires, but seeks to reintegrate individuals and groups into society, and States into the community of Nations. No punishment can suppress the inalienable dignity of those who have committed evil. The door to repentance and rehabilitation must always remain open.

Jesus Christ our reconciliation

6.   How many situations today call for reconciliation! In the face of this challenge, on which peace to a great extent depends, I appeal to all believers, and in a special way to the members of the Catholic Church, to devote themselves in an active and practical way to the work of reconciliation.

Believers know that *reconciliation comes from God*, who is always ready to forgive those who turn to him and turn their back on their sins (cf. *Is* 38:17). God's immense love goes far beyond human understanding, as Sacred Scripture says: 'Can a woman forget her suckling child, that she should have no compassion on the son of her womb? Even these may forget, yet I will not forget you' (*Is* 49:15).

Divine love is the foundation of the reconciliation to which all of us are called. 'It is he who forgives all your guilt, who heals every one of your ills; who redeems your life from the grave, who crowns you with love and compassion ... He does not treat us according to our sins nor repay us according to our faults' (*Ps* 102:3–4, 10).

In his loving readiness to forgive, God went even to the point of giving himself to the world in the Person of his Son, who came to bring redemption to every individual and all humanity. In the face of human offences, which culminated in his condemnation to death on the Cross, Jesus prayed: 'Father, forgive them; for they know not what they do' (*Lk* 23:34).

God's forgiveness is the expression of his loving kindness as our Father. In the Gospel parable of the prodigal son (cf. *Lk* 15:11–32), the father runs to meet his son as soon as he sees him coming home.

He does not even let the son apologize: everything is forgiven (cf. *Lk* 15:20–22). The intense joy of forgiveness, offered and received, heals seemingly incurable wounds, restores relationships and firmly roots them in God's inexhaustible love.

Throughout his life Jesus proclaimed God's forgiveness, but he also taught *the need for mutual forgiveness* as the condition for obtaining it. In the Lord's Prayer he makes us pray: 'Forgive us our trespasses, *as we forgive those who trespass against us*' (*Mt* 6:12). With that 'as', he places in our hands the measure with which we shall be judged by God. The parable of the unforgiving servant, punished for his hardness of heart towards his fellow servant (cf. *Mt* 18:23-35), teaches us that those who are unwilling to forgive exclude themselves by this very fact from divine forgiveness: 'So also my heavenly Father will do to every one of you, if you do not forgive your brother from your heart' (*Mt* 18:35).

Our prayer itself cannot be pleasing to the Lord unless it is preceded, and in a certain sense 'guaranteed' in its authenticity, by a sincere effort on our part to be reconciled with our brother who has 'something against us': only then will it be possible for us to present an offering pleasing to God (cf. *Mt* 5:23–24).

In the service of reconciliation

7.   Jesus not only taught his disciples the duty to forgive, but he also intended his Church to be the sign and instrument

of his plan of reconciliation, making her the sacrament 'of intimate union with God, and of the unity of all humanity'.[2] In the light of this responsibility, Saint Paul described the apostolic ministry as the 'ministry of reconciliation' (cf. *2 Cor* 5:18–20). But in a certain sense every baptized person must consider himself a 'minister of reconciliation' since, having been reconciled with God and the brethren, he is called to build peace with the power of truth and justice.

As I had occasion to state in my Apostolic Letter *Tertio Millennio Adveniente,* Christians, as they get ready to cross the threshold of a new millennium, are invited to renew their repentance for 'all those times in history when they departed from the spirit of Christ and his Gospel and, instead of offering to the world the witness of a life inspired by the values of faith, indulged in ways of thinking and acting which were truly *forms of counter-witness and scandal'.[3]*

Among these, *the divisions which harm the unity of Christians* are of singular importance. As we prepare to celebrate the Great Jubilee of the Year 2000, we must together seek Christ's forgiveness, beseeching the Holy Spirit to grant the grace of full unity. 'Unity, after all, is a gift of the Holy Spirit. We are asked to respond to this gift responsibly, without compromise to our witness to the truth'.[4] Fixing our gaze on *Jesus Christ, our reconciliation,* in this first year of preparation for the Jubilee, let us do everything we can, through prayer, witness and action, in order to advance towards greater unity. This cannot fail to exercise a positive influence on the peacemaking processes going on in different parts of the world.

In June 1997, the Churches of Europe will hold in Graz their second European Ecumenical Assembly on the theme *'Reconciliation, gift of God and source of new life'.* In preparation for this meeting, the Presidents of the Conference of European Churches and of the Council of European Episcopal Conferences have issued a joint message calling for a fresh commitment to reconciliation, the 'gift of God for us and for the whole of creation.' They have listed some of the

239

many tasks which await the Ecclesial Communities: the search for a more visible unity, and commitment to the reconciliation of peoples. May the prayer of all Christians sustain the preparations in the local Churches for this meeting and foster practical gestures of reconciliation throughout Europe, opening the way to similar efforts on other continents.

In the above-mentioned Apostolic Letter, I expressed the lively hope that along the way to the Year 2000 Christians will take the texts of Sacred Scripture as their constant inspiration and reference. An extremely relevant theme to guide this pilgrimage could be that of forgiveness and reconciliation, to be meditated upon and lived in the concrete circumstances of every person and community.

An appeal to all people of good will

8.   I wish to conclude this Message, which I am sending to believers and all people of good will for the coming World Day of Peace, with an appeal to every individual to become an instrument of peace and reconciliation.

In the first place I address myself to you, my Brother *Bishops and priests:* be mirrors of the merciful love of God not only in the ecclesial community, but also in civil society, especially where nationalistic and ethnic conflicts are raging. In spite of the sufferings you may have to endure, do not let hatred enter your hearts, but joyfully proclaim Christ's Gospel and dispense God's forgiveness through the Sacrament of Reconciliation.

To you *parents,* the first educators of your children in the faith, I ask you to help your children to look upon all people as their brothers and sisters, to reach out to others without prejudice, with an attitude of trust and acceptance. Be for your children a reflection of God's love and forgiveness; make every effort to create a united and harmonious family.

And you *educators,* called to teach young people the true values of life by introducing them to the complexity of history and human culture, help them to live in every situation the virtues of tolerance, understanding and respect; hold up to them as models those who have been artisans of peace and reconciliation.

You *young people,* who cherish great hopes in your hearts, learn to live with one another in peace, without building barriers which stop you from sharing the treasures of other cultures and traditions. Respond to violence with works of peace, in order to build a world which is reconciled and fully human.

You *men and women in public life,* called to serve the common good, exclude no one from your concerns; take special care of the weakest sectors of society. Do not put your personal advantage above all else; do not give in to the lure of corruption and, above all, face even the most difficult situations with the weapons of peace and reconciliation.

To you who *work in the mass media,* I ask you to consider the great responsibilities which your profession involves, and never to be promoters of messages marked by hatred, violence or falsehood. Always keep in mind the truth of the human person, whose welfare the powerful means of communication are meant to serve.

Finally, to all of you who *believe in Christ,* I address an invitation to walk faithfully on the path of forgiveness and reconciliation, uniting yourselves to his prayer to the Father that all may be one (cf. *Jn* 17:21). And I exhort you to accompany this unceasing prayer for peace with deeds of brotherhood and mutual acceptance.

To every person of good will, eager to work tirelessly in the building of a new civilization of love, I say once more:

Offer forgiveness and receive peace!

Notes

1   Cf. John Paul II, Encyclical Letter *Dives in Misericordia* (30 November 1980), 14: *AAS* 72 (1980), 1223.
2   Second Vatican Ecumenical Council, Dogmatic Constitution on the Church *Lumen Gentium,* 1.
3   No. 33: *AAS* 87 (1995), 25.
4   *Ibid.,* No. 34: *loc. cit.,* 26.

1 January 1998

FROM THE JUSTICE OF EACH COMES PEACE FOR ALL

On the fiftieth anniversary of the Universal Declaration of Human Rights, this message is addressed above all to Heads of State. Its focus is the close connection between justice for each individual and peace for everyone. It underlines how much justice rests on respect for human rights. The Pope quotes passages from the Universal Declaration commenting that this document 'must be observed integrally, in both its spirit and letter'. Two essential characteristics of human rights need to be kept in mind as essential guiding principles: the universality and the indivisibility of human rights. Cultural specificity can never be used to mask violations of human rights. The Pope comments on the 'revolutions' in the social, economic and technological fields since 1989 and says we are on the threshold of a new era. This brings great hopes but it puts before us the challenge of ensuring globalization is accompanied by solidarity so that united nations can become a 'family of nations'. The Pope draws particular attention to external debt and poverty in general. He refers too to the 'evil of corruption'. Other injustices listed include the poor not having the possibility of fair access to credit and the 'scourge of usury'. He refers to increasing violence against women and children as 'one of the most widespread violations of human rights'. He reminds Christians that what is due in justice should never be represented as the offering of a charitable gift. Finally, he refers to the 'Spirit of hope' at work in the world in those who promote peace and reconciliation.

✳ ✳ ✳

242

1.   Justice goes hand in hand with peace and is permanently and actively linked to peace. Justice and peace seek the good of one and all, and for this reason they demand order and truth. When one is threatened, both falter; when justice is offended, peace is also placed in jeopardy.

Precisely because there exists a very close connection between the justice of the individual and the peace of everyone, in the present Message for the World Day of Peace I wish to address above all the Heads of States, keeping in mind that today's world, though marked in many regions by tension, violence and conflict, is nevertheless seeking a new composition and a more balanced stability, with a view to a true and lasting peace for the whole of humanity.

Justice and peace are not abstract concepts or remote ideals. They are values which dwell, as a common patrimony, in the heart of every individual. Individuals, families, communities and nations, all are called to live in justice and to work for peace. No one can claim exemption from this responsibility.

At this moment my thoughts turn to those who, without wanting it, are caught in the midst of bitter conflicts. I also think of the marginalized, the poor, the victims of all kinds of exploitation. These are people who are experiencing in their own flesh the absence of peace and the terrible effects of injustice. Who can remain indifferent to their craving for a life rooted in justice and in genuine peace? It is everyone's responsibility to ensure that they achieve their desire: there can be no complete justice unless everyone shares in it equally.

Justice is, at one and the same time, a moral virtue and a legal concept. Sometimes it is represented as a blindfold figure; in effect though, it is the proper task of justice to be clear-sighted and vigilant in ensuring the balance between rights and duties, in fostering an equitable sharing of burdens and benefits. Justice makes whole, it does not destroy; it leads to reconciliation, not to revenge. Upon examination, at its deepest level it is rooted in love, which finds its most significant expression in mercy. Therefore justice, if separated from merciful love, becomes cold and cutting.

Justice is an active and life-giving virtue: it defends and promotes the inestimable dignity of every human person and is concerned for the common good, insofar as it is the guardian of relations between individuals and peoples. No one, in fact, ever lives in isolation. From the first moment of life, each human being exists in relationship to others, in such a way that the good of the individual and the good of society go hand in hand. Between the two there exists a delicate balance.

Justice rests on respect for human rights

2.   The human person is by nature endowed with universal, inviolable and inalienable rights. These rights do not however exist in isolation. In this respect my venerable predecessor Pope John XXIII taught that the person 'has rights and duties, flowing directly and simultaneously from his very nature'.[1] It is upon the correct anthropological foundation of these rights and duties, and upon their intrinsic correlation, that the true bulwark of peace rests.

In recent centuries, these human rights have been formulated in declarations of principles and binding legal instruments. In the history of peoples and nations in search of justice and freedom, the proclamation of these rights is remembered with rightful pride, also because it was often experienced as a turning-point after patent violations of the dignity of single individuals and whole peoples.

Fifty years ago, after a war characterized by the denial for certain peoples of the right even to exist, the General Assembly of the United Nations promulgated the Universal Declaration of Human Rights. That was a solemn act, arrived at after the sad experience of war, and motivated by the desire formally to recognize that *the same rights belong to every individual and to all peoples*. In that document we read the following statement, which has resisted the passage of time: 'Recognition of the inherent dignity and of the equal and inalienable rights of all members of the human family is the foundation of freedom, justice and peace in the world'.[2] The concluding words of the document deserve no less attention: 'Nothing in this Declaration may be interpreted as implying for any State, group or person any right to engage in any activity or to perform any act aimed at the destruction of any of the rights and freedoms set forth herein'.[3] It is a tragic fact that today this provision is still being blatantly violated through oppression, conflict and corruption, or, in a more subtle way, through an attempt to reinterpret, or wilfully misinterpret, the very definitions contained in the Universal Declaration. That document must be observed integrally, in both its spirit and letter. It remains – as Pope Paul VI of venerable memory declared – one of the United Nations' principal titles to glory, 'especially when we think of the importance which is attributed to it as a sure path to peace'.[4]

On the fiftieth anniversary of the Universal Declaration of Human Rights, being celebrated this year, it is fitting to recall that 'the promotion and protection of human rights is a matter of priority for the international community'.[5] Certain shadows however hover over the anniversary, consisting in the reservations being expressed in relation to two essential characteristics of the very idea of human rights: their *universality* and their *indivisibility*. These distinctive features must be strongly reaffirmed, in order to reject the criticisms of those who would use the argument of cultural specificity to mask violations of human rights, and the criticisms of those who weaken the concept of human dignity by denying juridical weight to social, economic and cultural rights. Universality and indivisibility are two guiding principles which at the same time demand that human rights be rooted in each culture and that their juridical profile be strengthened so as to ensure that they are fully observed.

Respect for human rights not only involves their protection in law. It must include all the other aspects which stem from the notion of human dignity, the very basis of rights. In this regard attention to education assumes great relevance. It is likewise important to attend to the promotion of human rights: a task which follows from love of the human person as such, 'since love goes beyond what justice can provide'.[6] In the context of promoting human rights, further efforts must be made to protect the rights of the family, which is 'the natural and basic unit of society'.[7]

Globalization with solidarity

3.   The vast geopolitical changes which have taken place since 1989 have been accompanied by veritable revolutions in the social and economic fields. The globalization of the economy and of finance is now a reality, and we are realizing more and more clearly the effects of the rapid progress related to information technologies. We are on the threshold of a new era which is the bearer of great hopes and disturbing questions. What will be the effect of the changes taking place? Will *everyone* be able to take advantage of a global market? Will *everyone* at last have a chance to enjoy peace? Will relations between States become more equitable, or will economic competition and rivalries between peoples and nations lead humanity towards a situation of even greater instability?

For a more equitable society and a more stable peace in a world on the way to globalization, it is an urgent task of the International Organizations to help promote a sense of responsibility for the common good. But to achieve this we must never lose sight of the human person, who must be at the centre of every social project. Only thus will the United Nations become a 'family of nations', in accordance with its original mandate of 'promoting social progress and better standards of life in larger freedom'.[8] This is the path for building a world community based on 'mutual trust, mutual support and sincere respect'.[9] The challenge, in short, is to ensure a globalization *in solidarity*, a globalization *without marginalization*. This is a clear duty in justice, with serious moral implications in the organization of the economic, social, cultural and political life of nations.

The heavy burden of external debt

4.   Nations and whole regions of the world, on account of their fragile financial or economic potential, risk being excluded from an economy which is becoming globalized. Others have greater resources, but unfortunately cannot take advantage of them for various reasons: unrest, internal conflicts, a lack of adequate structures, environmental degradation, widespread corruption, criminality and other reasons as well. Globalization has to be linked with solidarity. Special aid must be forthcoming so that countries which are unable to enter the market successfully on their own strength alone can in fact overcome their present situation of disadvantage.

This is something owed to them in justice. In a true 'family of nations' no one can be excluded; on the contrary, it is the weakest, the most fragile which must be supported, so that they too can develop their full potential.

My thoughts go here to one of the greatest difficulties which the poorer nations have to face today. I refer to the heavy burden of *external debt*, which compromises the economies of whole peoples and hinders their social and political progress. In this regard, the international financial institutions have recently initiated significant attempts to secure a coordinated reduction of this debt. I earnestly hope that progress will continue to be made in this direction by applying conditions in a flexible way, so that all eligible nations can benefit before the year 2000. The wealthier nations can do much in this respect, by supporting the implementation of such measures.

The debt question is part of a vaster problem: that of the persistence of poverty, sometimes even extreme, and the emergence of new inequalities which are accompanying the globalization process. If the aim is globalization *without marginalization*, we can no longer tolerate a world in which there live side by side the immensely rich and the miserably poor, the have-nots deprived even of essentials and people who thoughtlessly waste what others so desperately need. Such contrasts are an affront to the dignity of the human person.

Certainly there is no lack of appropriate means for eliminating poverty, including the promotion of consistent social and productive investments on the part of world economic bodies. This presupposes that the international community intends to act with the necessary political determination. Praiseworthy steps in that direction have already been taken, but a lasting solution requires a concerted effort by everyone, including the States concerned.

A culture of respect for the rule of law is urgently needed

5.   And what are we to say of the grave inequalities existing *within* nations? Situations of *extreme poverty*, wherever they are found, constitute a prime injustice. Eliminating them ought to be a priority for everyone, at the national as well as the international level.

Nor can we pass over in silence the *evil of corruption* which is undermining the social and political development of so many peoples. It is a growing phenomenon insidiously infiltrating many sectors of society, mocking the law and ignoring the rules of justice and of truth. Corruption is hard to combat, because it takes many different forms: when it has been suppressed in one area, it springs up in another. Courage is needed just to denounce it. To eliminate it, together with the resolute determination of the Authorities, the generous support of all citizens is needed, sustained by a firm moral conscience.

A grave responsibility in this battle falls on people in public life. Theirs is the duty to work tirelessly for the equitable application of the law and for transparency in all acts of public administration. Being at the service of its citizens, the State is the steward of the people's resources, which it must administer with a view to the common good. Good government requires accurate controls and complete honesty in *all* economic transactions. In no way can it be permitted that resources intended for the public good are used for other interests of a private or even criminal nature.

The fraudulent use of public monies penalizes above all the poor, who are the first to be deprived of the basic services essential for personal development. And when corruption creeps into the administration of justice, it is again the poor who pay the heaviest price: delays, inefficiency, structural insufficiencies, the lack of an adequate defence. They often have no choice but to suffer the abuse of power.

Particularly offensive forms of injustice

6. There are other forms of injustice which put peace at risk. Here, I wish to mention two. First, *not having the possibility of fair access to credit*. The poor are often obliged to remain outside the normal financial system or to place themselves in the hands of unscrupulous money-lenders who charge exorbitant rates of interest. The end result is the aggravation of an already precarious situation. For this reason it is everyone's duty to work to ensure that the poor have access to credit on equitable terms and at affordable interest rates. Actually, financial agencies offering mini-credit on terms favouring the poor already exist in various parts of the world. These are initiatives to be encouraged, for this is the path which can lead to the radical elimination of the shameful scourge of usury, by giving everyone access to the economic means needed for the dignified development of families and communities.

And what are we to say of *increasing violence against women and against children of both sexes?* Today this is one of the most widespread violations of human rights, and tragically it has even become a terror tactic: women taken hostage, children barbarously slaughtered. To this must be added the violence of forced prostitution and child pornography, and the exploitation of children in the workplace in conditions of veritable slavery. Practical steps are needed to try to stop the spread of these forms of violence. In particular, appropriate legal measures are needed at both the national and international level. If, as I have often stated in previous Messages, the dignity of every person is to be recognized and respected, the difficult task of education and cultural promotion must be faced. One element, in fact, absolutely must not be lacking in the ethical and cultural patrimony of the human family as a whole and of each individual person: awareness that human beings are all equal in dignity, deserve the same respect, and have the same rights and duties.

Building peace in justice is a task for one and all

7.   Peace for all of us comes from the justice of each of us. No one is excused from a task of such importance for the whole of humanity. It concerns every man and every woman, each according to his or her own competence and responsibility.

I appeal above all to you, *Heads of States and Leaders of Nations*, the principal guardians of the rule of law in your respective countries. Certainly this is not an easy task for you to fulfil, but it constitutes a primary obligation. May the codes which govern the States you serve be a guarantee of justice for the people and an incentive for an ever growing sense of civic responsibility.

Furthermore, building peace in justice calls for the cooperation of *every sector of society*, each in its own area of influence and in harmony with other groups within the community. In particular I encourage you, *educators* engaged at every level in training and educating the younger generation: form them in moral and civic values, instil in them a lively sense of rights and duties, beginning with the experience of the school community itself. Educate in justice in order to educate in peace: this is one of your primary tasks.

In the formative process, the *family* is indispensable. The family is the appropriate environment for the human formation of the younger generation. From your example, dear *parents*, depends to a large degree the moral character of your children: they assimilate it from the kind of relations which you foster within the family nucleus and towards those outside it. The family is the first school of living, and the influence received inside the family is decisive for the future development of the individual.

Finally, to you, *young people* of the world, who spontaneously aspire to justice and peace, I say: always keep

250

alive the quest for these ideals, and have the patience and persistence to pursue them whatever the concrete situation in which you find yourselves. Be quick to reject the temptation of unlawful short-cuts towards false mirages of success and wealth. On the contrary, value what is right and true, even when to do so requires sacrifice and commits you to going against the current. Thus it is that 'from the justice of each comes peace for all'.

Sharing, the way to peace

8.   The Jubilee of the Year 2000 is fast approaching, a time which for believers is devoted in a special way to God, the Lord of history, a reminder to all of the radical dependence of the creature on the Creator. But in the Biblical tradition it was also a time for freeing slaves, for returning land to its rightful owner, for forgiving debts, thus restoring the conditions of equality willed by God among all the members of the people. It is therefore a special time for seeking that justice which leads to peace.

By virtue of their faith in the God who is love and of their sharing in Christ's universal redemption, Christians are called to act justly and to live in peace with all, for 'Jesus does not merely give us peace. He gives us *his* Peace accompanied by *his* Justice. He *is* Peace and Justice. He becomes *our* Peace and *our* Justice'.[10] I said these words almost twenty years ago, but against the backdrop of the radical changes now taking place they assume an even more specific and vital meaning.

The distinctive mark of the Christian, today more than ever, must be love for the poor, the weak, the suffering. Living out this demanding commitment requires a total reversal of the alleged values which make people seek only their own good: power, pleasure, the unscrupulous accumulation of wealth. Yes, it is precisely to this radical conversion that Christ's disciples are called. Those who commit themselves to following this path will truly experience 'righteousness and peace and joy in the Holy Spirit' (*Rom* 14:17), and will taste 'the peaceful fruit of righteousness' (*Heb* 12:11).

I wish to repeat to the Christians of all continents the admonishment of the Second Vatican Council: 'The demands of justice should first be satisfied, lest the giving of what is due in justice be represented as the offering of a charitable gift'.[11] A society of genuine solidarity can be built only if the well-off, in helping the poor, do not stop at giving from what they do not need. Moreover, offering material things is not enough: what is needed is *a spirit of sharing*, so that we consider it an honour to be able to devote our care and attention to the needs of our brothers and sisters in difficulty. Christians, the followers of other religions and numberless men and women of good will today feel called to a simple lifestyle as a condition for making the just sharing of the fruits of God's creation a reality. Those living in poverty can wait no longer: they need help *now* and so have a right to receive *immediately* what they need.

The Holy Spirit at work in the world

9.   The First Sunday of Advent marked the beginning of the second year of immediate preparation for the Great Jubilee of the Year 2000, dedicated to the Holy Spirit. The Spirit of hope is at work in the world. He is present in the selfless service of those who work alongside the outcast and the suffering, those who welcome immigrants and refugees, those who bravely refuse to reject a person or a whole group for ethnic, cultural or religious reasons. He is especially present in the generous activity of all who patiently and perseveringly continue to promote peace and reconciliation between people who were once opponents and enemies. Indeed, these are signs of hope which encourage us to seek the justice which leads to peace.

The heart of the Gospel message is Christ, who is everyone's peace and reconciliation. May his countenance shine upon the path of humanity as it prepares to cross the threshold of the Third Millennium!

May his justice and his peace become a gift for all, without distinction!

'Then shall the wilderness be fertile land and fertile land become forest.
In the wilderness justice will come to live, and integrity in the fertile land;
integrity will bring peace,
justice give everlasting security' (*Is* 32:15–17).

Notes

1   John XXIII, Encyclical Letter *Pacem in Terris* (11 April 1963), I, 1: *AAS* 55 (1963), 259.
2   *Universal Declaration of Human Rights*, Preamble.
3   *Ibid.*, Art. 30.
4   *Message to the President of the 28th General Assembly of the United Nations on the occasion of the 25th anniversary of the Universal Declaration of Human Rights* (10 December 1973): *AAS* 65 (1973), 674.
5   *Vienna Declaration*, The World Conference on Human Rights (June 1993), Preamble I.
6   Second Ecumenical Vatican Council, Pastoral Constitution *Gaudium et Spes*, 78.
7   *Universal Declaration of Human Rights*, No. 16, § 3; cf. *Charter of the Rights of the Family* (22 October 1983), presented by the Holy See.
8   *Charter of the United Nations*, Preamble.
9   John Paul II, *Address to the 50th General Assembly of the United Nations Organization* (5 October 1995), 14: *L'Osservatore Romano*, 6 October 1995, p. 7.
10   John Paul II, *Homily at Yankee Stadium, New York* (2 October 1979), 1: *AAS* 71 (1979), 1169.
11   Decree on the Apostolate of the Laity, *Apostolicam Actuositatem*, 8.

1 January 1999

RESPECT FOR HUMAN RIGHTS:
THE SECRET OF TRUE PEACE

Promoting the right to peace implies respect for all other human rights. But in this message Pope John Paul identifies and examines certain specific rights that appear to be particularly exposed to violation today: the right to life, religious freedom, the right to participate in the life of their community, the denial of the fundamental right to exist to ethnic groups and national minorities, the right to self-fulfilment. Life can never be downgraded to the level of a thing, and to choose life involves rejecting every form of violence. The Pope deals with topics such as the sacredness of human life from conception to its natural end, discrimination on the basis of religious beliefs or ethnic belonging, the violent conflicts that can occur as a result, the problem of election manipulation and the obstacles that block sound democracy, the lack of adequate education in some regions of the world where primary school educational opportunities are actually decreasing, and the right to work. He offers the opinion that the new International Criminal Court could contribute to ensuring on a world scale an effective protection of human rights. He raises the question of who in today's globalization is responsible for guaranteeing the global common good and the exercise of economic and social rights. In the face of international debt of poorer nations, arms trafficking, economic crises, damage to creation, he pleads for 'a new vision of global progress in solidarity'.

✳ ✳ ✳

1.   In my first Encyclical *Redemptor Hominis*, addressed almost twenty years ago to all men and women of good will, I stressed the importance of respect for human rights. Peace flourishes when these rights are fully respected, but when they are violated what comes is war, which causes other still graver violations.[1]

At the beginning of a new year, the last before the Great Jubilee, I would like to dwell once more on this crucially important theme with all of you, the men and women of every part of the world, with you, the political leaders and religious guides of peoples, with you, who love peace and wish to consolidate it in the world.

Looking towards the World Day of Peace, let me state the conviction which I very much want to share with you: when the promotion of the dignity of the person is the guiding principle, and when the search for the common good is the overriding commitment, then solid and lasting foundations for building peace are laid. But when human rights are ignored or scorned, and when the pursuit of individual interests unjustly prevails over the common good, then the seeds of instability, rebellion and violence are inevitably sown.

Respect for human dignity, the heritage of humanity

2.   The dignity of the human person is a transcendent value, always recognized as such by those who sincerely search for the truth. Indeed, the whole of human history should be interpreted in the light of this certainty. Every person, created in the image and likeness of God (cf. *Gen* 1:26–28) and therefore radically oriented towards the Creator, is constantly in relationship with those possessed of the same dignity. To promote the good of the individual is thus to serve the common good, which is that point where rights and duties converge and reinforce one another.

The history of our time has shown in a tragic way the danger which results from forgetting the truth about the human person. Before our eyes we have the results of ideologies such as Marxism, Nazism and Fascism, and also of myths like racial superiority, nationalism and ethnic exclusivism. No less pernicious, though not always as obvious, are the effects of materialistic consumerism, in which the exaltation of the individual and the selfish satisfaction of personal aspirations become the ultimate goal of life. In this outlook, the negative effects on others are considered completely irrelevant. Instead it must be said again that no affront to human dignity can be ignored, whatever its source, whatever actual form it takes and wherever it occurs.

The universality and indivisibility of human rights

3.   The year 1998 has marked the fiftieth anniversary of the adoption of the Universal Declaration of Human Rights. The Declaration was intentionally linked to the United Nations Charter, since it shares a common inspiration. As its fundamental premise, it affirms that the recognition of the innate dignity of all members of the human family, as also the equality and inalienability of their rights, is the foundation of liberty, justice and peace in the world.[2] All the subsequent international documents on human rights declare this truth anew, recognizing and affirming that human rights stem from the inherent dignity and worth of the human person.[3]

The Universal Declaration is clear: it acknowledges the rights which it proclaims but does not confer them, since they are inherent in the human person and in human dignity. Consequently, no one can legitimately deprive another person, whoever they may be, of these rights, since this would do violence to their nature. All human beings, without exception, are equal in dignity. For the same reason, these rights apply to every stage of life and to every political, social, economic and cultural situation. Together they form a single whole, directed unambiguously towards the promotion of every aspect of the good of both the person and society.

Human rights are traditionally grouped into two broad categories, including on the one hand civil and political rights and on the other economic, social and cultural rights. Both categories, although to different degrees, are guaranteed by international agreements. All human rights are in fact closely connected, being the expression of different dimensions of a single subject, the human person. The integral promotion of every category of human rights is the true guarantee of full respect for each individual right.

Defence of the universality and indivisibility of human rights is essential for the construction of a peaceful society and for the overall development of individuals, peoples and nations. To affirm the universality and indivisibility of rights is not to exclude legitimate cultural and political differences in the exercise of individual rights, provided that in every case the levels set for the whole of humanity by the Universal Declaration are respected.

With these fundamental presuppositions clearly in mind, I would now like to identify certain specific rights which appear to be particularly exposed to more or less open violation today.

The right to life

4.   The first of these is the basic right to life. Human life is sacred and inviolable from conception to its natural end. 'Thou shalt not kill' is the divine commandment which states the limit beyond which it is never licit to go. 'The deliberate decision to deprive an innocent human being of life is always morally evil'.[4]

The right to life is inviolable. This involves a positive choice, a choice for life. The development of a culture of this kind embraces all the circumstances of life and ensures the promotion of human dignity in every situation. A genuine culture of life, just as it guarantees to the unborn the right to come into the world, in the same way protects the newly born, especially girls, from the crime of infanticide. Equally, it assures the handicapped that they can fully develop their capacities, and ensures adequate care for the sick and the elderly.

Recent developments in the field of genetic engineering present a profoundly disquieting challenge. In order that scientific research in this area may be at the service of the person, it must be accompanied at every stage by careful ethical reflection, which will bring about adequate legal norms safeguarding the integrity of human life. Life can never be downgraded to the level of a thing.

To choose life involves rejecting every form of violence: the violence of poverty and hunger, which afflicts so many human beings; the violence of armed conflict; the violence of criminal trafficking in drugs and arms; the violence of mindless damage to the natural environment.[5] In every circumstance, the right to life must be promoted and safeguarded with appropriate legal and political guarantees, for no offence against the right to life, against the dignity of any single person, is ever unimportant.

Religious freedom, the heart of human rights

5.   Religion expresses the deepest aspirations of the human person, shapes people's vision of the world and affects their relationships with others: basically it offers the answer to the question of the true meaning of life, both personal and communal. Religious freedom therefore constitutes the very heart of human rights. Its inviolability is such that individuals must be recognized as having the right even to change their religion, if their conscience so demands. People are obliged to follow their conscience in all circumstances and cannot be forced to act against it.[6] Precisely for this reason, no one can be compelled to accept a particular religion, whatever the circumstances or motives.

The Universal Declaration of Human Rights recognizes that the right to religious freedom includes the right to manifest personal beliefs, whether individually or with others, in public or in private.[7] In spite of this, there still exist today places where the right to gather for worship is either not recognized or is limited to the members of one religion alone. This grave violation of one of the fundamental rights of the person is a source of enormous suffering for believers. When a State grants special status to one religion, this must not be to the detriment of the others. Yet it is common knowledge that there are nations in which individuals, families and entire groups are still being discriminated against and marginalized because of their religious beliefs.

Nor should we pass over in silence another problem indirectly linked to religious freedom. It sometimes happens that increasing tensions develop between communities or peoples of different religious convictions and cultures, which, because of the strong passions involved, turn into violent conflict. Recourse to violence in the name of religious belief is a perversion of the very teachings of the major religions. I reaffirm here what many religious figures have repeated so often: the use of violence can never claim a religious justification, nor can it foster the growth of true religious feeling.

The right to participate

6.   All citizens have the right to participate in the life of their community: this is a conviction which is generally shared today. But this right means nothing when the democratic process breaks down because of corruption and favouritism, which not only obstruct legitimate sharing in the exercise of power but also prevent people from benefitting equally from community assets and services, to which everyone has a right. Even elections can be manipulated in order to ensure the victory of certain parties or persons. This is an affront to democracy and has serious consequences, because citizens have not only the right but also the responsibility to participate: when they are prevented from exercising this responsibility, they lose hope of playing any effective role and succumb to an attitude of passive indifference. The development of a sound democratic system then becomes practically impossible.

In recent times various measures have been adopted to ensure legitimate elections in States which are struggling to move from a totalitarian form of government to a democratic one. However useful and effective these may be in emergencies, such initiatives cannot dispense from the effort to create in the citizens a basis of shared convictions, thanks to which

259

manipulation of the democratic process would be rejected once and for all.

In the context of the international community, nations and peoples have the right to share in the decisions which often profoundly modify their way of life. The technical details of certain economic problems give rise to the tendency to restrict the discussions about them to limited circles, with the consequent danger that political and financial power is concentrated in a small number of governments and special interest groups. The pursuit of the national and international common good requires the effective exercise, even in the economic sphere, of the right of all people to share in the decisions which affect them.

A particularly serious form of discrimination

7.   One of the most tragic forms of discrimination is the denial to ethnic groups and national minorities of the fundamental right to exist as such. This is done by suppressing them or brutally forcing them to move, or by attempting to weaken their ethnic identity to such an extent that they are no longer distinguishable. Can we remain silent in the face of such grave crimes against humanity? No effort must be judged too great when it is a question of putting an end to such abuses, which are violations of human dignity.

A positive sign of the growing willingness of States to recognize their responsibility to protect victims of such crimes and to commit themselves to preventing them is the recent initiative of a United Nations Diplomatic Conference: it specifically approved the Statute of an International Criminal Court, the task of which it will be to identify guilt and to punish those responsible for crimes of genocide, crimes against humanity and crimes of war and aggression. This new institution, if built upon a sound legal foundation, could gradually contribute to ensuring on a world scale the effective protection of human rights.

The right to self-fulfilment

8.   Every human being has innate abilities waiting to be developed. At stake here is the full actualization of one's own person and the appropriate insertion into one's social environment. In order that this may take place, it is necessary above all to provide adequate education to those who are just beginning their lives: their future success depends on this.

From this perspective, how can we not be concerned when we see that in some of the poorest regions of the world educational opportunities are actually decreasing, especially in the area of primary education? This is sometimes due to the economic situation of the particular country, which prevents teachers from receiving a proper salary. In other cases, money seems to be available for prestigious projects and for secondary education, but not for primary schools. When educational opportunities are limited, particularly for young girls, there will surely arise discriminatory structures which adversely affect the overall development of society. The world could find itself divided according to a new criterion: on the one side, States and individuals endowed with advanced technologies; on the other, countries and people with extremely limited knowledge and abilities. As one can easily guess, this would simply reinforce the already acute economic inequalities existing not only between States but also within them. In developing countries, education and professional training must be a primary concern, just as they are in the urban and rural renewal programmes of more economically advanced peoples.

Another fundamental right, upon which depends the attainment of a decent level of living, is the right to work. Otherwise how can people obtain food, clothing, a home, health care and the many other necessities of life? The lack of work, however, is a serious problem today: countless people in many parts of the world find themselves caught up in the devastating reality of unemployment. It is urgently necessary on the part of everyone, and particularly on the part of those who exercise political or economic power, that everything possible be done to resolve this difficult situation. Emergency

261

interventions, necessary as they are, are not enough in cases of unemployment, illness or similar circumstances which are beyond the control of the individual,[8] but efforts must also be made to enable the poor to take responsibility for their own livelihood and to be freed from a system of demeaning assistance programmes.

Global progress in solidarity

9.   The rapid advance towards the globalization of economic and financial systems also illustrates the urgent need to establish who is responsible for guaranteeing the global common good and the exercise of economic and social rights. The free market by itself cannot do this, because in fact there are many human needs which have no place in the market. 'Even prior to the logic of a fair exchange of goods and the forms of justice appropriate to it, there exists something which is due to man because he is man, by reason of his lofty dignity'.[9]

The effects of the recent economic and financial crises have had heavy consequences for countless people, reduced to conditions of extreme poverty. Many of them had only just reached a position which allowed them to look to the future with optimism. Through no fault of their own, they have seen these hopes cruelly dashed, with tragic results for themselves and their children. And how can we ignore the effects of fluctuations in the financial markets? We urgently need a new vision of global progress in solidarity, which will include an overall and sustainable development of society, so as to enable all people to realize their potential.

In this context, I make a pressing appeal to all those with responsibility for financial relations on the worldwide level. I ask them to make a sincere effort to find a solution to the frightening problem of the international debt of the poorest nations. International financial institutions have initiated concrete steps in this regard which merit appreciation. I appeal to all those involved in this problem, especially the more affluent nations, to provide the support necessary to ensure the full success of this initiative. An immediate and vigorous effort is needed, as we look to the year 2000, to ensure that the greatest possible number of nations will be able to extricate themselves from a now intolerable situation. Dialogue among the institutions involved, if prompted by a sincere willingness to reach agreement, will lead – I am certain – to a satisfactory and definitive solution. In this way, lasting development will become a possibility for those Nations facing the greatest difficulties, and the millennium now before us will become for them too a time of renewed hope.

Responsibility for the environment

10.   The promotion of human dignity is linked to the right to a healthy environment, since this right highlights the dynamics of the relationship between the individual and society. A body of international, regional and national norms on the environment is gradually giving juridic form to this right. But juridic measures by themselves are not sufficient. The danger of serious damage to land and sea, and to the climate, flora and fauna, calls for a profound change in modern civilization's typical consumer lifestyle, particularly in the richer countries. Nor can we underestimate another risk, even if it is a less drastic one: people who live in poverty in rural areas can be driven by necessity to exploit beyond sustainable limits the little land which they have at their disposal. Special training aimed at teaching them how to harmonize the cultivation of the land with respect for the environment needs to be encouraged.

The world's present and future depend on the safeguarding of creation, because of the endless interdependence between human beings and their environment. Placing human well-being at the centre of concern for the environment is actually the surest way of safeguarding creation; this in fact stimulates the responsibility of the individual with regard to natural resources and their judicious use.

The right to peace

11.   In a sense, promoting the right to peace ensures respect for all other rights, since it encourages the building of a society in which structures of power give way to structures of cooperation, with a view to the common good. Recent history clearly shows the failure of recourse to violence as a means for resolving political and social problems. War destroys, it does not build up; it weakens the moral foundations of society and creates further divisions and long-lasting tensions. And yet the news continues to speak of wars and armed conflicts, and of their countless victims. How often have my Predecessors and I myself called for an end to these horrors! I shall continue to do so until it is understood that war is the failure of all true humanism.[10]

Thanks be to God, steps have been taken in some regions towards the consolidation of peace. Great credit must go to those courageous political leaders who are resolved to continue negotiations even when the situation seems impossible. But at the same time how can we not denounce the massacres still taking place in other regions, with the uprooting of entire peoples from their lands and the destruction of homes and crops? Mindful of the innumerable victims, I call on the leaders of the Nations and on all people of good will to come to the aid of those involved – especially in Africa – in cruel conflicts, sometimes prompted by external economic interests, and to help them to bring these conflicts to an end. A concrete step in this regard is certainly the eradication of trafficking in arms destined for countries at war, and the support of the leaders of those peoples in their quest for the path of dialogue. This is the path worthy of the human person, this is the path of peace!

I think with sorrow of those living and growing up against a background of war, of those who have known nothing but conflict and violence. Those who survive will carry the scars of this terrible experience for the rest of their lives. And what shall we say about children forced to fight? Can we ever accept that lives which are just beginning should be ruined in this way? Trained to kill and often compelled to do so, these children cannot fail to have serious problems in their future insertion into civil society. Their education is interrupted and their chances of employment are stifled: what a terrible legacy for their future! Children need peace; they have a right to it.

To the thought of these children I also wish to add a mention of the children who are victims of land mines and other devices of war. Despite efforts already being made to remove mines, we are now witnessing an unbelievable and inhuman paradox: with disregard for the clearly expressed will of governments and peoples to put a final end to the use of such an insidious weapon, mines are still being laid even in places which had already been cleared.

Seeds of war are also being spread by the massive and uncontrolled proliferation of small arms and light weapons, which it seems are passing freely from one area of conflict to another, increasing violence along the way. Governments must adopt appropriate measures for controlling the production, sale, importation and exportation of these instruments of death. Only in this way will it be possible to deal effectively and completely with the problem of the massive illegal traffic in arms.

A culture of human rights, the responsibility of all

12.   It is not possible to discuss this topic more fully here. I would however like to emphasize that no human right is safe if we fail to commit ourselves to safeguarding all of them. When the violation of any fundamental human right is accepted without reaction, all other rights are placed at risk. It is therefore essential that there should be a global approach to the subject of human rights and a serious commitment to defend them. Only when a culture of human rights which respects different traditions becomes an integral part of humanity's moral patrimony shall we be able to look to the future with serene confidence.

In effect, how could there be war if every human right were respected? Complete observance of human rights is the surest road to establishing solid relations between States. The culture of human rights cannot fail to be a culture of peace. Every violation of human rights carries within it the seeds of possible conflict. My Venerable Predecessor, the Servant of God Pius XII, at the end of the Second World War asked the question: 'If one people is crushed to death by force, who will dare promise the rest of the world security in a lasting peace?'.[11]

The promotion of a culture of human rights which engages consciences requires all sectors of society to work together. I would like to mention specifically the role of the mass media, which is so important in forming public opinion, and consequently in influencing people's behaviour. Just as we could not deny their responsibility in cases of the violation of human rights arising from any exaltation of violence on their part, so it is right to give them credit for the noble initiatives of dialogue and solidarity which have come about thanks to their insistence on promoting mutual understanding and peace.

A time of decision, a time of hope

13.   The new millennium is close at hand, and its approach has filled the hearts of many with hope for a more just and fraternal world. This is an aspiration which can, and indeed must, become a reality!

It is in this context that I now address you, dear Brothers and Sisters in Christ, who in all parts of the world take the Gospel as the pattern of your lives: become heralds of human dignity! Faith teaches us that every person has been created in the image and likeness of God. Even when man refuses it, the Heavenly Father's love remains steadfast; his is a love without limits. He sent his Son Jesus to redeem every individual, restoring each one's full human dignity.[12] With this in mind, how can we exclude anyone from our care? Rather, we must recognize Christ in the poorest and the most marginalized, those whom the Eucharist – which is communion in the body and blood of Christ given up for us – commits us to serve.[13] As the parable of the rich man, who will remain for ever without a name, and the poor man called Lazarus clearly shows, 'in the stark contrast between the insensitive rich man and the poor in need of everything, God is on the latter's side'.[14] We too must be on this same side.

The third and final year of preparation for the Jubilee is marked by a spiritual pilgrimage to the Father's house: all are invited to walk the path of authentic conversion, which involves rejecting evil and making a positive choice for good. On the threshold of the year 2000, it is our duty to renew our commitment to safeguarding the dignity of the poor and the marginalized, and to recognize in a practical way the rights of those who have no rights. Let us raise our voices on their behalf, by living in its fullness the mission which Christ entrusted to his disciples! This is the spirit of the now imminent Jubilee.[15]

Jesus taught us to call God 'Father', *Abba*, thus revealing to us the depth of our relationship with him. Infinite and eternal is his love for every person and for all humanity. Eloquent in this regard are God's words found in the book of the Prophet Isaiah:

'Can a woman forget her baby at the breast,
or fail to cherish the child of her womb?
Yet even if these forget,
I will never forget you.
See, upon the palms of my hands
I have written your name' (49:15–16).

Let us accept the invitation to share this love! In it is found the secret of respect for the rights of every woman and every man. The dawn of the new millennium will thus find us more ready to build peace together.

Notes

1   Cf. *Redemptor Hominis* (4 March 1979), 17: *AAS* 71 (1979), 296.

2   Cf. *Universal Declaration of Human Rights*, Preamble.

3   Cf. in particular the *Vienna Declaration* (25 June 1993), Preamble, 2.

4   John Paul II, Encyclical Letter *Evangelium Vitae* (25 March 1995), 57: *AAS* 87 (1995), 465.

5   Cf. *ibid.*, 10, *loc. cit.*, 412.

6   Cf. Second Vatican Ecumenical Council, Declaration on Religious Freedom *Dignitatis Humanae*, 3.

7   Cf. Article 18.

8   Cf. *Universal Declaration of Human Rights*, Article 25, 1.

9   John Paul II, Encyclical Letter *Centesimus Annus* (1 May 1991), 34: *AAS* 83 (1991), 836.

10 Cf. In this regard the *Catechism of the Catholic Church*, 2307–2317.

11 Address to a group of representatives from the Congress of the United States of America (21 August 1945): *Discorsi e Radiomessaggi di Sua Santità Pio XII*, VII (1945–1946), 141.

12 Cf. John Paul II, Encyclical Letter *Redemptor Hominis* (4 March 1979), 13–14: *AAS* 71 (1979), 282–286.

13 Cf. *Catechism of the Catholic Church*, 1397.

14 John Paul II, Angelus Address, 27 September 1998, 1: *L'Osservatore Romano*, 28–29 September 1998, p. 5.

15 Cf. John Paul II, Apostolic Letter *Tertio Millennio Adveniente* (10 November 1994), 49–51: *AAS* 87 (1995), 35–36.

1 January 2000
'PEACE ON EARTH TO THOSE WHOM GOD LOVES!'

In the Jubilee Year celebrating Jesus, gift of peace, the Pope's message proclaims: God loves all, we are all one family and so as brothers and sisters we are called to renew relationships in peace between individuals and peoples. Promoting a culture of peace involves openness to the Transcendent, promotion of the human person and respect for the world of nature. The Pope repeats his conviction that 'war is a defeat for humanity' and 'there will be peace only to the extent that humanity as a whole rediscovers its soul in its fundamental calling to be one family'. In a wide-ranging review, he lists the possibilities and conditions underlining the possibility of taking measures to disarm an unjust aggressor. He also calls for renewal of the UN (whose work he esteems) and international institutions. He recalls the many who have spoken and worked on behalf of peace in the twentieth century even to the point of martyrdom. He also praises those in science and technology who brought about great advances for enhancing and prolonging human life. Highlighting once again the increasing North–South divide, the Pope points out that it is a demand not only of ethics but also of sound economy to rethink the economy and its purposes, especially the concept of prosperity. With one billion four hundred million people living in dire poverty, there is a need also to reconsider (without falling into ideological mistakes) the models which inspire developmental policies. International cooperation in a new culture of solidarity is needed.

✳ ✳ ✳

1.   This is the proclamation of the Angels which greeted the birth of Jesus Christ two thousand years ago (cf. *Lk* 2:14), and which we will hear re-echoing joyfully on the holy night of Christmas, when the Great Jubilee will be solemnly inaugurated.

At the dawn of the new Millennium, we wish to propose once more the message of hope which comes from the stable of Bethlehem: God loves all men and women on earth and gives them the hope of a new era, an era of peace. His love, fully revealed in the Incarnate Son, is the foundation of universal peace. When welcomed in the depths of the human heart, this love reconciles people with God and with themselves, renews human relationships and stirs that desire for brotherhood capable of banishing the temptation of violence and war.

The Great Jubilee is inseparably linked to this message of love and reconciliation, a message which gives voice to the truest aspirations of humanity today.

2.   Looking to a year so filled with meaning, I once more offer everyone my good wishes for peace. To everyone I affirm that peace is possible. It needs to be implored from God as his gift, but it also needs to be built day by day with his help, through works of justice and love.

To be sure, the problems which make the path to peace difficult and often discouraging are many and complex, but peace is a need deeply rooted in the heart of every man and woman. The will to seek peace must not therefore be allowed to weaken. This seeking must be based on the awareness that humanity, however much marred by sin, hatred and violence, is called by God to be *a single family*. This divine plan needs to be recognized and carried out through the search for harmonious relationships between individuals and peoples, in a culture where openness to the Transcendent, the promotion of the human person and respect for the world of nature are shared by all.

This is the message of Christmas, this is the message of the Jubilee, this is my hope at the beginning of a new Millennium.

War is a defeat for humanity

3.   In the century we are leaving behind, humanity has been sorely tried by an endless and horrifying sequence of wars, conflicts, genocides and 'ethnic cleansings' which have caused unspeakable suffering: millions and millions of victims, families and countries destroyed, an ocean of refugees, misery, hunger, disease, underdevelopment and the loss of immense resources. At the root of so much suffering there lies a logic of supremacy fuelled by the desire to dominate and exploit others, by ideologies of power or totalitarian utopias, by crazed nationalisms or ancient tribal hatreds. At times brutal and systematic violence, aimed at the very extermination or enslavement of entire peoples and regions, has had to be countered by armed resistance.

The twentieth century bequeaths to us above all else a warning: *wars are often the cause of further wars* because they fuel deep hatreds, create situations of injustice and trample upon people's dignity and rights. Wars generally do not resolve the problems for which they are fought and therefore, in addition to causing horrendous damage, they prove ultimately futile. *War is a defeat for humanity.* Only in peace and through peace can respect for human dignity and its inalienable rights be guaranteed.[1]

4.   Against the backdrop of war in the twentieth century, *humanity's honour has been preserved by those who have spoken and worked on behalf of peace.*

We cannot fail to remember the countless men and women who have contributed to the affirmation and the solemn proclamation of human rights, and who have helped to defeat the various forms of totalitarianism, to put an end to colonialism, to develop democracy and to establish the great international organizations. Those who built their lives on the value of non-violence have given us a luminous and prophetic example. Their example of integrity and loyalty, often to the point of martyrdom, has provided us with rich and splendid lessons.

271

Among those who have acted in the name of peace we should not forget those men and women whose dedication has brought about great advances in every field of science and technology, making it possible to overcome dreadful diseases and to enhance and prolong human life.

Nor can I fail to mention my own venerable Predecessors who have guided the Church in the twentieth century. By their lofty teaching and their tireless efforts they have given direction to the Church in the promotion of a culture of peace. Emblematic of this many-sided effort was the timely and prophetic intuition of Pope Paul VI, who on 8 December 1967 instituted the World Day of Peace. With the passing of the years, the World Day of Peace has become more firmly established as a fruitful experience of reflection and shared vision for the future.

Called to be one family

5.   *'Peace on earth to those whom God loves!'* The Gospel greeting prompts a heart-felt question: will the new century be one of peace and a renewed sense of brotherhood between individuals and peoples? We cannot of course foresee the future. But we can set forth one certain principle: *there will be peace only to the extent that humanity as a whole rediscovers its fundamental calling to be one family,* a family in which the dignity and rights of individuals – whatever their status, race or religion – are accepted as prior and superior to any kind of difference or distinction.

This recognition can give the world as it is today – marked by the process of globalization – a soul, a meaning and a direction. Globalization, for all its risks, also offers exceptional and promising opportunities, precisely with a view to enabling humanity to become a single family, built on the values of justice, equity and solidarity.

6.   For this to happen, a complete change of perspective will be needed: it is no longer the well-being of any one political, racial or cultural community that must prevail, but rather the

good of humanity as a whole. The pursuit of the common good of a single political community cannot be in conflict with *the common good of humanity,* expressed in the recognition of and respect for human rights sanctioned by the Universal Declaration of Human Rights of 1948. It is necessary, then, to abandon ideas and practices – often determined by powerful economic interests – which subordinate every other value to the absolute claims of the nation and the State. In this new perspective, the political, cultural and institutional divisions and distinctions by which humanity is ordered and organized are legitimate in so far as they are compatible with membership in the one human family, and with the ethical and legal requirements which stem from this.

Crimes against humanity

7.　　This principle has an immensely important consequence: *an offense against human rights is an offense against the conscience of humanity as such,* an offence against humanity itself. The duty of protecting these rights therefore extends beyond the geographical and political borders within which they are violated. *Crimes against humanity cannot be considered an internal affair of a nation.* Here an important step forward was taken with the establishment of an International Criminal Court to try such crimes, regardless of the place or circumstances in which they are committed. We must thank God that in the conscience of peoples and nations there is a growing conviction that human rights have no borders, because they are universal and indivisible.

8.　　In our time, the number of wars between States has diminished. This fact, albeit consoling, appears in a very different light if we consider the armed conflicts taking place *within States*. Sadly these are quite numerous on practically every continent, and often very violent. For the most part, they are rooted in long-standing historical motives of an ethnic, tribal or even religious character, to which must be added nowadays other ideological, social and economic causes.

These internal conflicts, usually waged through the large-scale use of small-calibre weapons and so-called 'light' arms – arms which in are fact extraordinarily lethal – often have grave consequences which spill over the borders of the country in question, involving outside interests and responsibilities. While it is true that the extreme complexity of these conflicts makes it very difficult to understand and evaluate the causes and interests at play, one fact cannot be disputed: it is the *civilian population* which suffers most tragically, since neither ordinary laws nor the laws of warfare are respected in practice. Far from being protected, civilians are often the prime target of the conflicting forces, when they themselves are not directly involved in armed activity as a result of a perverse spiral which makes them both victims and assassins of other civilians.

All too many and horrifying are the macabre scenarios in which innocent children, women, and unarmed older people have become intentional targets in the bloody conflicts of our time; too many, in fact, for us not to feel that the moment has come to change direction, decisively and with a great sense of responsibility.

The right to humanitarian assistance

9.   In every case, in the face of such tragic and complex situations and contrary to all alleged 'reasons' of war, there is a need to affirm the *preeminent value of humanitarian law and the consequent duty to guarantee the right to humanitarian aid* to suffering civilians and refugees.

The recognition of these rights and their effective implementation must not be allowed to depend on the interests of any of the parties in conflict. On the contrary, there is a duty to identify all the means, institutional or otherwise, which can best serve in a practical way to meet humanitarian objectives. The moral and political legitimacy of these rights is in fact based on the principle that the good of the human person comes before all else and stands above all human institutions.

10.   Here I wish to restate my conviction that, in the face of modern armed conflicts, negotiation between parties, with *appropriate attempts at mediation and pacification by international and regional bodies*, is of the greatest importance. Negotiation is necessary in order to prevent such conflicts and to end them once they have broken out, restoring peace through an equitable settlement of the rights and interests involved.

This conviction concerning the positive role played by mediation and pacification agencies should be extended to the non-governmental humanitarian organizations and religious bodies which, discreetly and without ulterior motives, promote peace between opposed groups and help to overcome age-old rivalries, reconcile enemies, and open the way to a new and shared future. While honouring their noble dedication to the cause of peace, I wish to remember with profound esteem all who have given their lives so that others might live: I lift up my prayers to God for them and I invite other believers to do the same.

'Humanitarian intervention'

11.   Clearly, when a civilian population risks being overcome by the attacks of an unjust aggressor and political efforts and non-violent defence prove to be of no avail, it is legitimate and even obligatory to take concrete measures to disarm the aggressor. These measures however must be limited in time and precise in their aims. They must be carried out in full respect for international law, guaranteed by an authority that is internationally recognized and, in any event, never left to the outcome of armed intervention alone.

The fullest and the best use must therefore be made of all the provisions of the United Nations Charter, further defining effective instruments and modes of intervention within the framework of international law. In this regard, the United Nations Organization itself must offer all its Member States an equal opportunity to be part of the decision-making process, eliminating privileges and discriminations which weaken its role and its credibility.

12.   This opens a new field of reflection and discussion both for politics and for law, a field which we all hope will be earnestly and wisely cultivated. What is needed without delay is a *renewal of international law and international institutions*, a renewal whose starting-point and basic organizing principle should be the primacy of the good of humanity and of the human person over every other consideration. Such a renewal is all the more urgent if we consider the paradox of contemporary warfare in which, as recent conflicts have shown, armies enjoy maximum security while the civilian population lives in frightening situations of danger. In no kind of conflict is it permissible to ignore the right of civilians to safety.

Beyond legal and institutional considerations, there remains a fundamental duty for all men and women of good will, called to commit themselves personally to the cause of peace: that of educating for peace, setting in place structures of peace and methods of non-violence, and making every possible effort to bring parties in conflict to the negotiating table.

Peace in solidarity

13.   *'Peace on earth to those whom God loves!'* From the problem of war, our gaze naturally turns to another closely related issue: *the question of solidarity*. The lofty and demanding task of peace, deeply rooted in humanity's vocation to be one family and to recognize itself as such, has one of its foundations in the principle of the universal destination of the earth's resources. This principle does not delegitimize private property; instead it broadens the understanding and management of private property to embrace its indispensable social function, to the advantage of the common good and in particular the good of society's weakest members.[2] Unfortunately, this basic principle is widely disregarded, as shown by the persistent and growing gulf in the world between a North filled with abundant commodities and resources and increasingly made up of older people, and a South where the

great majority of younger people now live, still deprived of credible prospects for social, cultural and economic development.

No one should be deceived into thinking that the simple absence of war, as desirable as it is, is equivalent to lasting peace. There is no true peace without fairness, truth, justice and solidarity. Failure awaits every plan which would separate *two indivisible and interdependent rights: the right to peace and the right to an integral development born of solidarity.* 'Injustice, excessive economic or social inequalities, envy, distrust and pride raging among men and nations constantly threaten peace and cause wars. Everything done to overcome these disorders contributes to building up peace and avoiding war'.[3]

14.   At the beginning of a new century, the one issue which most challenges our human and Christian consciences is *the poverty of countless millions of men and women.* This situation becomes all the more tragic when we realize that the major economic problems of our time do not depend on a lack of resources but on the fact that present economic, social and cultural structures are ill-equipped to meet the demands of genuine development.

Rightly then the poor, both in developing countries and in the prosperous and wealthy countries, 'ask for the right to share in enjoying material goods and to make good use of their capacity to work, thus creating a world that is more just and prosperous for all. The advancement of the poor constitutes a great opportunity for the moral, cultural and even economic growth of all humanity'.[4] Let us look at the poor not as a problem, but as people who can become the principal builders of a new and more human future for everyone.

The urgent need to rethink the economy

15.   In this context we also need to examine the growing concern felt by many economists and financial professionals when, in considering new issues involving poverty, peace,

ecology and the future of the younger generation, they reflect on the role of the market, on the pervasive influence of monetary and financial interests, on the widening gap between the economy and society, and on other similar issues related to economic activity.

Perhaps the time has come for *a new and deeper reflection on the nature of the economy and its purposes*. What seems to be urgently needed is a reconsideration of the concept of 'prosperity' itself, to prevent it from being enclosed in a narrow utilitarian perspective which leaves very little space for values such as solidarity and altruism.

16.   Here I would like to invite economists and financial professionals, as well as political leaders, to recognize the urgency of the need to ensure that economic practices and related political policies have as their aim the good of every person and of the whole person. This is not only a demand of ethics but also of a sound economy. Experience seems to confirm that economic success is increasingly dependent on a more genuine appreciation of individuals and their abilities, on their fuller participation, on their increased and improved knowledge and information, on a stronger solidarity.

These are values which, far from being foreign to economics and business, help to make them a fully 'human' science and activity. An economy which takes no account of the ethical dimension and does not seek to serve the good of the person – of every person and the whole person – cannot really call itself an 'economy', understood in the sense of a rational and constructive use of material wealth.

Which models of development?

17.   The very fact that humanity, called to form a single family, is still tragically split in two by poverty – at the beginning of the twenty-first century, more than a billion four hundred million people are living in a situation of dire poverty – means that there is urgent need to *reconsider the models which inspire development policies*.

In this regard, the legitimate requirements of economic efficiency must be better aligned with the requirements of political participation and social justice, without falling back into the ideological mistakes made during the twentieth century. In practice, this means making solidarity an integral part of the network of economic, political and social interdependence which the current process of globalization is tending to consolidate.

These processes call for *rethinking international cooperation in terms of a new culture of solidarity*. When seen as a sowing of peace, cooperation cannot be reduced to aid or assistance, especially if given with an eye to the benefits to be received in return for the resources made available. Rather, it must express a concrete and tangible commitment to solidarity which makes the poor the agents of their own development and enables the greatest number of people, in their specific economic and political circumstances, to exercise the creativity which is characteristic of the human person and on which the wealth of nations too is dependent.[5]

In particular it is necessary to find definitive solutions to the long-standing problem of the international debt of poor countries, while at the same time making available the financial resources necessary for the fight against hunger, malnutrition, disease, illiteracy and the destruction of the environment.

18.   Today more than in the past there is an urgent need to *foster a consciousness of universal moral values* in order to face the problems of the present, all of which are assuming an increasingly global dimension. The promotion of peace and human rights, the settling of armed conflicts both within States and across borders, the protection of ethnic minorities and immigrants, the safeguarding of the environment, the battle against terrible diseases, the fight against drug and arms traffickers, and against political and economic corruption: these are issues which nowadays no nation is in a position to face alone. They concern the entire human

community, and thus they must be faced and resolved through common efforts.

A way must be found to discuss the problems posed by the future of humanity in a comprehensible and common language. The basis of such a dialogue is *the universal moral law* written upon the human heart. By following this 'grammar' of the spirit, the human community can confront the problems of coexistence and move forward to the future with respect for God's plan.[6]

The encounter between faith and reason, between religion and morality, can provide a decisive impulse towards dialogue and cooperation between peoples, cultures and religions.

Jesus, gift of peace

19.   *'Peace on earth to those whom God loves!'* Looking to the Great Jubilee, Christians throughout the world are committed to the solemn commemoration of the Incarnation. Listening again to the proclamation of the Angels in the heavens above Bethlehem (cf. *Lk* 2:14), they commemorate the Incarnation in the knowledge that Jesus 'is our peace' (*Eph* 2:14), the gift of peace for all people. His first words to the disciples after the Resurrection were: 'Peace be with you'(*Jn* 20:19, 21, 26). Christ came to unite what was divided, to destroy sin and hatred, and to reawaken in humanity the vocation to unity and brotherhood. Therefore, he is 'the source and model of that renewed humanity, imbued with brotherly love, sincerity, and a peaceful spirit, to which all aspire'.[7]

20.   During this Jubilee Year, the Church vividly remembers her Lord and intends to confirm her vocation and mission to be in Christ a 'sacrament' or *sign and instrument of peace in the world and for the world*. For the Church, to carry out her evangelizing mission means to work for peace. 'The Church, then, God's only flock, like a standard lifted high for the nations to see, ministers the Gospel of peace to all mankind as she makes her pilgrim way in hope towards her goal, the fatherland above'.[8]

For the Catholic faithful, the commitment to build peace and justice is not secondary but essential. It is to be undertaken in openness towards their brothers and sisters of other Churches and Ecclesial Communities, towards the followers of other religions, and towards all men and women of good will, with whom they share the same concern for peace and brotherhood.

Working generously for peace

21.   It is a sign of hope that, despite many serious obstacles, initiatives for peace continue to spring up day by day, with the generous cooperation of many people. Peace is a building constantly under construction. The building up of peace involves:

- parents who are examples and witnesses of peace in their families, and who educate their children for peace;
- teachers who are able to pass on the genuine values present in every field of knowledge and in the historical and cultural heritage of humanity;
- working men and women, who are committed to extending their age-old struggle for the dignity of work to those present-day situations which, at the international level, cry out for justice and solidarity;
- political leaders who put at the heart of their own political activity and of that of their countries a firm and unwavering determination to promote peace and justice;
- those in International Organizations who, often with scarce resources, work in the front line where being 'peace-makers' can involve risking their own personal safety;
- the members of Non-Governmental Organizations who, in different parts of the world and in the most varied situations, are dedicated to preventing and resolving conflicts through research and activity;
- believers who, convinced that authentic faith is never a source of war or violence, spread convictions of peace and love through ecumenical and interreligious dialogue.

281

22.   I am thinking particularly of you, dear young people, who experience in a special way the blessing of life and have a duty not to waste it. In your schools and universities, in the work-place, in leisure and sports, in all that you do, let yourselves be guided by this constant thought: peace within you and peace around you, peace always, peace with everyone, peace for everyone.

To the young people who, unfortunately, have known the tragic experience of war and who harbour sentiments of hatred and resentment I address this plea: make every effort to rediscover the path of reconciliation and forgiveness. It is a difficult path, but it is the only one which will enable you to look to the future with hope for yourselves, your children, your countries and all humanity.

I will have an opportunity to return to this dialogue with you, dear young people, when we meet in Rome next August for the Jubilee celebration of World Youth Day.

Pope John XXIII in one of his last public addresses spoke once more to 'men of good will', asking them to commit themselves to a programme of peace *based on 'the Gospel of obedience to God, mercy and forgiveness'*. He went on to say: 'without a doubt the bright torch of peace will run its course, igniting joy and pouring light and grace into the hearts of people throughout the world, helping them to discover beyond all frontiers the faces of brothers and sisters, the faces of friends'.[9] May you, young people of the Year 2000, see in others, and help them to see, the faces of brothers and sisters, the faces of friends!

In this Jubilee Year, when the Church will commit herself to prayer for peace through solemn intercessions, we turn with filial devotion to the Mother of Jesus. Invoking her as the Queen of Peace, we ask that she generously bestow on us the gifts of her maternal goodness and help the human race to become one family, in solidarity and peace.

Notes

1 Cf. John Paul II, *Message for the World Day of Peace 1999*, 1.

2 Cf. John Paul II, Encyclical Letter *Centesimus Annus* (1 May 1991), 30–43: *AAS* 83 (1991), 830–848.

3 *Catechism of the Catholic Church*, 2317.

4 John Paul II, Encyclical Letter *Centesimus Annus* (1 May 1991), 28: *AAS* 83 (1991), 827–828.

5 Cf. John Paul II, Address to the Fiftieth General Assembly of the United Nations Organization (5 October 1995), 13: *Insegnamenti* XVIII, 2 (1995), 739–740.

6 Cf. *ibid.*, 3: *loc. cit.* 732.

7 Second Vatican Ecumenical Council, Decree on the Missionary Activity of the Church *Ad Gentes*, 8.

8 Second Vatican Ecumenical Council, Decree on Ecumenism *Unitatis Redintegratio*, 2.

9 Address on the occasion of the award of the Balzan Prize (10 May 1963): *AAS* 55 (1963), 455.

1 January 2001

DIALOGUE BETWEEN CULTURES FOR A CIVILISATION OF LOVE AND PEACE

In this message prompted by the UN 'International Year of Dialogue Among Civilizations' the Pope is clearly happy to grapple with the complex issues involved. Culture is defined as 'the form of man's self-expression in his journey through history'. Every person lives within a specific culture and normally the sociological and psychological forces of one's culture are constructive in giving solid roots to one's identity and human development. Love for one's country is a value to be fostered but it must include love for the whole human family and not xenophobia. Getting to know each other's cultures leads to mutual respect and integral humanism. Each particular community's cultural experience needs to be examined in its basic ethical orientations because 'cultures, like the people who give rise to them, are marked by the "mystery of evil" at work in human history.' Pope John Paul also points to the danger of slavish conformity of cultures, especially to cultural models deriving from the Western world that can erode from within other cultures and civilizations. He points to the culture of death and the despising of life that emerged in the West in the twentieth century. True dialogue between cultures is the privileged means for building a civilization of love and peace. And that is urgent today due to the impact both of new communications technology that is transforming our understanding of the world and the phenomenon of migration. Remembering the 2000 World Youth Day the Pope concludes with warm words to young people.

* * *

1. At the dawn of a new millennium, there is growing hope that relationships between people will be increasingly inspired by the ideal of a truly universal brotherhood. Unless this ideal is shared, there will be no way to ensure a stable peace. There are many signs which suggest that this conviction is becoming more deeply rooted in people's minds. The importance of fraternity is proclaimed in the great 'charters' of human rights; it is embodied in great international institutions, particularly the United Nations; and it is called for, as never before, by the process of globalization which is leading to a progressive unification of the economy, culture and society. For their part, the followers of the different religions are ever more conscious of the fact that a relationship with the one God, the common Father of all, cannot fail to bring about a greater sense of human brotherhood and a more fraternal life together. In God's revelation in Christ, this principle finds a radical expression: 'He who does not love does not know God; for God is love' (*1 Jn* 4:8).

2. At the same time, however, it cannot be denied that thick clouds overshadow these bright hopes. Humanity is beginning this new chapter of its history with still open wounds. In many regions it is beset by bitter and bloody conflicts, and is struggling with increasing difficulty to maintain solidarity between people of different cultures and civilizations living together in the same territory. We all know how hard it is to settle differences between parties when ancient hatreds and serious problems which admit of no easy solution create an atmosphere of anger and exasperation. But no less dangerous for the future of peace would be the inability to confront intelligently the problems posed by a new social configuration resulting in many countries from accelerated migration and the unprecedented situation of people of different cultures and civilizations living side by side.

3. I therefore consider it urgent to invite believers in Christ, together with all men and women of good will, to *reflect on the*

theme of dialogue between cultures and traditions. This dialogue is the obligatory path to the building of a reconciled world, a world able to look with serenity to its own future. This is a theme which is crucial to the pursuit of peace. I am pleased that the United Nations Organization has called attention to this urgent need by declaring 2001 the 'International Year of Dialogue Among Civilizations'.

Naturally, I do not believe that there can be easy or readily applicable solutions to a problem like this. It is difficult enough to undertake an analysis of the situation, which is in constant flux and defies all preconceived models. There is also the difficulty of combining principles and values which, however reconcilable in the abstract, can prove on the practical level to be resistant to any easy synthesis. In addition, at a deeper level, there are always the demands which ethical commitment makes upon individuals, who are not free of self-interest and human limitations.

But for this very reason I see the usefulness of a shared reflection on these issues. With this intention I confine myself here to offering some guidelines, listening to what the Spirit of God is saying to the Churches (cf. *Rev* 2:7) and to all of humanity at this decisive hour of its history.

Mankind and its different cultures

4.   Reflecting upon the human situation, one is always amazed at the complexity and diversity of human cultures. Each of them is distinct by virtue of its specific historical evolution and the resulting characteristics which make it a structurally unique, original and organic whole. *Culture is the form of man's self-expression in his journey through history,* on the level of both individuals and social groups. For man is driven incessantly by his intellect and will to 'cultivate natural goods and values',[1] to incorporate in an ever higher and more systematic cultural synthesis his basic knowledge of all aspects of life, particularly those involving social and political life, security and economic development, and to foster those existential values and perspectives, especially in the religious

sphere, which enable individual and community life to develop in a way that is authentically human.[2]

5.   A culture is always marked by stable and enduring elements, as well as by changing and contingent features. At first glance, in examining a culture we are struck above all by those aspects which distinguish it from our own culture; these give each culture a face of its own, as an amalgam of quite distinctive elements. In most cases, a culture develops in a specific place, where geographical, historical and ethnic elements combine in an original and unique way. The 'uniqueness' of each culture is reflected more or less clearly in those individuals who are its bearers, in a constant process whereby individuals are influenced by their culture and then, according to their different abilities and genius, contribute to it something of their own. In any event, *a person necessarily lives within a specific culture*. People are marked by the culture whose very air they breathe through the family and the social groups around them, through education and the most varied influences of their environment, through the very relationship which they have with the place in which they live. There is no determinism here, but rather a constant dialectic between the strength of the individual's conditioning and the workings of human freedom.

Human development and being part of a culture

6.   The need to accept one's own culture as a structuring element of one's personality, especially in the initial stages of life, is a fact of universal experience whose importance can hardly be overestimated. Without a firm rooting in a specific 'soil', individuals risk being subjected at a still vulnerable age to an excess of conflicting stimuli which could impair their serene and balanced development. It is on the basis of this essential relationship with one's own 'origins' – on the level of the family, but also of territory, society and culture – that people acquire *a sense of their nationality*, and culture tends to take on, to a greater or lesser degree in different places, a 'national' configuration. The Son of God himself, by becoming

man, acquired, along with a human family, a country. He remains for ever Jesus of Nazareth, the Nazarean (cf. *Mk* 10:47; *Lk* 18:37; *Jn* 1:45; 19:19). This is a natural process, in which sociological and psychological forces interact, with results that are normally positive and constructive. Love for one's country is thus *a value to be fostered*, without narrow-mindedness but with love for the whole human family[3] and with an effort to avoid those pathological manifestations which occur when the sense of belonging turns into selfexaltation, the rejection of diversity, and forms of nationalism, racism and xenophobia.

7.   Consequently, while it is certainly important to be able to appreciate the values of one's own culture, there is also a need to recognize that every culture, as a typically human and historically conditioned reality, necessarily has its limitations. In order to prevent the sense of belonging to one particular culture from turning into isolation, an effective antidote is a serene and unprejudiced knowledge of other cultures. Moreover, when cultures are carefully and rigorously studied, they very often reveal beneath their outward variations *significant common elements*. This can also be seen in the historical sequence of cultures and civilizations. The Church, looking to Christ, who reveals man to himself,[4] and drawing upon her experience of two thousand years of history, is convinced that 'beneath all that changes, there is much that is unchanging'.[5] This continuity is based upon the essential and universal character of God's plan for humanity.

Cultural diversity should therefore be understood *within the broader horizon of the unity of the human race*. In a real way, this unity constitutes the primordial historical and ontological datum in the light of which the profound meaning of cultural diversity can be grasped. In fact, only an overall vision of both the elements of unity and the elements of diversity makes it possible to understand and interpret the full truth of every human culture.[6]

Cultural differences and mutual respect

8.   In the past, cultural differences have often been a source of misunderstanding between peoples and the cause of conflicts and wars. Even now, sad to say, in different parts of the world we are witnessing with growing alarm *the aggressive claims of some cultures against others*. In the long run, this situation can end in disastrous tensions and conflicts. At the very least it can make more difficult the situation of those ethnic and cultural minorities living in a majority cultural context which is different from their own and prone to hostile and racist ways of thinking and acting.

In light of this, people of good will need to examine the basic ethical orientations which mark a particular community's cultural experience. Cultures, like the people who give rise to them, are marked by the 'mystery of evil' at work in human history (cf. *1 Th* 2:7), and they too are in need of purification and salvation. The authenticity of each human culture, the soundness of its underlying ethos, and hence the validity of its moral bearings, can be measured to an extent by its commitment to *the human cause* and *by its capacity to promote human dignity* at every level and in every circumstance.

9.   The radicalization of identity which makes cultures resistant to any beneficial influence from outside is worrying enough; but no less perilous is *the slavish conformity of cultures*, or at least of key aspects of them, to cultural models deriving from the Western world. Detached from their Christians origins, these models are often inspired by an approach to life marked by secularism and practical atheism and by patterns of radical individualism. This is a phenomenon of vast proportions, sustained by powerful media campaigns and designed to propagate lifestyles, social and economic programmes and, in the last analysis, a comprehensive world-view which erodes from within other estimable cultures and civilizations. Western cultural models are enticing and alluring because of their remarkable scientific and technical cast, but

regrettably there is growing evidence of their deepening human, spiritual and moral impoverishment. The culture which produces such models is marked by the fatal attempt to secure the good of humanity by eliminating God, the Supreme Good. Yet, as the Second Vatican Council warned, 'without the Creator the creature comes to nothing!'[7] A culture which no longer has a point of reference in God loses its soul and loses its way, becoming a culture of death. This was amply demonstrated by the tragic events of the twentieth century and is now apparent in the nihilism present in some prominent circles in the Western world.

Dialogue between cultures

10.   Individuals come to maturity through receptive openness to others and through generous self-giving to them; so too do cultures. Created by people and at the service of people, they have to be perfected through dialogue and communion, on the basis of the original and fundamental unity of the human family as it came from the hands of God who 'made from one stock every nation of mankind' (*Acts* 17:26).

In this perspective, *dialogue between cultures* – the theme of this World Day of Peace Message – *emerges as an intrinsic demand of human nature itself, as well as of culture.* It is dialogue which protects the distinctiveness of cultures as historical and creative expressions of the underlying unity of the human family, and which sustains understanding and communion between them. The notion of communion, which has its source in Christian revelation and finds its sublime prototype in the Triune God (cf. *Jn* 17:11, 21), never implies a dull uniformity or enforced homogenization or assimilation; rather it expresses the convergence of a multiform variety, and is therefore a sign of richness and a promise of growth.

Dialogue leads to a recognition of diversity and opens the mind to the mutual acceptance and genuine collaboration demanded by the human family's basic vocation to unity. As such, dialogue is a privileged means for building *the civilization of love and peace* that my revered predecessor Pope

Paul VI indicated as the ideal to inspire cultural, social, political and economic life in our time. At the beginning of the Third Millennium, it is urgent that *the path of dialogue* be proposed once again to a world marked by excessive conflict and violence, a world at times discouraged and incapable of seeing signs of hope and peace.

Possibilities and risks of global communication

11.   Dialogue between cultures is especially needed today because of *the impact of new communications technology* on the lives of individuals and peoples. Ours is an era of global communication, which is shaping society along the lines of new cultural models which more or less break with past models. At least in principle, accurate and up-to-date information is available to anyone in any part of the world.

The free flow of images and speech on a global scale is transforming not only political and economic relations between peoples, but even our understanding of the world. It opens up a range of hitherto unthinkable possibilities, but it also has certain negative and dangerous aspects. The fact that a few countries have a monopoly on these cultural 'industries' and distribute their products to an ever growing public in every corner of the earth can be a powerful factor in undermining cultural distinctness. These products include and transmit implicit value-systems and can therefore lead to a kind of dispossession and loss of cultural identity in those who receive them.

The challenge of migration

12.   A style and culture of dialogue are especially important when it comes to *the complex question of migration*, which is an important social phenomenon of our time. The movement of large numbers of people from one part of the planet to another is often a terrible odyssey for those involved, and it brings with it the intermingling of traditions and customs, with notable repercussions both on the countries from which people

come and on those in which they settle. How migrants are welcomed by receiving countries and how well they become integrated in their new environment are also an indication of how much effective dialogue there is between the various cultures.

The question of cultural integration is much debated these days, and it is not easy to specify in detail how best to guarantee, in a balanced and equitable way, the rights and duties of those who welcome and those who are welcomed. Historically, migrations have occurred in all sorts of ways and with very different results. In the case of many civilizations, immigration has brought new growth and enrichment. In other cases, the local people and immigrants have remained culturally separate but have shown that they are able to live together, respecting each other and accepting or tolerating the diversity of customs. Regrettably, situations still exist in which the difficulties involved in the encounter of different cultures have never been resolved, and the consequent tensions have become the cause of periodic outbreaks of conflict.

13. In such a complex issue there are no 'magic' formulas; but still we must identify some basic ethical principles to serve as points of reference. First of all, it is important to remember the principle that *immigrants must always be treated with the respect due to the dignity of every human person*. In the matter of controlling the influx of immigrants, the consideration which should rightly be given to the common good should not ignore this principle. The challenge is to combine the welcome due to every human being, especially when in need, with a reckoning of what is necessary for both the local inhabitants and the new arrivals to live a dignified and peaceful life. The cultural practices which immigrants bring with them should be respected and accepted, as long as they do not contravene either the universal ethical values inherent in the natural law or fundamental human rights.

Respect for cultures and the 'cultural profile' of different regions

14.   It is a much more difficult thing to determine the extent to which immigrants are entitled to public legal recognition of the particular customs of their culture, which may not be readily compatible with the customs of the majority of citizens. The solution to this question, within a climate of genuine openness, *calls for a realistic evaluation of the common good* at any given time in history and in any given place and social context. Much depends upon whether people embrace a spirit of openness that, without yielding to indifferentism about values, can combine the concern for identity with the willingness to engage in dialogue.

On the other hand, as I noted above, one cannot underestimate the capacity of the characteristic culture of a region to produce a balanced growth, especially in the delicate early stages of life, in those who belong to that culture from birth. From this point of view, a reasonable way forward would be to ensure a certain 'cultural equilibrium' in each region, by reference to the culture which has prevalently marked its development. This equilibrium, even while welcoming minorities and respecting their basic rights, would allow the continued existence and development of a particular 'cultural profile', by which I mean that basic heritage of language, traditions and values which are inextricably part of a nation's history and its national identity.

15.   Clearly, though, the need to ensure an equilibrium in a region's cultural profile cannot be met by legislative measures alone, since these would prove ineffectual unless they were grounded in the ethos of the population. They would also be inevitably destined to change should a culture lose its ability to inspire a people and a region, becoming no more than a legacy preserved in museums or in artistic and literary monuments.

In effect, as long as a culture is truly alive, it need have no fear of being displaced. And no law could keep it alive if it were already dead in people's hearts. In the dialogue between cultures, no side can be prevented from proposing to the other the values in which it believes, as long as this is done in a way that is respectful of people's freedom and conscience. 'Truth can be imposed only with the force of truth itself, which penetrates the mind both gently and powerfully'.[8]

The recognition of shared values

16. Dialogue between cultures, a privileged means for building the civilization of love, is based upon the recognition that *there are values which are common to all cultures* because they are rooted in the nature of the person. These values express humanity's most authentic and distinctive features. Leaving aside ideological prejudices and selfish interests, it is necessary to foster people's awareness of these shared values, in order to nurture that intrinsically universal cultural 'soil' which makes for fruitful and constructive dialogue. The different religions too can and ought to contribute decisively to this process. My many encounters with representatives of other religions – I recall especially the meeting in Assisi in 1986 and in Saint Peter's Square in 1999 – have made me more confident that mutual openness between the followers of the various religions can greatly serve the cause of peace and the common good of the human family.

The value of solidarity

17. Faced with growing inequalities in the world, *the prime value* which must be ever more widely inculcated is certainly that of *solidarity*. A society depends on the basic relations that people cultivate with one another in ever widening circles — from the family to other intermediary social groups, to civil society as a whole and to the national community. States in turn have no choice but to enter into relations with one another. The present reality of global interdependence makes it easier to appreciate the common destiny of the entire human family, and makes all thoughtful people increasingly appreciate the virtue of solidarity.

At the same time it is necessary to point out that this growing interdependence has brought to light many inequalities, such as the gap between rich and poor nations; the social imbalance within each nation between those living in opulence and those offended in their dignity since they lack even the necessities of life; the human and environmental degradation provoked and accelerated by the irresponsible use of natural resources. These social inequalities and imbalances have grown worse in certain places, and some of the poorest nations have reached a point of irreversible decline.

Consequently, *the promotion of justice* is at the heart of a true culture of solidarity. It is not just a question of giving one's surplus to those in need, but of 'helping entire peoples presently excluded or marginalized to enter into the sphere of economic and human development. For this to happen, it is not enough to draw on the surplus goods which in fact our world abundantly produces; it requires above all a change of lifestyles, of models of production and consumption, and of the established structures of power which today govern societies'.[9]

The value of peace

18.　The culture of solidarity is closely connected with *the value of peace*, the primary objective of every society and of national and international life. However, on the path to better understanding among peoples there remain many challenges which the world must face: these set before everyone choices which cannot be postponed. The alarming increase of arms, together with the halting progress of commitment to nuclear non-proliferation, runs the risk of feeding and expanding a culture of competition and conflict, a culture involving not only States but also non-institutional entities, such as paramilitary groups and terrorist organizations.

Even today the world is dealing with the consequences of wars past and present, as well as the tragic effects of anti-personnel mines and the use of frightful chemical and biological weapons. And what can be said about the permanent risk of conflicts between nations, of civil wars within some States and of widespread violence, before which international organizations and national governments appear almost impotent? Faced with such threats, everyone must feel the moral duty to take concrete and timely steps to promote the cause of peace and understanding among peoples.

The value of life

19.   An authentic dialogue between cultures cannot fail to nourish, in addition to sentiments of mutual respect, a lively sense of *the value of life itself*. Human life cannot be seen as an object to do with as we please, but as the most sacred and inviolable earthly reality. There can be no peace when this most basic good is not protected. *It is not possible to invoke peace and despise life.* Our own times have seen shining examples of generosity and dedication in the service of life, but also the sad sight of hundreds of millions of men and women whom cruelty and indifference have consigned to a painful and harsh destiny. I am speaking of a tragic spiral of death which includes murder, suicide, abortion, euthanasia, as well as practices of mutilation, physical and psychological torture, forms of unjust coercion, arbitrary imprisonment, unnecessary recourse to the death penalty, deportations, slavery, prostitution, trafficking in women and children. To this list we must add irresponsible practices of genetic engineering, such as the cloning and use of human embryos for research, which are justified by an illegitimate appeal to freedom, to cultural progress, to the advancement of mankind. When the weakest and most vulnerable members of society are subjected to such atrocities, the very idea of the human family, built on the value of the person, on trust, respect and mutual support, is dangerously eroded. A civilization based on love and peace must oppose these experiments, which are unworthy of man.

The value of education

20.   In order to build the civilization of love, dialogue between cultures must work to overcome all ethnocentric selfishness and make it possible to combine regard for one's own identity with understanding of others and respect for diversity. Fundamental in this respect is the *responsibility of education*. Education must make students aware of their own roots and provide points of reference which allow them to define their own personal place in the world. At the same time, it must be committed to teaching respect for other cultures. There is a need to look beyond one's immediate personal experience and accept differences, discovering the richness to be found in other people's history and in their values.

Knowledge of other cultures, acquired with an appropriate critical sense and within a solid ethical framework, leads to a deeper awareness of the values and limitations within one's own culture, and at the same time it reveals the existence of a patrimony that is common to the whole of humanity. Thanks precisely to this broadening of horizons, *education has a particular role to play in building a more united and peaceful world*. It can help to affirm that integral humanism, open to life's ethical and religious dimension, which appreciates the importance of understanding and showing esteem for other cultures and the spiritual values present in them.

Forgiveness and reconciliation

21.   During the Great Jubilee, two thousand years after the birth of Jesus, the Church has had a powerful experience of *the challenging call to reconciliation*. This call is significant also in the context of the complex issue of dialogue between cultures. Dialogue in fact is often difficult because it is weighed down by the tragic heritage of war, conflict, violence and hatred, which lives on in people's memory. For the barriers caused by noncommunication to be bridged, the path to take is the path of forgiveness and reconciliation. Many people, in the name of a disillusioned realism, maintain that this is a utopian and

naive path. From the Christian point of view it is the only path which leads to the goal of peace.

The eyes of believers contemplate the image of the Crucified One. Shortly before dying, Jesus exclaims: 'Father, forgive them, for they know not what they do' (*Lk* 23:34). The evil-doer crucified on his right, hearing these last words of the dying Redeemer, opens his heart to the grace of conversion, welcomes the Gospel of forgiveness and receives the promise of eternal happiness. The example of Christ makes us certain that the many impediments to communication and dialogue between people can indeed be torn down. Gazing upon the Crucified One we are filled with confidence that forgiveness and reconciliation can become the normal practice of everyday life and of every culture, and thus a real opportunity for building humanity's peace and future.

Mindful of the significant Jubilee experience of the purification of memory, I wish to make a specific appeal to Christians to become witnesses to and missionaries of forgiveness and reconciliation. In this way, through their active invocation of the God of peace, they will hasten the fulfilment of Isaiah's splendid prophecy, which can be applied to all the peoples of the earth: 'In that day there will be a highway from Egypt to Assyria, and the Assyrian will come into Egypt, and the Egyptian into Assyria, and the Egyptians will worship with the Assyrians. In that day Israel will be the third with Egypt and Assyria, a blessing in the midst of the earth, whom the Lord of hosts has blessed, saying, "Blessed be Egypt my people, and Assyria the work of my hands, and Israel my heritage"' (*Is* 19:23–25).

An appeal to young people

22. I wish to conclude this Message of peace with a special appeal to you, *young people of the whole world*, who are humanity's future and living stones in the building of the civilization of love. I treasure in my heart the memory of the emotional and hope-filled meetings which we had during the recent World Youth Day in Rome. Your participation was

joyous, sincere and reassuring. In your energy and vitality, and in your love of Christ, I was able to glimpse a more peaceful and human future for the world.

Feeling your closeness to me, I sensed a profound gratitude to the Lord who gave me the grace of contemplating – through the multicoloured mosaic of your different languages, cultures, customs and ways of thinking – *the miracle of the universality of the Church*, of her catholicity, of her unity. Through you I was able to admire *the marvellous coming together of diversity in the unity* of the same faith, the same hope, the same love. Here was an eloquent expression of the wondrous reality of the Church, sign and instrument of Christ for the salvation of the world and for the unity of mankind.[10] The Gospel calls you to rebuild the original unity of the human family, which has its source in God the Father, Son and Holy Spirit.

Dear young people of every language and culture, *a high and exhilarating task* awaits you: that of becoming men and women capable of solidarity, peace and love of life, with respect for everyone. Become craftsmen of a new humanity, where brothers and sisters – members all of the same family – are able at last to live in peace.

Notes

1   Second Vatican Ecumenical Council, Pastoral Constitution on the Church in the Modern World *Gaudium et Spes*, 53.
2   Cf. John Paul II, Address to the United Nations (15 October 1995).
3   Cf. Second Vatican Ecumenical Council, Pastoral Constitution on the Church in the Modern World *Gaudium et Spes*, 75.
4   Cf. *ibid.*, 22.
5   *Ibid.*, 10.
6   John Paul II, Address to UNESCO (2 June 1980), No. 6.
7   Pastoral Constitution on the Church in the Modern World *Gaudium et Spes*, 36.
8   Second Vatican Ecumenical Council, Declaration on Religious Freedom *Dignitatis Humanae*, 1.
9   John Paul II, Encyclical Letter *Centesimus Annus*, 58.
10   Cf. Second Vatican Ecumenical Council, Dogmatic Constitution on the Church *Lumen Gentium*, 1.

1 January 2002
NO PEACE WITHOUT JUSTICE, NO JUSTICE WITHOUT FORGIVENESS

Issued after the USA September 11 terrorist attack, this message is offered by a Pope who shares how, throughout his own life and in the light of his own experiences of Nazism and Communism, he has struggled with the question: 'how do we restore the moral and social order subjected to such horrific violence?' His 'reasoned conviction' confirmed by biblical revelation is that only a response that combines justice with the form of love that is forgiveness can restore shattered order. He knows it's difficult to talk of this. If peace is the work of justice and tranquillity of order, it needs forgiveness 'in all circumstances great and small' to heal and rebuild troubled human relations from their foundations. While affirming the right to defend oneself against terrorism he warns against extending criminal culpability to the nation, ethnic group or religion to which terrorists belong. He goes to the root of the fundamentalism that leads to terrorism and asserts that as well as being a hatred of humanity, such fundamentalism exploits God: 'consequently, no religious leader can condone terrorism, and must less preach it.' Forgiveness finds its perfect exemplar in Christ on the cross but even human reason asks: 'why not do to others what you would want them to do to you?' The Pope encourages Jewish, Christian and Islamic religious leaders to take the lead in publicly condemning terrorism and form morally sound public opinion. He writes of the forthcoming prayer for peace in Assisi.

* * *

1. The World Day of Peace this year is being celebrated in the shadow of the dramatic events of 11 September last. On that day, a terrible crime was committed: in a few brief hours thousands of innocent people of many ethnic backgrounds were slaughtered. Since then, people throughout the world have felt a profound personal vulnerability and a new fear for the future. Addressing this state of mind, the Church testifies to her hope, based on the conviction that evil, the *mysterium iniquitatis*, does not have the final word in human affairs. The history of salvation, narrated in Sacred Scripture, sheds clear light on the entire history of the world and shows us that human events are always accompanied by the merciful Providence of God, who knows how to touch even the most hardened of hearts and bring good fruits even from what seems utterly barren soil.

This is the hope which sustains the Church at the beginning of 2002: that, by the grace of God, a world in which the power of evil seems once again to have taken the upper hand will in fact be transformed into a world in which the noblest aspirations of the human heart will triumph, a world in which true peace will prevail.

Peace: the work of justice and love

2. Recent events, including the terrible killings just mentioned, move me to return to a theme which often stirs in the depths of my heart when I remember the events of history which have marked my life, especially my youth.

The enormous suffering of peoples and individuals, even among my own friends and acquaintances, caused by Nazi and Communist totalitarianism, has never been far from my thoughts and prayers. I have often paused to reflect on the persistent question: *how do we restore the moral and social order subjected to such horrific violence?* My reasoned conviction, confirmed in turn by biblical revelation, is that the shattered order cannot be fully restored except by a response that combines justice with forgiveness. *The pillars of true peace are justice and that form of love which is forgiveness.*

3.   But in the present circumstances, how can we speak of justice and forgiveness as the source and condition of peace? *We can and we must*, no matter how difficult this may be; a difficulty which often comes from thinking that justice and forgiveness are irreconcilable. But forgiveness is the opposite of resentment and revenge, not of justice. In fact, true peace is 'the work of justice' (*Is* 32:17). As the Second Vatican Council put it, peace is 'the fruit of that right ordering of things with which the divine founder has invested human society and which must be actualized by man thirsting for an ever more perfect reign of justice' (Pastoral Constitution *Gaudium et Spes*, 78). For more than fifteen hundred years, the Catholic Church has repeated the teaching of Saint Augustine of Hippo on this point. He reminds us that the peace which can and must be built in this world is the peace of right order – *tranquillitas ordinis*, the tranquillity of order (cf. *De Civitate Dei*, 19,13).

True peace therefore is the fruit of justice, that moral virtue and legal guarantee which ensures full respect for rights and responsibilities, and the just distribution of benefits and burdens. But because human justice is always fragile and imperfect, subject as it is to the limitations and egoism of individuals and groups, it must include and, as it were, be completed by the *forgiveness which heals and rebuilds troubled human relations from their foundations*. This is true in circumstances great and small, at the personal level or on a wider, even international scale. Forgiveness is in no way opposed to justice, as if to forgive meant to overlook the need to right the wrong done. It is rather the fullness of justice, leading to that tranquillity of order which is much more than a fragile and temporary cessation of hostilities, involving as it does the deepest healing of the wounds which fester in human hearts. Justice and forgiveness are both essential to such healing.

It is these two dimensions of peace that I wish to explore in this message. The World Day of Peace this year offers all humanity, and particularly the leaders of nations, the opportunity to reflect upon the demands of justice and the call to forgiveness in the face of the grave problems which continue to afflict the world, not the least of which is *the new level of violence introduced by organized terrorism.*

The reality of terrorism

4.   It is precisely peace born of justice and forgiveness that is under assault today by international terrorism. In recent years, especially since the end of the Cold War, terrorism has developed into a sophisticated network of political, economic and technical collusion which goes beyond national borders to embrace the whole world. Well-organized terrorist groups can count on huge financial resources and develop wide-ranging strategies, striking innocent people who have nothing to do with the aims pursued by the terrorists.

When terrorist organizations use their own followers as weapons to be launched against defenceless and unsuspecting people they show clearly the death-wish that feeds them. Terrorism springs from hatred, and it generates isolation, mistrust and closure. Violence is added to violence in a tragic sequence that exasperates successive generations, each one inheriting the hatred which divided those that went before. *Terrorism is built on contempt for human life.* For this reason, not only does it commit intolerable crimes, but because it resorts to terror as a political and military means it is itself *a true crime against humanity.*

5.   *There exists therefore a right to defend oneself against terrorism,* a right which, as always, must be exercised with respect for moral and legal limits in the choice of ends and means. The guilty must be correctly identified, since criminal culpability is always personal and cannot be extended to the nation, ethnic group or religion to which the terrorists may belong. International cooperation in the fight against terrorist activities must also include a courageous and resolute political, diplomatic and economic commitment to relieving situations of oppression and marginalization which facilitate the designs

of terrorists. The recruitment of terrorists in fact is easier in situations where rights are trampled upon and injustices tolerated over a long period of time.

Still, it must be firmly stated that the injustices existing in the world can never be used to excuse acts of terrorism, and it should be noted that the victims of the radical breakdown of order which terrorism seeks to achieve include above all the countless millions of men and women who are least well-positioned to withstand a collapse of international solidarity – namely, the people of the developing world, who already live on a thin margin of survival and who would be most grievously affected by global economic and political chaos. The terrorist claim to be acting on behalf of the poor is a patent falsehood.

You shall not kill in God's name!

6.   Those who kill by acts of terrorism actually despair of humanity, of life, of the future. In their view, everything is to be hated and destroyed. Terrorists hold that the truth in which they believe or the suffering that they have undergone are so absolute that their reaction in destroying even innocent lives is justified. Terrorism is often the outcome of that fanatic *fundamentalism* which springs from the conviction that one's own vision of the truth must be forced upon everyone else. Instead, even when the truth has been reached – and this can happen only in a limited and imperfect way – it can never be imposed. Respect for a person's conscience, where the image of God himself is reflected (cf. *Gen* 1:26–27), means that we can only propose the truth to others, who are then responsible for accepting it. To try to impose on others by violent means what we consider to be the truth is an offence against human dignity, and ultimately an offence against God whose image that person bears. For this reason, what is usually referred to as fundamentalism is an attitude radically opposed to belief in God. *Terrorism exploits not just people, it exploits God:* it ends by making him an idol to be used for one's own purposes.

7. *Consequently, no religious leader can condone terrorism, and much less preach it.* It is a profanation of religion to declare oneself a terrorist in the name of God, to do violence to others in his name. Terrorist violence is a contradiction of faith in God, the Creator of man, who cares for man and loves him. It is altogether contrary to faith in Christ the Lord, who taught his disciples to pray: *'Forgive us our debts, as we also have forgiven our debtors'* (Mt 6:12).

Following the teaching and example of Jesus, Christians hold that to show mercy is to live out the truth of our lives: we can and must be merciful because mercy has been shown us by a God who is Love (cf. *1 Jn* 4:7–12). The God who enters into history to redeem us, and through the dramatic events of Good Friday prepares the victory of Easter Sunday, is a God of mercy and forgiveness (cf. *Ps* 103:3–4, 10–13). Thus Jesus told those who challenged his dining with sinners: 'Go and learn what this means, "I desire mercy and not sacrifice". For I came not to call the righteous, but sinners' (*Mt* 9:13). The followers of Christ, baptized into his redeeming Death and Resurrection, must always be men and women of mercy and forgiveness.

The need for forgiveness

8. *But what does forgiveness actually mean? And why should we forgive?* A reflection on forgiveness cannot avoid these questions. Returning to what I wrote in my Message for the 1997 World Day of Peace ('Offer Forgiveness and Receive Peace'), I would reaffirm that forgiveness inhabits people's hearts before it becomes a social reality. Only to the degree that an ethics and a culture of forgiveness prevail can we hope for a 'politics' of forgiveness, expressed in society's attitudes and laws, so that through them justice takes on a more human character.

Forgiveness is above all a personal choice, a decision of the heart to go against the natural instinct to pay back evil with evil. The measure of such a decision is the love of God who draws us to himself in spite of our sin. It has its perfect exemplar in the forgiveness of Christ, who on the Cross prayed: 'Father, forgive them; for they know not what they do' (*Lk* 23:34).

Forgiveness therefore has a divine source and criterion. This does not mean that its significance cannot also be grasped in the light of human reasoning; and this, in the first place, on the basis of what people experience when they do wrong. They experience their human weakness, and they want others to deal leniently with them. Why not therefore do towards others what we want them to do towards us? All human beings cherish the hope of being able to start all over again, and not remain for ever shut up in their own mistakes and guilt. They all want to raise their eyes to the future and to discover new possibilities of trust and commitment.

9.   Forgiveness therefore, as a fully human act, is above all a personal initiative. But individuals are essentially social beings, situated within a pattern of relationships through which they express themselves in ways both good and bad. Consequently, *society too is absolutely in need of forgiveness*. Families, groups, societies, States and the international community itself need forgiveness in order to renew ties that have been sundered, go beyond sterile situations of mutual condemnation and overcome the temptation to discriminate against others without appeal. *The ability to forgive lies at the very basis of the idea of a future society marked by justice and solidarity.*

By contrast, the failure to forgive, especially when it serves to prolong conflict, is extremely costly in terms of human development. Resources are used for weapons rather than for development, peace and justice. What sufferings are inflicted on humanity because of the failure to reconcile! What delays in progress because of the failure to forgive! *Peace is essential for development, but true peace is made possible only through*

Forgiveness, the high road

10.   Forgiveness is not a proposal that can be immediately understood or easily accepted; in many ways it is a paradoxical message. Forgiveness in fact always involves an *apparent* short-term loss for a *real* long-term gain. Violence is the exact opposite; opting as it does for an apparent short-term gain, it involves a

real and permanent loss. Forgiveness may seem like weakness, but it demands great spiritual strength and moral courage, both in granting it and in accepting it. It may seem in some way to diminish us, but in fact it leads us to a fuller and richer humanity, more radiant with the splendour of the Creator.

My ministry at the service of the Gospel obliges me, and at the same time gives me the strength, to insist upon the necessity of forgiveness. I do so again today in the hope of stirring serious and mature thinking on this theme, with a view to *a far-reaching resurgence of the human spirit in individual hearts and in relations between the peoples of the world.*

11.   Reflecting on forgiveness, our minds turn naturally to certain situations of conflict which endlessly feed deep and divisive hatreds and a seemingly unstoppable sequence of personal and collective tragedies. I refer especially to what is happening in the Holy Land, that blessed place of God's encounter with man, where Jesus, the Prince of Peace, lived, died and rose from the dead.

The present troubled international situation prompts a more intense call to resolve the Arab-Israeli conflict, which has now been going on for more than fifty years, with alternate phases of greater or lesser tension. The continuous recourse to acts of terror and war, which aggravate the situation and diminish hope on all sides, must finally give way to a negotiated solution. The rights and demands of each party can be taken into proper account and balanced in an equitable way, if and when there is a will to let justice and reconciliation prevail. Once more I urge the beloved peoples of the Holy Land to work for a new era of mutual respect and constructive accord.

Interreligious understanding and cooperation

12.   In this whole effort, religious leaders have a weighty responsibility. The various Christian confessions, as well as the world's great religions, need to work together to eliminate the social and cultural causes of terrorism. They can do this by teaching the greatness and dignity of the human person, and by

spreading *a clearer sense of the oneness of the human family*. This is a specific area of ecumenical and interreligious dialogue and cooperation, a pressing service which religion can offer to world peace.

In particular, I am convinced that Jewish, Christian and Islamic religious leaders must now take the lead in publicly condemning terrorism and in denying terrorists any form of religious or moral legitimacy.

13. In bearing common witness to the truth that the deliberate murder of the innocent is a grave evil always, everywhere, and without exception, the world's religious leaders will help to form the morally sound public opinion that is essential for building an international civil society capable of pursuing the tranquillity of order in justice and freedom.

In undertaking such a commitment, the various religions cannot but pursue *the path of forgiveness*, which opens the way to mutual understanding, respect and trust. The help that religions can give to peace and against terrorism consists precisely in their *teaching forgiveness*, for those who forgive and seek forgiveness know that there is a higher Truth, and that by accepting that Truth they can transcend themselves.

Prayer for peace

14. Precisely for this reason, prayer for peace is not an afterthought to the work of peace. It is of the very essence of building the peace of order, justice, and freedom. To pray for peace is to open the human heart to the inroads of God's power to renew all things. With the life-giving force of his grace, God can create openings for peace where only obstacles and closures are apparent; he can strengthen and enlarge the solidarity of the human family in spite of our endless history of division and conflict. To pray for peace is to pray for justice, for a right-ordering of relations within and among nations and peoples. It is to pray for freedom, especially for the religious freedom that is a basic human and civil right of every individual. To pray for

peace is to seek God's forgiveness, and to implore the courage to forgive those who have trespassed against us.

For all these reasons I have invited representatives of the world's religions to come to Assisi, the town of Saint Francis, on 24 January 2002, to pray for peace. In doing so we will show that genuine religious belief is an inexhaustible wellspring of mutual respect and harmony among peoples; indeed it is the chief antidote to violence and conflict. At this time of great distress, the human family needs to be reminded of our unfailing reasons for hope. It is precisely this hope that we intend to proclaim in Assisi, *asking Almighty God*—in the beautiful phrase attributed to Saint Francis himself—*to make each of us a channel of his peace.*

15.   *No peace without justice, no justice without forgiveness*: this is what in this Message I wish to say to believers and non-believers alike, to all men and women of good will who are concerned for the good of the human family and for its future.

No peace without justice, no justice without forgiveness: this is what I wish to say to those responsible for the future of the human community, entreating them to be guided in their weighty and difficult decisions by the light of man's true good, always with a view to the common good.

No peace without justice, no justice without forgiveness: I shall not tire of repeating this warning to those who, for one reason or another, nourish feelings of hatred, a desire for revenge or the will to destroy.

On this World Day of Peace, may a more intense prayer rise from the hearts of all believers for the victims of terrorism, for their families so tragically stricken, for all the peoples who continue to be hurt and convulsed by terrorism and war. May the light of our prayer extend even to those who gravely offend God and man by these pitiless acts, that they may look into their hearts, see the evil of what they do, abandon all violent intentions, and seek forgiveness. In these troubled times, may the whole human family find true and lasting peace, born of the marriage of justice and mercy!

1 January 2003

PACEM IN TERRIS: A PERMANENT COMMITMENT

In the 2003 message Pope John Paul II proposes we revisit Pope John XXIII's encyclical, Pacem in terris issued forty years previously in 1963 and learn from its prophetic teaching. Pope John XXIII saw that despite many negative signs at that time, something more was at work in human affairs bringing about a spiritual revolution in history. He saw the world becoming increasingly conscious of the conviction that all human beings are equal by reason of their natural dignity and with this a growth in awareness of human rights. Pope John Paul comments that indeed human rights movements subsequently gave rise to one of the great dynamics of contemporary history: the quest for freedom as an indispensable component of work for peace. In a world becoming increasingly interdependent, Pope John XXIII looked with hope to the UN and its Universal Declaration of Human Rights. He spoke of the need for a public authority on the international plane with effective capacity to advance the universal common good. Pope John Paul II reviews both the many positive developments since 1963 and highlights some contemporary trends. He notes the failure to insist sufficiently on duties as well as rights. Taking up again St Augustine's notion of peace as 'tranquillity of order', John Paul II discusses the principles upon which new forms of world order are unfolding and calls for a new constitutional organization of the human family.

* * *

1.   Almost forty years ago, on Holy Thursday, 11 April 1963, Pope John XXIII published his epic Encyclical Letter *Pacem in Terris*. Addressing himself to 'all men of good will', my venerable predecessor, who would die just two months later, summed up his message of 'peace on earth' in the first sentence of the Encyclical: 'Peace on earth, which all men of every era have most eagerly yearned for, can be firmly established and sustained only if the order laid down by God be dutifully observed' (*Introduction: AAS, 55* [1963], 257).

Speaking peace to a divided world

2.   The world to which John XXIII wrote was then in a profound state of disorder. The twentieth century had begun with great expectations for progress. Yet within sixty years, that same century had produced two World Wars, devastating totalitarian systems, untold human suffering, and the greatest persecution of the Church in history.

Only two years before *Pacem in Terris*, in 1961, the Berlin Wall had been erected in order to divide and set against each other not only two parts of that City but two ways of understanding and building the earthly city. On one side and the other of the Wall, life was to follow different patterns, dictated by antithetical rules, in a climate of mutual suspicion and mistrust. Both as a world-view and in real life, that Wall traversed the whole of humanity and penetrated people's hearts and minds, creating divisions that seemed destined to last indefinitely.

Moreover, just six months before the Encyclical, and just as the Second Vatican Council was opening in Rome, the world had come to the brink of a nuclear war during the Cuban Missile Crisis. The road to a world of peace, justice and freedom seemed blocked. Humanity, many believed, was condemned to live indefinitely in that precarious condition of 'cold war', hoping against hope that neither an act of aggression nor an accident would trigger the worst war in human history. Available atomic arsenals meant that such a war would have imperiled the very future of the human race.

The four pillars of peace

3. Pope John XXIII did not agree with those who claimed that peace was impossible. With his Encyclical, *peace* – in all its demanding truth – came knocking on both sides of the Wall and of all the other dividing walls. The Encyclical spoke to everyone of their belonging to the one human family, and shone a light on the shared aspiration of people everywhere to live in security, justice and hope for the future.

With the profound intuition that characterized him, John XXIII identified the essential conditions for peace in four precise requirements of the human spirit: *truth, justice, love* and *freedom* (cf. *ibid.*, I: *l.c.*, 265–266). *Truth* will build peace if every individual sincerely acknowledges not only his rights, but also his own duties towards others. *Justice* will build peace if in practice everyone respects the rights of others and actually fulfils his duties towards them. *Love* will build peace if people feel the needs of others as their own and share what they have with others, especially the values of mind and spirit which they possess. *Freedom* will build peace and make it thrive if, in the choice of the means to that end, people act according to reason and assume responsibility for their own actions.

Looking at the present and into the future with the eyes of faith and reason, Blessed John XXIII discerned deeper historical currents at work. Things were not always what they seemed on the surface. Despite wars and rumours of wars, something more was at work in human affairs, something that to the Pope looked like the promising beginning of a spiritual revolution.

A new awareness of human dignity and inalienable human rights

4. Humanity, John XXIII wrote, had entered a new stage of its journey (cf. *ibid.*, I: *l.c.*, 267–269). The end of colonialism and the rise of newly independent States, the protection of workers' rights, the new and welcome presence of women in public life, all testified to the fact that the human race was

indeed entering a new phase of its history, one characterized by *'the conviction that all men are equal by reason of their natural dignity'* (*ibid.*, I: *l.c.*,268). The Pope knew that that dignity was still being trampled upon in many parts of the world. Yet he was convinced that, despite the dramatic situation, the world was becoming increasingly *conscious of certain spiritual values*, and increasingly open to the meaning of those *pillars of peace* – truth, justice, love, and freedom (cf. *ibid.*, I: *l.c.*, 268-269). Seeking to bring these values into local, national and international life, men and women were becoming more aware that their relationship with God, the source of all good, must be the solid foundation and supreme criterion of their lives, as individuals and in society (cf. *ibid.*). This evolving spiritual intuition would, the Pope was convinced, have profound public and political consequences.

Seeing the growth of awareness of human rights that was then emerging within nations and at the international level, Pope John XXIII caught the potential of this phenomenon and understood its singular power to change history. What was later to happen in central and eastern Europe would confirm his insight. The road to peace, he taught in the Encyclical, lay in the defence and promotion of basic human rights, which every human being enjoys, not as a benefit given by a different social class or conceded by the State but simply because of our humanity: 'Any human society, if it is to be well-ordered and productive, must lay down as a foundation this principle, namely, that every human being is a person, that is, his nature is endowed with intelligence and free will. Indeed, precisely because he is a person he has rights and obligations, flowing directly and simultaneously from his very nature. And as these rights and obligations are universal and inviolable so they cannot in any way be surrendered' (*ibid.*, 259).

As history would soon show, this was not simply an abstract idea; it was an idea with profound consequences. Inspired by the conviction that every human being is equal in dignity, and that society therefore had to adapt its form to that conviction, *human rights movements* soon arose and gave concrete political

313

expression to one of the great dynamics of contemporary history: the quest for freedom as an indispensable component of work for peace. Emerging in virtually every part of the world, these movements were instrumental in replacing dictatorial forms of government with more democratic and participatory ones. They demonstrated in practice that peace and progress could only be achieved by respecting *the universal moral law written on the human heart* (cf. John Paul II, *Address to the United Nations General Assembly*, 5 October 1995, No. 3).

The universal common good

5.   On another point too *Pacem in Terris* showed itself prophetic, as it looked to the next phase of the evolution of world politics. Because the world was becoming increasingly interdependent and global, the common good of humanity had to be worked out on the international plane. It was proper, Pope John XXIII taught, to speak of a *'universal common good'* (*Pacem in Terris*, IV: *l.c.*, 292). One of the consequences of this evolution was the obvious need for *a public authority, on the international level*, with effective capacity to advance the universal common good; an authority which could not, the Pope immediately continued, be established by coercion but only by the consent of nations. Such a body would have to have as its fundamental objective the 'recognition, respect, safeguarding, and promotion of the rights of the human person' (*ibid.*, IV: *l.c.*, 294).

Not surprisingly therefore John XXIII looked with hope and expectation to the United Nations Organization, which had come into being on June 26, 1945. He saw that Organization as a credible instrument for maintaining and strengthening world peace, and he expressed particular appreciation of its 1948 *Universal Declaration of Human Rights*, which he considered 'an approximation towards the establishment of a juridical and political organization of the world community' (*ibid.*, IV: *l.c.*, 295). What he was saying in fact was that the *Declaration* set out the moral foundations on which the evolution of a world characterized by order rather than disorder, and by dialogue rather than force, could proceed. He was suggesting that the vigorous defence of human rights by the United Nations Organization is the indispensable foundation for the development of that Organization's capacity to promote and defend international security.

Not only is it clear that Pope John XXIII's vision of an effective international public authority at the service of human rights, freedom and peace has not yet been entirely achieved, but there is still in fact much hesitation in the international community about the obligation to respect and implement human rights. This duty touches *all* fundamental rights, excluding that arbitrary picking and choosing which can lead to rationalizing forms of discrimination and injustice. Likewise, we are witnessing the emergence of an alarming gap between a series of new 'rights' being promoted in advanced societies – the result of new prosperity and new technologies – and other more basic human rights still not being met, especially in situations of underdevelopment. I am thinking here for example about the right to food and drinkable water, to housing and security, to self-determination and independence – which are still far from being guaranteed and realized. *Peace demands that this tension be speedily reduced and in time eliminated.*

Another observation needs to be made: the international community, which since 1948 has possessed a charter of the inalienable rights of the human person, has generally failed to *insist sufficiently on corresponding duties.* It is *duty* that establishes the limits within which *rights* must be contained in order not to become an exercise in arbitrariness. A greater awareness of *universal human duties* would greatly benefit the cause of peace, setting it on the moral basis of a shared recognition of *an order in things* which is not dependent on the will of any individual or group.

A new international moral order

6.   Nevertheless it remains true that, despite many difficulties and setbacks, *significant progress has been made*

315

over the past forty years towards the implementation of Pope John's noble vision. The fact that States throughout the world feel obliged to honour the idea of human rights shows how powerful are the tools of moral conviction and spiritual integrity, which proved so decisive in the revolution of conscience that made possible the 1989 non-violent revolution that displaced European communism. And although distorted notions of freedom as licence continue to threaten democracy and free societies, it is surely significant that, in the forty years since *Pacem in Terris*, much of the world has become more free, structures of dialogue and cooperation between nations have been strengthened, and the threat of a global nuclear war, which weighed so heavily on Pope John XXIII, has been effectively contained.

Boldly, but with all humility, I would like to suggest that the Church's fifteen-hundred-year-old teaching on peace as *'tranquillitas ordinis* – the tranquillity of order' as Saint Augustine called it (*De Civitate Dei*, 19, 13), which was brought to a new level of development forty years ago by *Pacem in Terris,* has a deep relevance for the world today, for the leaders of nations as well as for individuals. That there is serious disorder in world affairs is obvious. Thus the question to be faced remains: *What kind of order can replace this disorder*, so that men and women can live in freedom, justice, and security? And since the world, amid its disorder, continues nevertheless to be 'ordered' and organized in various ways – economic, cultural, even political – there arises another equally urgent question: On what principles are these new forms of world order unfolding?

These far-reaching questions suggest that the problem of order in world affairs, which is the problem of peace rightly understood, cannot be separated from issues of moral principle. This is another way of saying that the question of peace cannot be separated from the question of human dignity and human rights. That is one of the enduring truths taught by *Pacem in Terris*, which we would do well to remember and reflect upon on this fortieth anniversary.

Is this not the time for all to *work together for a new constitutional organization of the human family*, truly capable of ensuring peace and harmony between peoples, as well as their integral development? But let there be no misunderstanding. This does not mean writing the constitution of a global super-State. Rather, it means continuing and deepening processes already in place to meet the almost universal *demand for participatory ways of exercising political authority, even international political authority, and for transparency and accountability at every level of public life*. With his confidence in the goodness he believed could be found in every human person, Pope John XXIII called the entire world to a nobler vision of public life and public authority, even as he boldly challenged the world to think beyond its present state of disorder to new forms of international order commensurate with human dignity.

The bond between peace and truth

7.   Against those who think of politics as a realm of necessity detached from morality and subject only to partisan interests, Pope John XXIII, in *Pacem in Terris*, outlined a truer picture of human reality and indicated the path to a better future for all. Precisely because human beings are created with the capacity for moral choice, *no human activity takes place outside the sphere of moral judgment*. Politics is a human activity; therefore, it too is subject to a distinctive form of moral scrutiny. This is also true of international politics. As the Pope wrote: 'The same natural law that governs the life and conduct of individuals must also regulate the relations of political communities with one another' (*Pacem in Terris*, III: *l.c.*, 279). Those who imagine that international public life takes place somewhere outside the realm of moral judgment need only reflect on the impact of *human rights movements* on the national and international politics of the twentieth century just concluded. These developments, anticipated by the teaching of the Encyclical, decisively refute the claim that international politics must of necessity be a 'free zone' in which the moral law holds no sway.

317

Perhaps nowhere today is there a more obvious need for the correct use of political authority than in *the dramatic situation of the Middle East and the Holy Land*. Day after day, year after year, the cumulative effect of bitter mutual rejection and an unending chain of violence and retaliation have shattered every effort so far to engage in serious dialogue on the real issues involved. The volatility of the situation is compounded by the clash of interests among the members of the international community. Until those in positions of responsibility undergo a veritable revolution in the way they use their power and go about securing their peoples' welfare, it is difficult to imagine how progress towards peace can be made. The fratricidal struggle that daily convulses the Holy Land and brings into conflict the forces shaping the immediate future of the Middle East shows clearly the need for men and women who, out of conviction, will implement policies firmly based on the principle of respect for human dignity and human rights. Such policies are incomparably more advantageous to everyone than the continuation of conflict. A start can be made on the basis of this truth, which is certainly more liberating than propaganda, especially when that propaganda serves to conceal inadmissible intentions.

The premises of a lasting peace

8.   There is an unbreakable bond between *the work of peace* and *respect for truth*. Honesty in the supply of information, equity in legal systems, openness in democratic procedures give citizens a sense of security, a readiness to settle controversies by peaceful means, and a desire for genuine and constructive dialogue, all of which constitute *the true premises of a lasting peace*. Political summits on the regional and international levels serve the cause of peace only if joint commitments are then honoured by each party. Otherwise these meetings risk becoming irrelevant and useless, with the result that people believe less and less in dialogue and trust more in the use of force as a way of resolving issues. The negative repercussions on peace resulting from commitments made and then not

honoured must be carefully assessed by State and government leaders.

Pacta sunt servanda, says the ancient maxim. If at all times commitments ought to be kept, *promises made to the poor should be considered particularly binding*. Especially frustrating for them is any breach of faith regarding promises which they see as vital to their well-being. In this respect, the failure to keep commitments in the sphere of aid to developing nations is a serious moral question and further highlights the injustice of the imbalances existing in the world. *The suffering caused by poverty is compounded by the loss of trust.* The end result is hopelessness. The existence of trust in international relations is *a social capital of fundamental value*.

A culture of peace

9.   In the end, peace is not essentially about *struc*tures but about *people*. Certain structures and mechanisms of peace – juridical, political, economic – are of course necessary and do exist, but they have been derived from nothing other than the accumulated wisdom and experience of *innumerable gestures of peace* made by men and women throughout history who have kept hope and have not given in to discouragement. *Gestures of peace* spring from the lives of people who *foster peace first of all in their own hearts*. They are the work of the heart and of reason in those who are peacemakers (cf. *Mt* 5:9). *Gestures of peace* are possible when people *appreciate fully the community dimension of their lives*, so that they grasp the meaning and consequences of events in their own communities and in the world. *Gestures of peace* create a tradition and a culture of peace.

Religion has a vital role in fostering gestures of peace and in consolidating conditions for peace. It exercises this role all the more effectively if it concentrates on what is proper to it: attention to God, the fostering of universal brotherhood and the spreading of a culture of human solidarity. The *Day of Prayer for Peace* which I promoted in Assisi on 24 January 2002, involving representatives of many religions, had this purpose. It expressed a desire to nurture peace by spreading a spirituality and a culture of peace.

The legacy of Pacem in Terris

10.   Blessed Pope John XXIII was a man unafraid of the future. He was sustained in his optimism by his deep trust in God and in man, both of which grew out of the sturdy climate of faith in which he had grown up. Moved by his trust in Providence, even in what seemed like a permanent situation of conflict, he did not hesitate to summon the leaders of his time to a new vision of the world. This is the legacy that he left us. On this World Day of Peace 2003, let us all resolve to have his same outlook: trust in the merciful and compassionate God who calls us to brotherhood, and confidence in the men and women of our time because, like those of every other time, they bear the image of God in their souls. It is on this basis that we can hope to build a world of peace on earth.

At the beginning of a new year in our human history, this is the hope that rises spontaneously from the depths of my heart: that in the spirit of every individual there may be a renewed dedication to the noble mission which *Pacem in Terris* proposed forty years ago to all men and women of good will. The task, which the Encyclical called 'immense', is that 'of establishing new relationships in human society, under the sway and guidance of truth, justice, love, and freedom'. Pope John indicated that he was referring to 'relations between individual citizens, between citizens and their respective States, between States, and finally between individuals, families, intermediate associations and States on the one hand, and the world community on the other'. He concluded by saying that 'to bring about true peace in accordance with divinely established order' was a 'most noble task' (*Pacem in Terris*, V: l.c., 301-302).

The fortieth anniversary of *Pacem in Terris* is an apt occasion to return to Pope John XXIII's prophetic teaching. Catholic communities will know how to celebrate this anniversary during the year with initiatives which, I hope, will have an ecumenical and interreligious character and be open to all those who have a heartfelt desire 'to break through the barriers which divide them, to strengthen the bonds of mutual love, to learn to understand one another and to pardon those who have done them wrong' (*l.c.*, 304).

I accompany this hope with a prayer to Almighty God, the source of all our good. May he who calls us from oppression and conflict to freedom and cooperation for the good of all help people everywhere to build a world of peace ever more solidly established on the four pillars indicated by Blessed Pope John XXIII in his historic Encyclical: *truth, justice, love, freedom.*

1 January 2004

AN EVER TIMELY COMMITMENT: TEACHING PEACE

In his twenty fifth Annual World Day of Peace Message, Pope John Paul comments firstly on the 'science of peace' contained in Pope Paul VI's messages and then his own messages defined as a 'kind of primer' containing 'the various colours of the prism of peace'. In continuing the Church's constant teaching that 'Peace is possible', the main focus of this year's message is the role of international law in favouring peace. He briefly traces the history of the emergence of the 'law of the nations'. He deals at length on the need for profound renewal of the international legal order. Referring to the UN, its Security Council and Charter, he examines the exceptions to the prohibition of the use of force. Despite the difficulties experienced by the UN, he notes the UN's 'notable contribution' to the promotion of respect for human dignity and peace-building. By way of encouraging reform, he underlines how the ideals of the UN have become widely diffused and in this context he mentions Non-Governmental Organizations and Movements for human rights. He calls on the UN to become 'a moral centre where all the nations of the world feel at home...a family of nations'. We are reminded of an ancient adage, 'preserve order and order will preserve you'. By way of conclusion the Pope develops the theme of the civilization of love where justice and love are two faces of a single reality. His final word is the ancient maxim: Omnia vincit amor (Love conquers all).

* * *

My words are addressed to you, the Leaders of the nations, who have the duty of promoting peace!

To you, Jurists, committed to tracing paths to peaceful agreement, preparing conventions and treaties which strengthen international legality!

To you, Teachers of the young, who on all continents work tirelessly to form consciences in the ways of understanding and dialogue!

And to you too, men and women tempted to turn to the unacceptable means of terrorism and thus compromise at its root the very cause for which you are fighting!

All of you, hear the humble appeal of the Successor of Peter who cries out: today too, at the beginning of the New Year 2004, *peace remains possible*. And if peace is possible, *it is also a duty!*

A practical initiative

1.   My first Message for the World Day of Peace, in the beginning of January 1979, was centred on the theme: *'To Reach Peace, Teach Peace'.*

That New Year's Message followed in the path traced by Pope Paul VI of venerable memory, who had wished to celebrate on January 1 each year a World Day of Prayer for Peace. I recall the words of the late Pontiff for the New Year 1968: 'It would be Our desire, then, that this celebration take place each year as a sign of hope and promise, at the beginning of the calendar which measures and guides the journey of human life through time, in order that Peace, with its just and salutary equilibrium, will dominate the unfolding of history yet to come'.[1]

Faithful to the wishes expressed by my venerable Predecessor on the Chair of Peter, each year I have continued this noble tradition by dedicating the first day of the civil year to reflection and to prayer for peace in the world.

In the twenty-five years of Pontificate which the Lord has thus far granted me, I have not failed to speak out before the Church and the world, inviting believers and all persons of good will to take up the cause of peace and to help bring about this fundamental good, thereby assuring the world a better future, one marked by peaceful coexistence and mutual respect.

Once more this year I feel bound to invite all men and women, on every continent, to celebrate a new World Day of Peace. Humanity needs now more than ever to rediscover the path of concord, overwhelmed as it is by selfishness and hatred, by the thirst for power and the lust for vengeance.

The science of peace

2.   The eleven Messages addressed to the world by Pope Paul VI progressively mapped out the path to be followed in attaining the ideal of peace. Slowly but surely the great Pontiff set forth the various chapters of a true 'science of peace'. It can be helpful to recall the themes of the Messages bequeathed to us by Pope Paul VI for this occasion.[2] Each of these Messages continues to be timely today. Indeed, before the tragedy of the wars which at the beginning of the Third Millennium are still causing bloodshed throughout the world, especially in the Middle East, they take on at times the tone of prophetic admonishments.

A primer of peace

3.   For my part, throughout these twenty-five years of my Pontificate, I have sought to advance along the path marked out by my venerable Predecessor. At the dawn of each new year I have invited people of good will to reflect, in the light of reason and of faith, on different aspects of an orderly coexistence.

The result has been a synthesis of teaching about peace which is *a kind of primer* on this fundamental theme: a primer easy to understand by those who are well-disposed, but at the same time quite demanding for anyone concerned for the future of humanity.[3]

The various colours of the prism of peace have now been amply illustrated. What remains now is to work to ensure that the ideal of a peaceful coexistence, with its specific requirements, will become part of the consciousness of individuals and peoples. We Christians see the commitment to educate ourselves and others to peace as something at the very heart of our religion. For Christians, in fact, to proclaim peace is to announce Christ who is 'our peace' (*Eph* 2:14); it is to announce his Gospel, which is a 'Gospel of peace' (*Eph* 6:15); it is to call all people to the beatitude of being 'peacemakers' (cf. *Mt* 5:9).

Teaching peace

4.   In my Message for the World Day of Peace on 1 January 1979 I made this appeal: *To Reach Peace, Teach Peace*. Today that appeal is more urgent than ever, because men and women, in the face of the tragedies which continue to afflict humanity, are tempted to yield to fatalism, as if peace were an unattainable ideal.

The Church, on the other hand, has always taught and continues today to teach a very simple axiom: *peace is possible*. Indeed, the Church does not tire of repeating that *peace is a duty*. It must be built on the four pillars indicated by Blessed John XXIII in his Encyclical *Pacem in Terris*: truth, justice, love and freedom. A duty is thus imposed upon all those who love peace: that of *teaching these ideals to new generations*, in order to prepare a better future for all mankind.

Teaching legality

5.   In this task of teaching peace, there is a particularly urgent need to lead individuals and peoples to *respect the international order* and to respect the commitments assumed by the Authorities which legitimately represent them. Peace and international law are closely linked to each another: *law favours peace*.

the very dawn of civilization, developing human communities sought to establish agreements and pacts which would avoid the arbitrary use of force and enable them to seek a peaceful solution of any controversies which might arise. Alongside the legal systems of the individual peoples there progressively grew up another set of norms which came to be known as *ius gentium* (the law of the nations). With the passage of time, this body of law gradually expanded and was refined in the light of the historical experiences of the different peoples.

This process was greatly accelerated with the birth of modern States. From the sixteenth century on, jurists, philosophers and theologians were engaged in developing the various headings of international law and in grounding it in the fundamental postulates of the natural law. This process led with increasing force to the formulation of *universal principles which are prior to and superior to the internal law of States*, and which take into account the unity and the common vocation of the human family.

Central among all these is surely the principle that *pacta sunt servanda*: accords freely signed must be honoured. This is the pivotal and exceptionless presupposition of every relationship between responsible contracting parties. The violation of this principle necessarily leads to a situation of illegality and consequently to friction and disputes which would not fail to have lasting negative repercussions. It is appropriate to recall this fundamental rule, especially at times when there is a temptation to appeal to the *law of force* rather than to the *force of law*.

One of these moments was surely the drama which humanity experienced during the Second World War: an abyss of violence, destruction and death unlike anything previously known.

Respect for law

6.   That war, with the horrors and the appalling violations of human dignity which it occasioned, led to *a profound renewal of the international legal order*. The defence and promotion of peace were set at the centre of a broadly modernized system of

norms and institutions. The task of watching over global peace and security and with encouraging the efforts of States to preserve and guarantee these fundamental goods of humanity was entrusted by Governments to an organization established for this purpose – the *United Nations Organization* – with a *Security Council* invested with broad discretionary power. Pivotal to the system was *the prohibition of the use of force*. This prohibition, according to the well-known Chapter VII of the *United Nations Charter*, makes provision for only two exceptions. The first confirms the *natural right to legitimate defence*, to be exercised in specific ways and in the context of the United Nations: and consequently also within the traditional limits of *necessity* and *proportionality*.

The other exception is represented by the *system of collective security*, which gives the Security Council competence and responsibility for the preservation of peace, with power of decision and ample discretion.

The system developed with the *United Nations Charter* was meant 'to save succeeding generations from the scourge of war, which twice in our lifetime has brought untold sorrow to mankind'.[4] In the decades which followed, however, the division of the international community into opposing blocs, the cold war in one part of the world, the outbreak of violent conflicts in other areas and the phenomenon of terrorism produced a growing break with the ideas and expectations of the immediate post-war period.

A new international order

7.   It must be acknowledged, however, that the United Nations Organization, even with limitations and delays due in great part to the failures of its members, has made a notable contribution to the promotion of respect for human dignity, the freedom of peoples and the requirements of development, thus preparing the cultural and institutional soil for the building of peace.

The activity of national Governments will be greatly encouraged by the realization that the ideals of the United

Nations have become widely diffused, particularly through the practical gestures of solidarity and peace made by the many individuals also involved in *Non-Governmental Organizations* and in *Movements* for human rights.

This represents a significant incentive for a reform which would enable the United Nations Organization to function effectively for the pursuit of its own stated ends, which remain valid: 'humanity today is in a new and more difficult phase of its genuine development. It needs a *greater degree of international ordering*'.[5] States must consider this objective as a clear moral and political obligation which calls for prudence and determination. Here I would repeat the words of encouragement which I spoke in 1995: 'The United Nations Organization needs to rise more and more above the cold status of an administrative institution and to become a moral centre where all the nations of the world feel at home and develop a shared awareness of being, as it were, a *family of nations*'.[6]

The deadly scourge of terrorism

8.   Today international law is hard pressed to provide solutions to situations of conflict arising from the changed landscape of the contemporary world. These situations of conflict frequently involve *agents which are not themselves States* but rather entities derived from the collapse of States, or connected to independence movements, or linked to trained criminal organizations. A legal system made up of norms established down the centuries *as a means of disciplining relations between sovereign States* finds it difficult to deal with conflicts which also involve *entities incapable of being considered States in the traditional sense*. This is particularly the case with terrorist groups.

The scourge of terrorism has become more virulent in recent years and has produced brutal massacres which have in turn put even greater obstacles in the way of dialogue and negotiation, increasing tensions and aggravating problems, especially in the Middle East.

Even so, if it is to be won, *the fight against terrorism cannot be limited solely to repressive and punitive operations*. It is essential that the use of force, even when necessary, be accompanied by a courageous and lucid analysis of the *reasons behind terrorist attacks*. The fight against terrorism must be conducted also on the *political and educational* levels: on the one hand, by eliminating the underlying causes of situations of injustice which frequently drive people to more desperate and violent acts; and on the other hand, by insisting on an education inspired by respect for human life in every situation: the unity of the human race is a more powerful reality than any contingent divisions separating individuals and people.

In the necessary fight against terrorism, international law is now called to develop legal instruments provided with effective means for the prevention, monitoring and suppression of crime. In any event, democratic governments know well that the use of force against terrorists *cannot justify a renunciation of the principles of the rule of law*. Political decisions would be unacceptable were they to seek success without consideration for fundamental human rights, since *the end never justifies the means*.

The contribution of the Church

9. 'Blessed are the peacemakers, for they shall be called sons of God' (*Mt* 5:9). How could this saying, which is a summons to work in the immense field of peace, find such a powerful echo in the human heart if it did not correspond to an irrepressible yearning and hope dwelling within us? And why else would peacemakers be called children of God, if not because God is by nature the God of peace? Precisely for this reason, in the message of salvation which the Church proclaims throughout the world, there are doctrinal elements of fundamental importance for the development of the principles needed for peaceful coexistence between nations.

History teaches that the building of peace cannot prescind from respect for an ethical and juridical order, in accordance with the ancient adage: *'Serva ordinem et ordo servabit te'* (preserve order and order will preserve you). International law must ensure that the law of the more powerful does not prevail. Its essential purpose is to replace 'the material force of arms with the moral force of law',[7] providing appropriate sanctions for transgressors and adequate reparation for victims. This must also be applicable to those government leaders who violate with impunity human dignity and rights while hiding behind the unacceptable pretext that it is a matter of questions internal to their State.

In an Address which I gave to the Diplomatic Corps accredited to the Holy See on 13 January 1997, I observed that *international law* is a primary means for pursuing peace: 'For a long time international law has been a law of war and peace. I believe that it is called more and more to become exclusively a law of peace, conceived in justice and solidarity. And in this context *morality must inspire law*; morality can even assume a preparatory role in the making of law, to the extent that it shows the path of what is right and good'.[8]

Down the centuries, the teaching of the Church, drawing upon the philosophical and theological reflection of many Christian thinkers, has made a significant contribution in directing international law to the common good of the whole human family. Especially in more recent times the Popes have not hesitated to stress the importance of international law as a pledge of peace, in the conviction that 'the harvest of justice is sown in peace by those who make peace' (*Jas* 3:18). This is the path which the Church, employing the means proper to her, is committed to following, in the perennial light of the Gospel and with the indispensable help of prayer.

The civilization of love

10. At the conclusion of these considerations, I feel it necessary to repeat that, for the establishment of true peace in the world, *justice must find its fulfilment in charity*. Certainly law is the first road leading to peace, and people need to be taught to respect that law. Yet one does not arrive at the end of this road unless justice is complemented by love. Justice and

love sometimes appear to be *opposing forces*. In fact they are but *two faces of a single reality*, two dimensions of human life needing to be mutually integrated. Historical experience shows this to be true. It shows how justice is frequently unable to free itself from rancour, hatred and even cruelty. *By itself, justice is not enough*. Indeed, it can even betray itself, unless it is open to that deeper power which is love.

For this reason I have often reminded Christians and all persons of good will that *forgiveness is needed* for solving the problems of individuals and peoples. *There is no peace without forgiveness!* I say it again here, as my thoughts turn in particular to the continuing crisis in Palestine and the Middle East: a solution to the grave problems which for too long have caused suffering for the peoples of those regions will not be found until a decision is made to transcend the logic of simple *justice* and to be open also to the logic of *forgiveness*.

Christians know that love is the reason for God's entering into relationship with man. And it is love which he awaits as man's response. Consequently, love is also *the loftiest and most noble form of relationship* possible between human beings. Love must thus enliven every sector of human life and extend to the international order. Only a humanity in which there reigns the 'civilization of love' will be able to enjoy authentic and lasting peace.

At the beginning of a New Year I wish to repeat to women and men of every language, religion and culture the ancient maxim: *'Omnia vincit amor'* (Love conquers all). Yes, dear Brothers and Sisters throughout the world, in the end love will be victorious! Let everyone be committed to hastening this victory. For it is the deepest hope of every human heart.

Notes

1   *Insegnamenti*, V (1967), 620.

2   1968: *1 January: World Day of Peace*
     1969: *The Promotion of Human Rights, the Road to Peace*
     1970: *Education for Peace Through Reconciliation*
     1971: *Every Man is My Brother*
     1972: *If You Want Peace, Work for Justice*
     1973: *Peace is Possible*
     1974: *Peace Depends on You Too*
     1975: *Reconciliation, The Way to Peace*
     1976: *The Real Weapons of Peace*
     1977: *If You Want Peace, Defend Life*
     1978: *No to Violence, Yes to Peace*

3   These are the themes of the successive twenty-five World Days of
     Peace:
     1979: *To Reach Peace, Teach Peace*
     1980: *Truth, the Power of Peace*
     1981: *To Serve Peace, Respect Freedom*
     1982: *Peace: A Gift of God Entrusted to Us!*
     1983: *Dialogue for Peace, A Challenge for Our Time*
     1984: *From a New Heart, Peace is Born*
     1985: *Peace and Youth Go Forward Together*
     1986: *Peace is a Value with No Frontiers North–South,
     East–West: Only One Peace*
     1987: *Development and Solidarity: Two Keys to Peace*
     1988: *Religious Freedom, Condition for Peace*
     1989: *To Build Peace, Respect Minorities*
     1990: *Peace with God the Creator, Peace with All of Creation*
     1991: *If You Want Peace, Respect the Conscience of Every
     Person*
     1992: *Believers United in Building Peace*
     1993: *If You Want Peace, Reach Out to the Poor*
     1994: *The Family Creates the Peace of the Human Family*
     1995: *Women: Teachers of Peace*
     1996: *Let Us Give Children a Future of Peace*
     1997: *Offer Forgiveness and Receive Peace*
     1998: *From the Justice of Each Comes Peace for All*
     1999: *Respect for Human Rights: The Secret of True Peace*
     2000: *'Peace on Earth to Those Whom God Loves!'*
     2001: *Dialogue Between Cultures for a Civilization of Love and
     Peace*
     2002: *No Peace Without Justice, No Justice Without Peace*
     2003: *'Pacem in Terris': A Permanent Commitment*

4   *Preamble.*

5   JOHN PAUL II, Encyclical Letter *Sollicitudo Rei Socialis,* 43: *AAS* 80 (1988), 575.

6   *Address to the Fiftieth General Assembly of the United Nations,* New York (5 October 1995), 14: *Insegnamenti,* XVIII/2 (1995), 741.

7   BENEDICT XV, *Appeal to the Leaders of the Warring Nations,* 1 August 1917: *AAS* 9 (1917), 422.

8   No. 4: *Insegnamenti,* XX/1 (1997), 97.

1 January 2005

DO NOT BE OVERCOME BY EVIL BUT OVERCOME EVIL WITH GOOD

In this final message of his pontificate, Pope John Paul meditates upon St Paul's words in the letter to the Romans: overcome evil with good. The Pope draws our attention to several places of violence: Africa (he calls 'for a radically new direction for Africa'), Palestine, Iraq and terrorist violence in general. The message itself is something of a summary of many themes mentioned in previous years. It highlights how peace is linked to the 'grammar' of the universal moral law that inspires common values and principles in an increasingly interdependent world. We are reminded of the need to form consciences, educate for peace and promote fundamental rights. He re-visits the issue of the ethical requirements surrounding the use of the earth's goods including those deriving from science and technology. He reflects on the need for the international community to take on greater responsibility for 'public goods' such as the fight against poverty, promotion of peace and security, concern for climate change and disease control. Once more he raises his voice in a preferential love for the poor by highlighting the tragedy of poverty closely linked to the issue of foreign debt of poor countries. In a year dedicated to the Eucharist, the 'supreme sacrament of love' of God's family, the Pope urges greater 'creativity in charity'. Overcoming evil with good is a fight that can be fought effectively only with the 'weapons of love': 'When good overcomes evil, love prevails and where love prevails, there peace prevails'.

* * *

334

1.   At the beginning of the New Year, I once again address the leaders of nations and all men and women of good will, who recognize the need to build peace in the world. For the theme of this 2005 World Day of Peace I have chosen Saint Paul's words in the Letter to the Romans: *'Do not be overcome by evil, but overcome evil with good'* (12:21). Evil is never defeated by evil; once that road is taken, *rather than defeating evil, one will instead be defeated by evil.*

The great Apostle brings out a fundamental truth: peace is the outcome of a long and demanding battle which is only won when evil is defeated by good. If we consider the tragic scenario of violent fratricidal conflicts in different parts of the world, and the untold sufferings and injustices to which they have given rise, the only truly constructive choice is, as Saint Paul proposes, to *flee what is evil and hold fast to what is good* (cf. *Rom* 12:9).

Peace is a good to be promoted with good: it is a good for individuals, for families, for nations and for all humanity; yet it is one which needs to be maintained and fostered by decisions and actions inspired by good. We can appreciate the profound truth of another saying of Saint Paul: *'Repay no one evil for evil'* (*Rom* 12:17). The one way out of the vicious circle of requiting evil for evil is to accept the Apostle's words: *'Do not be overcome by evil, but overcome evil with good'* (*Rom* 12:21).

Evil, good and love

2.   From the beginning, humanity has known the tragedy of evil and has struggled to grasp its roots and to explain its causes. Evil is not some impersonal, deterministic force at work in the world. It is the result of human freedom. Freedom, which distinguishes human beings from every other creature on earth, is ever present at the heart of the drama of evil. *Evil always has a name and a face:* the name and face of those men and women who freely choose it. Sacred Scripture teaches that at the dawn of history Adam and Eve rebelled against God, and Abel was killed by Cain, his brother (cf. *Gen* 3–4). These

were the first wrong choices, which were succeeded by countless others down the centuries. Each of these choices has an *intrinsic moral dimension*, involving specific individual responsibilities and the fundamental relationship of each person with God, with others and with all of creation.

At its deepest level, *evil is a tragic rejection of the demands of love*[1]. Moral good, on the other hand, is born of love, shows itself as love and is directed towards love. All this is particularly evident to Christians, who know that their membership in the one mystical Body of Christ sets them in a particular relationship not only with the Lord but also with their brothers and sisters. The inner logic of Christian love, which in the Gospel is the living source of moral goodness, leads even to the love of one's enemies: *'If your enemy is hungry, feed him; if he is thirsty, give him something to drink'* (*Rom* 12:20).

The 'grammar' of the universal moral law

3.   If we look to the present state of the world, we cannot help but note the disturbing spread of *various social and political manifestations of evil:* from social disorders to anarchy and war, from injustice to acts of violence and killing. To steer a path between the conflicting claims of good and evil, the human family urgently needs to preserve and esteem that *common patrimony of moral values* bestowed by God himself. For this reason, Saint Paul encourages all those determined to overcome evil with good *to be noble and disinterested in fostering generosity and peace* (cf. *Rom* 12:17–21).

Ten years ago, in addressing the General Assembly of the United Nations about the need for common commitment to the service of peace, I made reference to the *'grammar' of the universal moral law*(2), to which the Church appeals in her various pronouncements in this area. By inspiring common values and principles, this law unites human beings, despite their different cultures, and is itself unchanging: 'it subsists under the flux of ideas and customs and supports their progress... Even when it is rejected in its very principles, it cannot be destroyed or removed from the heart of man. It always rises again in the life of individuals and societies'[3].

4.   This common *grammar of the moral law* requires ever greater commitment and responsibility in ensuring that the life of individuals and of peoples is respected and advanced. In this light, the evils of a social and political nature which afflict the world, particularly those provoked by *outbreaks of violence*, are to be vigorously condemned. I think immediately of the beloved continent of *Africa*, where conflicts which have already claimed millions of victims are still continuing. Or the dangerous *situation of Palestine*, the Land of Jesus, where the fabric of mutual understanding, torn by a conflict which is fed daily by acts of violence and reprisal, cannot yet be mended in justice and truth. And what of the troubling phenomenon of *terrorist violence*, which appears to be driving the whole world towards a future of fear and anguish? Finally, how can we not think with profound regret of the *drama unfolding in Iraq*, which has given rise to tragic situations of uncertainty and insecurity for all?

To attain the good of peace there must be a clear and conscious acknowledgment that violence is an unacceptable evil and that it never solves problems. 'Violence is a lie, for it goes against the truth of our faith, the truth of our humanity. Violence destroys what it claims to defend: the dignity, the life, the freedom of human beings'[4]. What is needed is *a great effort to form consciences* and to educate the younger generation to goodness by upholding that *integral and fraternal humanism* which the Church proclaims and promotes. This is the foundation for a social, economic and political order respectful of the dignity, freedom and fundamental rights of each person.

The good of peace and the common good

5.   Fostering peace by overcoming evil with good requires careful reflection *on the common good*[5] and on its social and political implications. When the common good is promoted at every level, peace is promoted. Can an individual find

complete fulfilment without taking account of his social nature, that is, his being 'with' and 'for' others? The common good closely concerns him. It closely concerns every expression of his social nature: the family, groups, associations, cities, regions, states, the community of peoples and nations. *Each person, in some way, is called to work for the common good*, constantly looking out for the good of others as if it were his own. This responsibility belongs in a particular way to political authorities at every level, since they are called to create that sum of social conditions which permit and foster in human beings the integral development of their person[6].

The common good therefore demands respect for and the integral promotion of the person and his fundamental rights, as well as respect for and the promotion of the rights of nations on the universal plane. In this regard, the Second Vatican Council observed that 'the increasingly close interdependence gradually encompassing the entire world is leading to an increasingly universal common good... and this involves rights and duties with respect to the whole human race. Every social group must take account of the needs and legitimate aspirations of other groups and the common good of the entire human family'[7]. The good of humanity as a whole, including future generations, calls for true international cooperation, to which every nation must offer its contribution[8].

Certain reductive visions of humanity tend to present the common good as a purely *socio-economic state of well-being* lacking any transcendent purpose, thus emptying it of its deepest meaning. Yet the *common good* has a *transcendent dimension*, for God is the ultimate end of all his creatures[9]. Christians know that Jesus has shed full light on how the true common good of humanity is to be achieved. History journeys towards Christ and in him finds its culmination: because of Christ, through Christ and for Christ, every human reality can be led to complete fulfilment in God.

The good of peace and the use of the world's goods

6.   Since the good of peace is closely linked to the development of all peoples, the *ethical requirements for the use of the earth's goods* must always be taken into account. The Second Vatican Council rightly recalled that 'God intended the earth and all it contains for the use of everyone and of all peoples; so that the good things of creation should be available equally to all, with justice as guide and charity in attendance'[10].

As a member of the human family, each person becomes as it were a *citizen of the world*, with consequent duties and rights, since all human beings are united by *a common origin and the same supreme destiny*. By the mere fact of being conceived, a child is entitled to rights and deserving of care and attention; and someone has the duty to provide these. The condemnation of racism, the protection of minors, the provision of aid to displaced persons and refugees, and the mobilization of international solidarity towards all the needy are nothing other than consistent applications of the principle of world citizenship.

7.   The good of peace should be seen today as closely related to the *new goods* derived from progress in science and technology. These too, in application of the principle of the universal destination of the earth's goods, need to be *put at the service of humanity's basic needs*. Appropriate initiatives on the international level can give full practical implementation to the principle of the universal destination of goods by guaranteeing to all – individuals and nations – the basic conditions for sharing in development. This becomes possible once the barriers and monopolies that marginalize many peoples are removed[11].

The good of peace will be better ensured if the international community takes on greater responsibility for what are commonly called *public goods*. These are goods which all citizens automatically enjoy, without having consciously chosen them or contributed to them in any way. Such is the case, for example, at the national level, with such goods as the judiciary system, the defence system and the network of highways and railways. In our world the phenomenon of increased globalization means that more and more public goods are taking on a global character, and as a result *common interests* are daily increasing. We need but think of the fight against poverty, the promotion of peace and security, concern for climate change and disease control. The international community needs to respond to these interests with a broader network of juridical accords aimed at *regulating the use of public goods* and inspired by universal principles of fairness and solidarity.

8.   The principle of the universal destination of goods can also make possible a more effective approach to *the challenge of poverty*, particularly when we consider the extreme poverty in which millions of people are still living. The international community, at the beginning of the new millennium, set the priority of halving their number by the year 2015. The Church supports and encourages this commitment and invites all who believe in Christ to show, practically and in every sector, a *preferential love for the poor*[12].

The tragedy of poverty remains closely linked to the issue of the *foreign debt of poor countries*. Despite significant progress in this area, the problem has not yet been adequately resolved. Fifteen years ago I called public attention to the fact that the foreign debt of poor countries 'is closely related to a series of other problems such as foreign investment, the proper functioning of the major international organizations, the price of raw materials and so forth'[13]. Recent moves in favour of debt reduction, centred mainly on the needs of the poor, have certainly improved the quality of *economic growth*. Yet, because of a number of factors, this growth is still quantitatively insufficient, especially in relation to the millennium goals. Poor countries remain trapped in a *vicious circle:* low income and weak growth limit savings and, in turn, weak investments and an inefficient use of savings do not favour growth.

9.   As Pope Paul VI stated and as I myself have reaffirmed, the only really effective means of enabling States to deal with the grave problem of poverty is to provide them with the necessary resources through *foreign financial aid* – public and private – granted under reasonable conditions, within the framework of international commercial relations regulated with fairness[14]. What is urgently needed is a *moral and economic mobilization,* one which respects agreements already made in favour of poor countries, and is at the same time prepared to review those agreements which have proved excessively burdensome for some countries. In this regard, new impulse should be given to *Public Aid for Development,* and new forms of financing for development should be explored, whatever the difficulties entailed[15]. Some governments are already looking carefully at promising mechanisms for this; these significant initiatives should be carried out in a spirit of authentic sharing, with respect for the *principle of subsidiarity.* The management of financial resources destined to the development of poor countries should also entail scrupulous adherence, on the part of both donors and recipients, to sound administrative practices. The Church encourages and contributes to these efforts. One need only mention the significant contribution made by the many Catholic agencies dedicated to aid and development.

10.   At the end of the Great Jubilee of the year 2000, in my Apostolic Letter *Novo Millennio Ineunte,* I spoke of the urgent need for a new *creativity in charity*[16], in order to spread the Gospel of hope in the world. This need is clearly seen when we consider *the many difficult problems standing in the way of development in Africa:* numerous armed conflicts, pandemic diseases aggravated by extreme poverty, and political instability leading to widespread insecurity. These are tragic situations which call for a *radically new direction for Africa:* there is a need to create *new forms of solidarity, at bilateral and multilateral levels,* through a more decisive commitment

on the part of all, with complete conviction that the well-being of the peoples of Africa is an indispensable condition for the attainment of the universal common good.

May the peoples of Africa become the protagonists of their own future and their own cultural, civil, social and economic development! May Africa cease to be a mere recipient of aid, and become a responsible agent of convinced and productive sharing! Achieving this goal calls for a new political culture, especially in the area of international cooperation. Once again I wish to state that failure to honour the repeated promises of *Public Aid for Development*, the still unresolved question of the heavy foreign debt of African countries and the failure to give those countries special consideration in international commercial relations, represent grave obstacles to peace which urgently need to be addressed and resolved. Today more than ever, a decisive condition for bringing peace to the world is an acknowledgement of the interdependence between wealthy and poor countries, such that 'development either becomes shared in common by every part of the world or it undergoes a process of regression even in zones marked by constant progress'[17].

The universality of evil and Christian hope

11.   Faced with the many tragic situations present in the world, Christians confess with humble trust that God alone can enable individuals and peoples to overcome evil and achieve good. By his death and resurrection, Christ has redeemed us and ransomed us 'with a price' (*1 Cor* 6:20; 7:23), gaining salvation for all. With his help, *everyone can defeat evil with good*.

Based on the certainty that evil will not prevail, Christians *nourish an invincible hope* which sustains their efforts to promote justice and peace. Despite the personal and social sins which mark all human activity, hope constantly gives new impulse to the commitment to justice and peace, as well as firm confidence in the possibility of *building a better world*.

Although the 'mystery of iniquity' (*2 Th* 2:7) is present and active in the world, we must not forget that redeemed humanity is capable of resisting it. Each believer, created in the image of God and redeemed by Christ, 'who in a certain way has united himself to each human being'[18], can cooperate in the triumph of good. The work of 'the Spirit of the Lord fills the earth' (cf. *Wis* 1:7). Christians, especially the lay faithful, 'should not, then, hide their hope in the depth of their hearts, but rather express it through the structures of their secular lives in continual conversion and in wrestling "against the world rulers of this darkness, against the spiritual forces of iniquity" (*Eph* 6:12)'[19].

12. No man or woman of good will can renounce the struggle to overcome evil with good. This fight can be fought effectively only with the weapons of love. *When good overcomes evil, love prevails and where love prevails, there peace prevails.* This is the teaching of the Gospel, restated by the Second Vatican Council: 'the fundamental law of human perfection, and consequently of the transformation of the world, is the new commandment of love'[20].

The same is true in the social and political spheres. In this regard, Pope Leo XIII wrote that those charged with preserving peace in relations between peoples should foster in themselves and kindle in others 'charity, the mistress and queen of all the virtues'[21]. Christians must be convinced witnesses of this truth. They should show by their lives that love is the only force capable of bringing fulfilment to persons and societies, the only force capable of directing the course of history in the way of goodness and peace.

During this year dedicated to the *Eucharist*, may the sons and daughters of the Church find in the *supreme sacrament of love* the wellspring of all communion: communion with Jesus the Redeemer and, in him, with every human being. By Christ's death and resurrection, made sacramentally present in each Eucharistic celebration, we are saved from evil and enabled to do good. Through the new life which Christ has bestowed on us, we can recognize one another as brothers and sisters, despite every difference of language, nationality and culture. In a word, by sharing in the one bread and the one cup, we come to realize that we are 'God's family' and that together we can make our own effective contribution to building a world based on the values of justice, freedom and peace.

Notes

1   In this regard, Saint Augustine observed that 'two loves have established two cities: love of self, carried to contempt for God, has given rise to the earthly city; love of God, carried to contempt for self, has given rise to the heavenly city' (*De Civitate Dei*, XIV:28).

2   Cf. *Address to the General Assembly of the United Nations for its Fiftieth Anniversary* (5 October 1995), 3: *Insegnamenti* XVIII/2 (1995), 732.

3   *Catechism of the Catholic Church*, No. 1958.

4   John Paul II, *Homily at Drogheda*, Ireland (29 September 1979), 9: *AAS* 71 (1979), 1081.

5   The *common good* is widely understood to be 'the sum of those conditions of social life which enable groups and individuals to achieve their fulfilment more completely and readily'. Second Vatican Ecumenical Council, Pastoral Constitution *Gaudium et Spes*, 26.

6   Cf. John XXIII, Encyclical Letter *Mater et Magistra: AAS* 53 (1961), 417.

7   Pastoral Constitution *Gaudium et Spes*, 26.

8   Cf. John XXIII, Encyclical Letter *Mater et Magistra: AAS* 53 (1961), 421.

9   Cf. John Paul II, Encyclical Letter *Centesimus Annus*, 41: *AAS* 83 (1991), 844.

10 Pastoral Constitution *Gaudium et Spes*, 69.

11 Cf. John Paul II, Encyclical Letter *Centesimus Annus*, 35: *AAS* 83 (1991), 837.

12 Cf. John Paul II, Encyclical Letter *Sollicitudo Rei Socialis*, 42: *AAS* 80 (1988), 572.

13 *Address to Participants in the Study Week of the Pontifical Academy of Sciences* (27 October 1989), 6: *Insegnamenti* XII/2 (1989), 1050.

14 Cf. Paul VI, Encyclical Letter *Populorum Progressio*, 56–61: *AAS* 59 (1967), 285–287; John Paul II, Encyclical Letter *Sollicitudo Rei Socialis*, 33–34: *AAS* 80 (1988), 557–560.

15   Cf. John Paul II, *Message to the President of the Pontifical Council for Justice and Peace: L'Osservatore Romano*, 10 July 2004, p. 5.

16   Cf. No. 50: *AAS* 93 (2001), 303.

17   John Paul II, Encyclical Letter *Sollicitudo Rei Socialis*, 17: *AAS* 80 (1988) 532.

18   Second Vatican Ecumenical Council, Pastoral Constitution *Gaudium et Spes*, 22.

19   Second Vatican Ecumenical Council, Dogmatic Constitution *Lumen Gentium*, 35.

20   Pastoral Constitution *Gaudium et Spes*, 38.

21   Encyclical Letter *Rerum Novarum: Acta Leonis XIII* 11 (1892), 143; cf. Benedict XV, Encyclical Letter *Pacem Dei: AAS* 12 (1920), 215.